Shakespearean

Shakespearean

On Life and Language in Times of Disruption

ROBERT McCRUM

PEGASUS BOOKS

NEW YORK LONDON

SHAKESPEAREAN

Pegasus Books, Ltd.
148 West 37th Street, 13th Floor
New York, NY 10018

ISBN: 978-1-64313-789-6

10 9 8 7 6 5 4 3 2 1

Printed in the United States of America
Distributed by Simon & Schuster
www.pegasusbooks.com

For Emma

I hear new news every day, and those ordinary rumours of war, plagues, fires, inundations, thefts, murders, massacres, meteors, comets, spectrums, apparitions, of towns taken, cities besieged, daily musters and preparations, and such like, which these tempestuous times afford . . . To-day we hear of new Lords and officers created, to-morrow of some great men deposed, and then again of fresh honours conferred; one is let loose, another imprisoned; one thrives, his neighbour turns bankrupt; now plenty, then again dearth and famine.

Robert Burton, *The Anatomy of Melancholy* (1621)

Contents

PART ONE, 1564–2016:
'Who's There?'

Prologue: 'Was This the Face?' *3*
One: 'The Book of Life' *8*
Two: 'To Be, or Not To Be' *14*
Three: 'The Whirligig of Time' *24*
Four: 'Something Is Rotten in the State' *40*

PART TWO, 1585–1593:
'Shake-scene'

Five: 'The Very Cunning of the Scene' *49*
Six: 'Hot Ice' *62*
Seven: 'The Death of Kings' *77*
Eight: 'Upstart Crow' *92*
Nine: 'Dead Shepherd' *103*

PART THREE, 1594–1599:
'Words, Words, Words'

Ten: 'Sin of Self-Love' *121*
Eleven: 'Wood' *140*
Twelve: 'W. Shake-speare' *154*
Thirteen: 'A Kingdom for a Stage' *168*

PART FOUR, 1600–1609:
Shakespearean

Fourteen: 'Distracted Globe' *191*

Fifteen: 'What You Will' *207*

Sixteen: 'Tell Me Who I Am' *218*

Seventeen: 'Shameful Conquest' *234*

Eighteen: 'Brave New World' *253*

Nineteen: 'A World Elsewhere' *258*

PART FIVE, 1610–1616:
'Exit Ghost'

Twenty: 'Chaos Is Come Again' *271*

Twenty-One: 'Our Revels Now Are Ended' *284*

Twenty-Two: 'Sans Everything' *299*

Twenty-Three: 'The Undiscover'd Country' *308*

Epilogue: 'Remember Me' *316*

Postscript *325*

Notes *329*

Acknowledgements *363*

Select Book List *365*

Index *367*

PART ONE, 1564–2016:

'Who's There?'

Shakespeare then and now. How he's always modern, and why we turn to his 'book of life' in years of crisis and disruption.

Prologue

'WAS THIS THE FACE?'

The Portrait of a Young Man, 1585

1.

Through the darkness, under a brilliant spotlight, the enigmatic portrait of the anonymous young man glows like an icon in the dining hall of the Cambridge college where I grew up. After more scrutiny, this late-Tudor treasure, painted on wood, will furnish two dates – *Aetatis suae 21 Anno Domini 1585*, the sitter's age, plus the year in which he was posing – and a sombre, transgressive motto, *Quod me nutrit me detruit*, meaning, 'That which nourishes me also destroys me.'

The young man's costume is rich and fashionable, a gorgeous midnight-black velour doublet, cut to flash some peachy silk, and studded with exquisite gold buttons. His expression is confident but opaque. Pausing in front of this eye-catching scholar, we might be drawn to his face, framed by that androgynous mane of auburn hair. His lips are full and sensual. Do they express a smile? Possibly we are still guessing. Is there, in those dark-brown eyes, at once fearless and provocative, a challenge or an invitation? Perhaps he doesn't know, either. The shadow of his beard and that wispy moustache tells us he's barely out of adolescence. In the England of 1585, his inky costume alludes to Machiavellian thought, atheism and fashionable melancholy. *Quod me nutrit me detruit.* What unrequited love does this effeminate youth refer to? What existential torment? Who is he, and what are his circumstances?

Slowly, as we study this inscrutable image, he comes into focus as a university scholar, born in 1564, the same year as William Shakespeare. Further investigation, which now morphs into informed guesswork, even wishful thinking, yields an Elizabethan high-flyer, a godless poet, a homosexual, a secret agent – and finally, a name.

The most famous playwright in Elizabethan England, Christopher Marlowe is still remembered for the lyrical rhetoric of 'Was this the face that launched a thousand ships?', and perhaps for revolutionizing English theatre. Familiar to Shakespeare and his contemporaries as 'Kit', he is the author of poems like 'The Passionate Shepherd to his Love', and plays such as *Dr Faustus* and *The Jew of Malta*. Yet, more than four centuries on, Marlowe and his work can seem as antique as oil-paint on wood.

This 'putative portrait' is an image I grew up with. My father, Michael McCrum, was the senior tutor of Corpus Christi College when, in 1954, an undergraduate brought him some dusty pieces of scrap he'd rescued from a skip, an obscure picture of a young man in sixteenth-century dress, which he thought might be of interest. 'Since Marlowe was born in 1564,' my father later recalled, 'the dates fitted, and the Latin motto seemed appropriate. So it was possible that this was a portrait of the playwright, an alumnus of the college. We took the picture to our resident medievalist, who insisted that it should be cleaned and restored.'

Since then, although there has been no further proof

of identity, the picture, which hung for many years in the college hall, has become the accepted likeness of Christopher Marlowe. It's a haunting work of art, widely reproduced, that acts as a poignant reminder of a life cut short by sinister violence. Marlowe's melancholy image also suggests a greater truth: namely, that the deeper we enter this singular universe, the more remote it becomes. Indeed, it's chiefly the language and literature of Renaissance England which links us to a society so distant, strange and potent as to be simultaneously enthralling yet unknowable.

This anonymous portrait, which is almost contemporary with the year of Will Shakespeare's hasty wedding to Anne Hathaway, provokes many questions. None is bigger than this: how is it that one sixteenth-century English writer no longer enjoys even a fraction of the acclaim he knew in his prime, while another continues to speak to us, from day to day, almost as our contemporary? Today, Marlowe and his work are familiar mainly to specialists. The dangerous aesthete, who is a perennial topic of conspiracy theory, remains a tantalizing source of academic speculation, whereas Shakespeare will always be . . . Shakespeare.

2.

My question is: how did this happen? Why does Shakespeare live on as one of us, not merely in Britain, but across the globe? Posterity is fickle, and literary afterlives capricious, but Shakespeare's universal fame is spectacular and unprecedented. What is his secret as a vibrant part of modern culture, as well as a touchstone of English, American, and even the world's literature? How did a young man who grew up in rural Warwickshire, who did not go to university, who forged his early career paying Marlowe the sincere tribute of imitation, and who died at the age of fifty-two, far from court or cloister, become not merely 'Shakespeare' but also the global icon for something far more influential: namely, that quality we call 'Shakespearean'? What follows is a highly personal inquiry into the making, and perpetual remaking, of the greatest writer who ever lived, in relation to his time and our own. This investigation explores the paradox that, where Marlowe subordinated much of his art to his life – and is remembered accordingly – Shakespeare sublimated experience through art: in his plays, indeed, art and life become inextricable and timeless.

I will argue that today, in finding so many points of relevance and sympathy, we are closer than ever to Shakespeare and his world. His name conjures a universe of characters, poetry, scenes and ideas undergoing constant reinterpretation by audiences, actors and artists across the world, for more than four hundred years. It's through the dialogue of these incessant metamorphoses that, now more than ever, this 'Shakespeare' is as much a part of our time as of his. Moreover, it's as our contemporary that he remains modern, a writer with whom we inevitably engage, often not knowing precisely how or why. I am also concerned to examine the mystery of that transaction, by anatomizing the nature of the dialogue Shakespeare always sponsors with those, like me, who attend his plays or read his poetry, poised between the two worlds of then and now.

To write *Shakespearean*, I have immersed myself in the Elizabethan age of Marlowe and Shakespeare, although this remains a moving target. Pre-modern, and on the cusp of change, it does not always answer to the kinds of biographical inquiry we are used to. There are tantalizing gaps in the record of both lives, and in the many mysteries surrounding their work. Plays, players, and playwrights had neither the recognition nor the status they enjoy today. Yet both men left behind a treasure house of poetry and prose. Accordingly, I have grounded my argument in black and white – the words on the page – those surviving texts from a world now otherwise lost.

These words remain as fraught with significance as ever. In his essay, 'Shakespeare Four Hundredth', the scholar and critic George Steiner once wrote:

The words with which we seek to do him homage are his. We look for new celebration and find echo. Shakespeare has his mastering grip on the marrow of our speech. The shapes of life which he created give voice to our inward needs. We catch ourselves crooning desire like street-corner Romeos; we fall to jealousy in the cadence of Othello; we make Hamlets of our enigmas; old men rage and dodder like Lear.

Steiner acknowledged that he was only echoing 'the din of commemoration'. If you exclaim, 'How noble he was in reason, how infinite in faculty, in form and moving how express and admirable,' he conceded, you are simply quoting. But the question remains: is his genius a sufficient explanation for the reverence towards Shakespeare? Yes, of course. But how was it – to address the matter another way – that he became, and still becomes, 'Shakespearean'?

To start with, there are his arresting first lines, which always dive in at the deep end.

One

'THE BOOK OF LIFE'

When sometime-lofty towers I see down razed.
Sonnet 64, 3

1.

'Who's there?'

Bernardo the watchman's terror-struck challenge in the opening line of *Hamlet* signals an emergency. It's a question which reverberates throughout the drama that follows, alerting the audience to something life-threatening at stake. More universally, it is a question for everyone in dramatic and disturbing times. With so many dangers on hand at every turn, 'Who's there?' becomes a chyron for the way we live now. Spontaneous expressions of fear will become the first clue in my search for the meaning of *Shakespearean*, a quest that starts with the new millennium.

Not one thousand days into the twenty-first century, the sky came crashing down. For a few apocalyptic hours, on 11 September 2001, the earth itself seemed to explode in fire and fury. With hindsight, the inferno at the foot of Manhattan, a snapshot of American trauma televised across the world, became the fiery emblem of millennial catastrophe. Worse still, these upheavals were being experienced, in various iterations of chaos and disruption, throughout many different countries across the world.

Once upon a time, in 1989, we had been instructed in 'the end of history'. Now we were living with a time 'out of joint', and a history which seemed to fast-forward so precipitously that we could scarcely draw breath before the next crisis, still less make sense of what was happening. As I write, in the shadow of Covid-19, these first twenty-one years of the twenty-first century have become long decades of imminent dread, an age of profound anxiety, a state of mind Shakespeare would understand.

Against a backdrop of the Internet boom, the biggest communications revolution in five hundred years, 9/11 morphed into the war on terror, which in turn inspired the invasion and then the horrors of the war in Iraq, the tortures of Abu Ghraib, and the medieval atrocities of ISIS. Then, just as the next US election seemed to offer new hope for change in the skinny, rhetorical figure of Barack Obama, the roof fell in, almost literally, with the bursting of the American housing bubble, and the 'credit crunch' of 2007–8. In *1Q84*, his 2011 novel, the writer Haruki Murakami captured the mood of the moment: 'Everyone, deep in their hearts, is waiting for the end of the world to come.'

For a while, Obama's silver oratory was able to spin an elevated narrative line, until even his words were not enough. Other great communicators – from Bill Clinton to Nelson Mandela – withdrew, or fell silent. In the past, it would have been the voices of the world's leaders who provided the most comfort. Now, it seemed, there was only a rogues' gallery of rabble-rousers, a jarring and raucous Babel, while the economies of the West set about rebuilding their shattered banking systems.

As the Obama presidency stumbled to an end in race

riots, there was at least the prospect, for progressives, of the first woman president in the Democratic candidate Hillary Rodham Clinton. Simultaneously, on the other side of the Atlantic, the daily news was unfolding in more traditional ways. In Scotland, a knife-edge referendum on independence confounded many pollsters when the Scots decided, by a clear margin, not to leave the United Kingdom. For a moment, we could begin to breathe again.

History and hubris are cousins, however. After the Scottish vote, having barely broken a sweat during the Brexit referendum, the British political class went to bed on the night of 23 June 2016 secure in the expectation that there would be no change to the status quo. In the first of many rude awakenings that year, the next morning brought the news that a fiercely committed majority of insular Britons wanted to 'take back control'. By the end of the day, the prime minister had resigned. Within weeks, a new government was in power, the old order in the dustbin of history, and the progressive commentariat dumbfounded.

Not since its army of redcoats marched out of Yorktown to the tune of 'The World Turned Upside Down' in 1781 had the British establishment suffered such a humiliating defeat. In the bitter aftermath, 'Brexit' became the shorthand for a universal expression of utter incomprehension: a profound national dismay about Britain's prospects, with almost nobody – apart from a few deluded Brexiteers – having any clarity about the future, in an angry clash of tribes.

Lack of certainty was one thing. Unthinkable outcomes were something else. In November 2016, Mrs Clinton's failure to reach the White House was, for democrats in the United States, a seismic political event commensurate to the UK's Brexit vote. On college campuses across America, a generation of young voters phoned their parents, wept, threw up, suffered panic attacks, and launched a tsunami of tweets, a harbinger of things to come.

On Friday 20 January 2017, at the inauguration of the new president, this bafflement reached to the very top. When the former host of *Celebrity Apprentice* concluded his first address to the American people, a raw expression of domestic 'nativism', ex-president George W. Bush turned to his neighbour on the podium and muttered, 'That was some weird shit.'

Henceforward, the headline news, in Britain and America, throughout Europe and across the developed world, was the growing recognition of a deeper and more pervasive disruption – to some 'the new normal' – that seemed to threaten the established order of things. Worst of all, for many, even once-familiar paths into the future seemed obscure and uncertain.

This was especially true in the bitterly disputed world of climate change, whose debates became turbocharged by the appearance of Greta Thunberg. After 2015, the Paris Accord, which had seemed to offer a glimmer of hope for the future, was rejected by US republicans, but vindicated by some apocalyptic weather conditions in 2018–19. Elsewhere in the public arena, there was only confusion and mistrust. Finally, amid the cacophony, there was a familiar voice, one that seemed to understand our predicament, a voice of vision and clarity that offered a secure narrative line through the constancy of its focus on states of risk: the words of William Shakespeare.

2.

As it turned out, Shakespeare had already anticipated this moment of disruption in sonnet 64:

When I have seen by time's fell hand defaced
The rich proud cost of outworn buried age,
When sometime-lofty towers I see down razed,
And brass eternal slave to mortal rage,
When I have seen the hungry ocean gain
Advantage on the kingdom of the shore,
And the firm soil win of the wat'ry main,
Increasing store with loss and loss with store;
When I have seen such interchange of state,
Or state itself confounded to decay;
Ruin hath taught me thus to ruminate:
That time will come and take my love away.
   This thought is as a death, which cannot choose
   But weep to have that which it fears to lose.

Not only had Shakespeare already painted a picture of a world in terrifying flux; further, he'd addressed many multiplying anxieties in the words of the king in 2 *Henry IV*, 'O, God! That one might read the book of fate, And see the revolution of the times [3.1.44–6]'.

Amid a rising sea of troubles, as every generation in society came to terms with the challenges of the present, from populist nationalism to 'Fake News' and #MeToo, the plays of William Shakespeare were once again finding an audience in answer to the needs of the moment. Some two hundred years earlier, the great American critic Ralph Waldo Emerson had saluted Shakespeare as the author of 'the book of life', and a sublime master of literary omniscience: 'What mystery has he not signified his knowledge of? What office, or function, or district of man's work, has he not remembered? What sage has he not outseen?' Bewildered progressives today, possibly resistant towards such quasi-ecstatic sentiments, could still share the idea. After 2016, 'Shakespearean' became a buzzword that surged back into the language in two senses:

1. *Adjective*, 'relating to William Shakespeare or his works'; and
2. *Noun*, 'an expert on or student of Shakespeare's writings'.

Those were Romantic terms, coined by Keats and Coleridge, poets for whom Shakespeare was a secular god. In our peculiar emergency, however, both meanings are more practical, speaking to a new kind of desperation. In May 2020, the actor Robert De Niro, in conversation with BBC TV's *Newsnight*, seemed at a loss to describe American politics. Finally, he exclaimed, 'It's like Shakespearean, the whole thing,' to summarize the crisis as he saw it. 'So Shakespearean', an unexamined cultural shorthand, has now become a strangely comforting assurance that says, 'You are not alone.' For some contemporary readers, the work collected in Shakespeare's First Folio does indeed become such 'a book of life'. The questions we have to address are: how does he execute this consolation? Why does he never fail to speak to us? Whence is he always so modern? And, finally, what holds the key to his enduring sympathy?

Two

'TO BE, OR NOT TO BE'

If it be now, 'tis not to come. If it be not to come,
it will be now. If it be not now, yet it will come.
The readiness is all.
Hamlet, 5.2.166

1.

Shakespeare revels in the dramatic present. No fewer than
three of his plays begin with 'Now'. He will always confront
the most overwhelming questions, and come to our rescue
in many guises, but imminence is his default position. This
is Elizabethan: Shakespeare's age lived in the 'now', from
sunrise to sunset. 'The readiness is all,' says Hamlet. All
or nothing is a challenge the playwright celebrates in his
resonant antitheses. 'To be, or not to be', his most famous
dramatic opposite, is at once Anglo-Saxon, existential, and
direct. Such immediacy is a constant thread in the tapestry
of thought and language that will become Shakespearean.

Was it the accident of his birth in Elizabethan Warwickshire that awoke him to the drama of everyday life? Was
it here that he learned to extract many nuances of meaning
from the quotidian detail of the turning world? At some
point, growing up in Stratford, or moving to London, he
discovered the wellspring of great drama: imminent peril.
In his imagination, this would blossom into a lifelong

dialogue between risk and originality, a creative exchange the writer seems to have kept to himself. We will never know. In the words of Jorge Luis Borges, the man remains an enigma, being simultaneously 'many, and no one'.

What was he like? This question, so important in the twenty-first, has little traction in the seventeenth century. Yet, despite the paucity of evidence, there is a striking unanimity among contemporary witnesses. Almost all the references to 'the man Shakespeare' concur on his decency, plain dealing, discretion, and politeness, none of which hint at the kind of dark side that might assist in our understanding of plays such as *Richard III*, *Macbeth* or *King Lear*. Long ago, at the beginning of his career, he had been described, under duress, by the writer Henry Chettle as 'civil' and 'upright', known for his 'honesty' and 'facetious grace of writing'. In *Brief Lives*, compiled during the Restoration, the gossip John Aubrey reports him to have been 'a handsome, well-shaped man, very good company, and of a very ready and smooth pleasant wit'. Crucially, in a clue to his astonishing output, Aubrey described him as 'not a company keeper'.

We can, nonetheless, place this elusive figure in a historical landscape. The Shakespeare who came of age during decades of crisis, dread and disorder, speaks to every generation that finds itself *in extremis*. England's national poet and playwright has long been known for his extraordinary hold over our thoughts and feelings, especially in dark times. It has been remarked that that we don't read Shakespeare; he reads us. But what does this mean, exactly? Is it enough to say that the solace of great literature becomes uniquely crystallized in his 'book of life', through the mystery of his art? What is the secret of his strange, uncanny empathy, and where the key to his insights? How and why is his work so evergreen?

Perhaps, if he had struck just one note – political or merely historical – as the author of *King John*, or *Coriolanus*, Shakespeare might have seemed a bore. The macrocosm can only hold an audience for so long. It's in the minutiae of the particular – the quotidian, and the personal – that he excels. At the opening of *The Merchant of Venice*, Bassanio counsels Antonio, who's worrying about his marital prospects and future trading losses, with an archery image drawn from childhood:

In my schooldays, when I had lost one shaft,
I shot his fellow of the selfsame flight
The selfsame way, with more advised watch
To find the other forth, and by adventuring both,
I oft found both.
[1.1.140–44]

Or consider this moment in *Love's Labour's Lost* when Moth, a page to Don Armado, advocates 'brawling in French' as the open sesame to the heart of 'the country maid, Jaquanetta':

To jig off a tune at the tongue's end, canary to it with your feet, humour it with turning up your eyelids, sigh a note and sing a note, sometime through the throat as if you swallowed love with singing love, sometime through the nose as if you snuffed up love by smelling love, with your hat penthouse-like o'er the shop of your eyes . . .
[3.1.10–20]

Shakespeare knows that's a zinger. Later, in the same scene, Don Armado, who is possibly based on Sir Walter Raleigh, will salute Moth's 'sweet smoke of rhetoric [3.1.61]', an in-joke that acknowledges a new smoke Shakespeare has richly inhaled. Here, in this scene, he does what the great masters of our literature always do: he speaks to his audience as if for the first time, with images that strike deep.

From my own personal history I know that, in states of psychological need or distress, Shakespeare's can become the voice to which we listen. In July 1995, I was poleaxed in my sleep by something the doctors would call 'a right hemisphere haemorrhagic infarct' – in plain English, a stroke – and pitched into an acute left-sided paralysis. At first, in the aftermath of this massive disruption, my writing arm happily unimpaired, I completed a worm's-eye view of this experience, *My Year Off*, 'rediscovering life after a stroke'. During convalescence, the *Complete Works* became my book of life. Almost the only words that made sense were snatches of Shakespeare, and next – as I began to recover – longer passages from *King Lear*, *The Winter's Tale*, and especially *Hamlet*, the play that rarely fails to supply a kind of running commentary to the inner dialogue of the self.

In retrospect, I rediscovered Shakespeare through ill health, and the slow return to wellness, to the point where, reflecting on Prospero's haunting valediction – 'every third thought shall be my grave' – one of many strange and memorable lines from *The Tempest*, I found the title for a sequel to *My Year Off*, to which, in turn, *Shakespearean* has become a coda. Just as *Every Third Thought* sponsored a reconciliation with issues of life and death, so rereading

Shakespeare can be a revelation. Virginia Woolf, who once compared this experience to discovering an informal auto-biography, launches into an ecstatic celebration of this quality in her *Diaries*:

> I read Shakespeare *directly* I have finished writing.
> When my mind is agape and red-hot. I never yet knew
> how amazing his stretch and speed and word-coining
> power is, until I felt it utterly outpace and outrace my
> own . . . I could say that Shakespeare surpasses
> literature altogether, if I knew what I meant.

In any rereading, some of Shakespeare's most direct and powerful lines come in simple old English mono-syllables. 'To be, or not to be,' is equalled by King Lear's 'Let me not be mad,' and Ira's sign-off (in *Antony and Cleopatra*): 'we are for the dark.'

I, too, had become familiar with 'the dark'. The human animal lives at the epicentre of its own life, especially when it falls ill. In this condition, Shakespeare's eerie intuition is deeply consoling. When, as a long-term convalescent, each day becomes a reminder of human frailty, Shakespeare's extraordinary power to connect with his audience's perplexity, and to evoke a thrilling sense of mystery in the human predicament, inspires a mixture of reverence, awe, and fascination.

For me, this became a prolonged internal dialogue. If I could no longer travel, or move at will, as before, then at least I could make journeys of the mind, within Shakespeare's 'book of life'. The buzzword of my recovery was 'plasticity'. One definition of 'plasticity' describes the phenomenon as 'the capacity for continuous alteration of the neural pathways and synapses of the living brain and nervous system in response to experience or injury'. Putting it another way, 'plasticity' is about cerebral adaptability, the kind of unconscious responsiveness that occurs in any rereading of Shakespeare. This is the experience Henry James celebrates in his 1907 introduction to *The Tempest*:

> The artist is so steeped in the abysmal objectivity of his characters and situations that the great billows of the medium itself play with him, to our vision, very much as, over a ship's side, in certain waters, we catch through transparent tides, the flash of strange sea-creatures.

I now have three editions of the *Complete Works*, and each bears the impressions of much study: coffee and wine stains, torn folios, ghostly pencil marks and turned-down corners. During twenty years of recovery, I slowly transformed a knowledge of the plays I had read at school into a wider acquaintance with the Shakespeare canon, and joined the 'Shakespeare Club', a dedicated play-going circle whose outings I will intermittently refer to throughout these pages.

The first recorded meetings of this fraternity began in 1999 with *The Taming of the Shrew*, *Troilus and Cressida*, and *Hamlet*. Since then, in the course of more than one hundred productions, we have seen at least nine *Dream*s, eight *Tempest*s and *Twelfth Night*s, seven *Lear*s, five versions of *Much Ado*, and four *Caesar*s. We have also watched no fewer than a dozen *Hamlet*s, variously starring David Tennant, Rory Kinnear, Jude Law, Benedict Cumberbatch and Andrew Scott. By chance, this was good timing. Not until the late twentieth century were London theatregoers able fully to experience the sensation of the Elizabethan playhouse. If you ask how we might become contemporary Shakespeareans, one answer might be: go to the Globe.

2.

In June 1997, as a correspondent for the *Observer*, I attended the gala opening of Shakespeare's Globe, the fulfilment of a dream first dreamed by the American showman P. T. Barnum. The play selected for the inauguration of the new theatre was *Henry V*, a reliable paean of patriotic pride. On that first night (actually, it was an afternoon) in Southwark, the play's performance roused the locals' collective unconscious. There was, for instance, an extraordinary moment during this inaugural production when time seemed to stand still.

Everyone remembers the Prologue's 'O for a muse of fire . . .' Less famous, towards the end of Act Two, there's the scene that shifts to the French court. Enter the king of France, the Dauphin, and assorted French dukes, gorgeously caparisoned in blue velvet, and preening in arrogant Gallic splendour:

Thus comes the English with full power upon us,
And more than carefully it us concerns
To answer royally in our defences.
[2.4.1–3]

The reaction from the pit was instinctive. At the entrance of 'that sweet enemy' the French, everyone hissed.

Here, at the intersection of past and present, the historical and the everyday, Shakespeare suddenly became a

powerful contemporary voice. Actors and directors understand his ability to get under the skin of his audience, and
experience the alchemy by which his words and characters
continue to exert a grip on our collective unconscious.
They experience it as a mix of ancient and modern, memory
and sensation. When Andrew Scott played Hamlet in 2017,
he told the *Observer* that he wanted to make the production 'a play that would ignite our fourteen-year-old selves.
The big thing was to try to speak the language in as
conversational way as possible.' Similarly, in *Balancing
Acts*, the director Nicholas Hytner writes: 'The reason to
do [the plays] is to discover them as if for the first time,
and to confront the competing claims of then and
now . . .' Hytner relishes that challenge. 'To perform his
plays,' he writes, 'is to invite universal participation.'

Is it this 'universal participation' that unlocks
Shakespeare's magic? Four centuries of Shakespearean
performance supply many kinds of response, many of them
contradictory. In 2018, as one answer, Hytner launched his
innovative Bridge Theatre, opposite the Tower of London,
with a sell-out production of *Julius Caesar* which conscripted
a younger audience into its exhilarating crowd scenes.
Hytner repeated this *coup de théâtre* in 2019 with a witty,
transgressive production of *A Midsummer Night's Dream*
that bewitched the imaginations of its teenage groundlings.
The Shakespeare Club, remembering some awkward school
productions, was dazzled by Hytner's vision.

It's possibly at this juncture that some elements of the
audience might prefer to head for the hills than endure
another moment of madness in the Athenian or Danish
courts. They will find themselves in good company.
Prominent bardo-phobes include Tolstoy, Thomas Carlyle,

and D. H. Lawrence, with George Bernard Shaw a crotchety nay-sayer. What's Polonius to them, or they to Polonius? Who cares for Ophelia? Or Gertrude, Claudius and Horatio? If Rosencrantz and Guildenstern are dead, so be it. 'Alas, poor Yorick.'

For some readers, indeed, the rest is silence. For others there will be excruciating memories of Shakespeare in the examination hall. If that's the case, then the world of *Shakespearean* is not your oyster. Who can ever be comfortable with conventional wisdom, and what thoughtful person wants to be part of an idolatrous cult?

Equally, if you question Shakespeare's authorship of the texts reproduced in the First Folio (some thirty-six plays* and two long poems), and if you believe they were written by Francis Bacon, Christopher Marlowe, or the Earl of Oxford (even, in one theory, by Elizabeth I), then you might be advised to stand not upon the order of your going, but to go at once. You will find yourself in good company. Sigmund Freud, Mark Twain, Henry James, and Charlie Chaplin, together with some contemporary British actors such as Vanessa Redgrave, have all questioned Shakespeare's identity and authorship.

If, however, you stay with *Shakespearean*, in the chapters that follow I will attempt to elucidate a narrative line,

---

* Shakespeare's thirty-six plays become forty if we include *Pericles* and *The Two Noble Kinsmen* (both omitted from the First Folio), and two 'lost' plays, *Cardenio* and *Love's Labour's Won*. Some critics have also begun to reassess a play called *Edward III*, which is currently grouped with a collection of eleven other plays sometimes known as the 'Shakespeare Apocrypha'. The totals for the canonical and apocryphal plays remain in flux, as 'attribution' and 'collaboration' studies yield different readings. In 1908, as many as forty-two apocryphal plays were listed; now there are scarcely ten.

based on a conjectural chronology of the plays, to achieve three principal objectives: first, I want to connect these complete works with audiences past and present, old and new. Second, my argument will strive to enlist the experience of these plays in performance to explore the secrets of literary inspiration, the magic of creativity itself. Finally, I want to vindicate the claim that Shakespeare's words and ideas are part of our shared humanity. All these themes will be animated by the catalyst of risk and originality to be found on almost every page of his *Complete Works*. This is a story, the tale of a 'book of life' that's now four hundred years old.

Three

'THE WHIRLIGIG OF TIME'

The isle is full of noises.
The Tempest, 3.2.138

1.

In 2016, the 400th anniversary of Shakespeare's death, the upheavals of that year became an apt climax to centuries of contemporary audience engagement with his life and work. The record of those historical responses remains an intriguing merry-go-round of reinterpretation.

Shakespeare's unique and lasting hold over the creative imagination crops up in strange places. In his 1998 novel *I Married A Communist*, for example, Philip Roth breaks into a spontaneous riff, inspired by Feste's pointed comment to Malvolio in *Twelfth Night* that 'the whirligig of time brings in his revenges [5.1.373]':

Those cryptogrammic g's, the subtlety of their de-intensification – those hard g's in whirligig followed by the nasalized g of 'brings' followed by the soft g of 'revenges' . . . The assertive lengthening of the vowel i just before the rhythm shifts from iambic to trochaic and the prose pounds round the turn for the stretch. Short i, short i, long i. Short i, short i, boom! Revenges.

The how and why of Shakespeare rarely ceases to enthral, baffle, and provoke each new generation. To start with, between the publication of the First Folio in 1623 and the restoration of the Stuarts in 1660, the Puritan revolution was hostile to the playhouses and would close the theatres in 1642. Sidestepping academic disputes about the effectiveness of this ban, it's clear that English theatre went underground. Some playwrights lost their livelihood. Players, who had begun to enjoy some kind of professional status, had to fall back on private patronage. Plays would now be staged, discreetly, and in private, at the Inns of Court, college dining halls, or in remote country houses. Charles I even took a copy of the Second Folio into captivity. Visitors to the royal collection can still see where the doomed king amended the title of *Twelfth Night* to 'Malvolio'.

Amid the repression of popular culture, it was Milton – whose copy of the First Folio, a momentous discovery, is extensively annotated – who saluted the 'Dear son of memory, great heir of fame', paying fervent tribute in his 1630 sonnet 'On Shakespeare' as to 'a live-long monument'. Later, in *L'Allegro*, Milton celebrated his fellow poet as 'Sweetest Shakespeare, Fancy's child' who warbles 'native wood-notes wild'. Despite Milton, the first centenary of the poet's birth in 1664 attracted only modest attention, although the critic and poet John Dryden had begun to champion Shakespeare's national importance as the un-tutored genius, 'a comprehensive soul' who 'needed not the spectacles of books to read Nature; he looked inwards and found her there'. Meanwhile, the Second, Third and Fourth Folios of 1632, 1663, and 1685 carried Shakespeare's reputation steadily forward. Seventeenth- and eighteenth-century productions of Shakespeare were often untethered from their originals. Even Dryden did not scruple to rewrite a tragedy like *Antony and Cleopatra* as *All For Love; or, The World Well Lost* (1678). Sir William Davenant's versions of many Shakespeare classics, including *Hamlet* and *The Tempest* (retitled *The Enchanted Island*), so popular in Restoration England, bore scant resemblance to the Folio's texts. Not everyone was enraptured. In 1662, for example, Samuel Pepys decided that *A Midsummer Night's Dream* was 'the most insipid, ridiculous play that ever I saw in my life'.

Despite these infractions, Shakespeare's renown prevailed. Slowly, with the renewal of theatre life during the Restoration, the phenomenon of 'bardolatry' began to catch on, especially during the next century, a boisterous age of British nationalistic pride. A golden age of Shakespeare criticism flourished with the work of Malone, Pope and, notably, Dr Johnson. For Johnson, in a famous passage, the plays deserved comparison with nature: 'the composition of Shakespeare is a forest, in which oaks extend their branches, and pines tower in the air . . . filling the eye with awful pomp, and gratifying the mind with endless diversity.'

Samuel Johnson's Shakespeare was a vernacular miracle, a prodigally gifted writer – inexhaustible but unrefined – who never lost touch with his homespun origins:

Other poets display cabinets of precious rarities, minutely finished . . . Shakespeare opens a mine which contains gold and diamonds in unexhaustible plenty, though clouded by incrustations, debased by impurities, and mingled with a mass of meaner metals.

More succinctly, Johnson declared the *Complete Works* to be a mirror to 'the manners of life'. In 1769 these, and many other, Shakespearean sentiments coalesced in a belated national celebration of Shakespeare's genius. This was the work of Johnson's friend and contemporary, David Garrick. Some five years after the bicentenary of the poet's birth, the actor led a group of bardolaters to launch a 'Shakespeare Jubilee' in Stratford. On 5 September 1769, Garrick stepped forward to declaim an appropriate verse:

Here Nature nurs'd her darling boy,
From whom all care and sorrow fly,
Whose harp the Muses strung:
From heart to heart, let joy rebound,
Now, now, we tread the sacred ground,
Here Shakespeare walk'd and sung!

The main Jubilee stage was an octagonal wooden amphitheatre, the Rotunda, erected nearby on the banks of the Avon, the scene of a public banquet, a costume ball (to which James Boswell came as a Corsican chief), and finally a dazzling firework display. Inevitably, the Englishness of the setting took a hand. On the second morning, it began to drizzle, and then to rain in earnest. Suddenly the 'soft-flowing Avon' threatened the Rotunda, which teemed with crowds sheltering from the downpour. Garrick would not be distracted. He delivered his Jubilee Oration in a melodramatic manner, culminating in a *coup de théâtre* where he pulled on the gloves – the very gloves! – that Shakespeare was said to have worn on stage.

By the third day of this bizarre occasion, many had fled both the weather and the bombast. Thereafter, Stratford became what it is today, the focus of a Shakespeare relics industry – gloves, mugs, sweetheart rings, bookmarks, neckties, and even pieces of 'Shakespeare's chair' (the fridge magnets came later). The *Gentleman's Magazine* published a fine engraving of the Birthplace, the house on Henley Street, but piously demurred from identifying the room in which 'Shakespeare first drew breath'.

This was ludicrous, but influential. The buzz surrounding these antics inspired Garrick to put together *The Jubilee*, a spin-off to cash in on the publicity, recycling the festival's expensive costumes. Not coincidentally, Garrick had the perfect venue on hand, his brand-new Theatre Royal, Drury Lane, which opened its doors to the public in November 1769. Garrick had hatched *The Jubilee* during a London-to-Stratford coach trip with the painter Benjamin Wilson, and used it, shamelessly, to play to the gallery. Instead of a theatrical performance such as his much-admired *Richard III*, Garrick offered a glittering procession of nineteen 'scenes from Shakespeare', including the great actor-manager as Benedick in a tableau from *Much Ado About Nothing*. The show ended with Garrick's 'Ode to Shakespeare' and an exhilarating chorus in which, if the stage directions can be believed, 'Every character joins in the chorus &c., and the Audience applaud – Bravo, Jubilee, Shakespeare forever!'

Throughout the Augustan age, Shakespeare's characters became part of the national conversation. 'How many a time,' writes Jane Austen in *Mansfield Park,* 'have we *to be'd* and *not to be'd* in this very room.' She also describes Edmund Bertram observing: 'We all talk Shakespeare.' To which Henry Crawford, the fashionable and dangerous bachelor, responds: 'Shakespeare one gets acquainted with without knowing how. It is part of an Englishman's constitution . . . one is intimate with him by instinct.'

2.

At the beginning of the nineteenth century, three prominent Romantics – Coleridge, Keats and Hazlitt – further transformed traditional ways of reading Shakespeare, finding undreamed-of depths of psychological meaning in the 'imagination'. For the obsessive Keats, who declared himself 'very near agreeing with Hazlitt that Shakespeare is enough for us', the *Collected Works* became 'a book of life'.

Shakespeare had become a universal theme. Blake, Turner and Millais looked to Macbeth, Mercutio and Ophelia almost as obsessively as Berlioz and Verdi exploited *Romeo and Juliet* and *Othello*. In Britain, he became co-opted as an unofficial sponsor of the civilizing mission. Together, Shakespeare and the British Empire became the global production on which the sun would never set. Imperialism translated his most memorable characters – from Falstaff and Lady Macbeth to Bottom and Prince Hal – into various archetypes.

However remote their language, Shakespeare's people came to represent something essential about Englishness. As in a reflecting mirror – Dr Johnson's image – several national types, values, and instincts have become embodied in the figures of Falstaff, Touchstone, Romeo, Rosalind, King Lear, Portia, Prospero, and many others. This element of 'Shakespearean' has deep roots: since Victorian times, our references to these classic characters have become a quotidian habit.

One plausible test of any great English writer might be

their creation of timeless roles: Charles Dickens? (Oliver Twist, Ebenezer Scrooge, Mr Gradgrind, Little Nell, Bob Cratchit, and Mr Pickwick.) Jane Austen? (Emma Woodhouse, Mr and Mrs Bennet; Mr Collins, Miss Bates, and Lady Catherine de Burgh.) And later, perhaps: P. G. Wodehouse? (Bertie Wooster, Jeeves, Psmith, Aunt Agatha, and Lord Emsworth.) Shakespeare's tally of immortals effortlessly betters these.

During 1864, deep in Victorian Britain, a chaotic and farcical tercentenary replaced the obsessive grandstanding of Garrick's 'Jubilee' with a kind of mad Victorian self-importance. First, in the tourist town of Stratford, came a worthy local initiative, led by the Midlands brewer Edward Flower, whose declared intention was to erect an 'enduring monument' to Stratford's famous son.

In London, however, the editor of the *Athenaeum* had other ideas. W. Hepworth Dixon was determined to launch a rival project for an alternative statue. A culture war of a very English kind now broke out between shire and city. Stratford insisted on its primacy. Dixon retaliated, using his magazine as the megaphone for a pet project. The metropolitan press feasted on this absurd public spat, coining an ironical verb, to 'tercentenerate', in mockery.

Finally, when the poet's birthday, Saturday 23 April, dawned, Stratford's celebrations were rescued from imminent catastrophe by Nature herself. The spring sun shone, and thousands flocked from Birmingham. Meanwhile, in London, an attempt to plant a commemorative oak sapling on Primrose Hill somehow got mixed up in a pro-Garibaldi demonstration to which the police were summoned by agitated locals. The subsequent headlines were about Garibaldi, not Shakespeare. 'Notwithstanding this 300th anniversary,' commented *The Times*, 'Shakespeare is not a whit more admired this year than he was last year, or will be next year.'

In the aftermath of this quintessentially English cultural farce, a new mood settled on the next generation. There would always be fresh new productions with the latest stars, actors such as Henry Irving and Ellen Terry, but now among young writers like Oscar Wilde, Shakespeare became reinterpreted yet again as the raw material for new aesthetic ambitions. Wilde's scintillating short story, 'The Portrait of Mr W. H.', contemporary with *The Picture of Dorian Gray*, elegantly transforms a 'pseudo-scholarly controversy' about the sonnets into a homoerotic fantasy, in Wildean cadenzas of quasi-literary exaggeration.

By the turn of the twentieth century, Shakespeare had become the figure we recognize today, a ubiquitous mirror for the anxieties of the moment. A hundred years before, Keats had identified something about Shakespeare's character – a lack of 'personality' – which would always inspire a variety of responses, ranging from the hopelessly fixated to the merely fanatical. In *The Waste Land*, a great Anglo-American poet spoke for the new age:

But
O O O O that Shakespeherian Rag –
It's so elegant
So intelligent.
[*The Game of Chess*, 127–30]

Some predictable terms of this bardolatry resurfaced in 1934, when the young Orson Welles published the introduction to a book, *Everybody's Shakespeare*, that also promoted his identification with the playwright. 'Shakespeare said everything,' exclaimed Welles. 'Brain to belly; every mood and minute of a man's season. His language is starlight and fireflies, and the sun and the moon.'

A generation later, in 1964, Shakespeare's 400th birthday, nothing like its eccentric precursors, would become a worldwide celebration that was part of the cultural reawakening associated with the Sixties. Shakespeare was once again another contemporary writer, sharing top billing with Sylvia Plath, Samuel Beckett, R. D. Laing, and Ted Hughes. Within a youthful counterculture, his most magical characters – Oberon, Ariel and Miranda – became emblematic of a new sensibility. Vanessa Redgrave's 1961 performance as Rosalind was followed by Franco Zeffirelli's film of *Romeo and Juliet*, another expression of post-war romanticism. In 1970, Peter Brook transformed *A Midsummer Night's Dream* into breathtaking circus magic for the next generation. Darker, and more sinister, Jean-Luc Godard and Akira Kurosawa located cinematic versions of *King Lear* in the existential crises of old age. In his theatre classic, *The Empty Space*, Brook expressed a view of Shakespeare I first encountered as a Cambridge student in the Sixties:

In the second half of the twentieth century in England where I am writing these words, we are faced with the infuriating fact that Shakespeare is still our model. In this respect, our work on Shakespeare production is always to make the plays 'modern', because it is only when the audience comes into direct contact with the plays' themes that time and conventions vanish.

Even the academics were getting wowed by this new Elizabethan spirit. The Shakespeare scholar Samuel Schoenbaum described how, standing in Stratford on 1 September 1964, the mood of the moment had inspired him to embark on his magnum opus, *Shakespeare's Lives*. Like Edward Gibbon, who had dreamed of *Decline and Fall* in the Forum, Schoenbaum 'pondered the inconceivable mystery of creation . . . mad folk drawn, moth-like, to the Shakespearean flame'.

Other critics and scholars, notably George Steiner, became roused to awestruck speculation: 'Will the Shakespeare anniversary of 2064,' he wondered, 'find laser beams carrying the sight and rejoicing of Stratford bells to all stations in space?' At the same time, Steiner struck a prescient warning note: 'Any prophecy is rash . . . Mass education has immensely widened Shakespeare's audience. Never before have so many human beings had some measure of acquaintance with the plays.'

3.

In the half-century since those words were written, and far beyond the English-speaking world, Shakespeare and his works have become the catalyst for a global revolution in theatrical theory and practice, a cross-fertilization of stage and screen, opera, ballet, cinema, and television, with video and new technology being used to reimagine these classics for new audiences, especially in the innovative use of lasers during the 2013 RSC production of *The Tempest*.

Elsewhere, in the words of the *New York Times*, reporting on the new relationship between theatre and immersive technology, 'Hamlet is in a bathtub with water up to his neck delivering "To be, or not to be". Look to your right and you'll see his mother, Gertrude, in her bedroom putting on makeup. Look in the distance, and you'll see Laertes, practicing with his sword.' In this virtual-reality version, the audience becomes the ghost of Hamlet's murdered father. *Hamlet 360: Thy Father's Spirit* was a joint production from two different outfits: the Commonwealth Shakespeare Company, which is known for staging free Shakespeare on Boston Common, and the tech giant Google.

Shakespeare, actor and playwright, is perfectly suited to these innovations. He offers inspiring scripts, magical poetry and compelling plots, entertaining and inventive comedy; above all a loosely unified vision of the world, built around the five-act structure of his plays. At the same time, he is ideal for all kinds of performance – from work-shop to circus tent to open air. There is no dramatic space imaginable in which his work does not flourish. Actors can stage his work in five hours or fifty minutes, or even five, mashed-up, multicultural, or gender-fluid.

For another British director, Adrian Noble, one key to Shakespeare is that he's not only 'a great visionary' but also a 'practical man of the theatre'. He wrote plays to be performed 'to an audience that consisted of a broad cross-section of society: from the highly educated and well-read to the illiterate'. Noble goes on, 'The protean audience that crammed inside the walls of the Globe Theatre was hard to please and pretty volatile. Shakespeare had to grab their attention and keep it.'

Cut off a hand, gouge out an eye, bring on a wild bear, uproot a forest, slit an artery: Shakespeare will do anything to seize the attention of the playhouse. Four centuries later, the British rapper Stormzy, a champion of disadvantaged black students, used a Shakespearean echo in his chart-topping 2019 album *Heavy is the head* (*h.i.t.h*), a nod to *2 Henry IV* [3.1.31]. In this vein, Andrew Scott sees his job as an actor as 'electrifying' an audience. He also says he found his own way into the text of *Hamlet* through rap music. 'I just hate the idea of Shakespeare being put in a glass box, like something that's dead.'

Even when you put him under glass, he breaks away: millennial Shakespeare is more than ever free from the traditional constraints of time and place. In 2012, the British Library held an exhibition of its treasures. The singular volume that aroused most public and media excitement was not an illuminated medieval manuscript but a mass-produced edition of a book formerly owned by a convicted terrorist, inked with his marginalia.

In prison, by some disputed accounts, Nelson Mandela had kept *The Complete Works of William Shakespeare* by his bedside for more than twenty years. It is part of Mandela's 'myth' that its poetry had sustained him through his darkest hours on Robben Island. Typically, a line from *Julius Caesar* – 'the valiant never taste of death but once [2.2.33]' – is identified as one of Mandela's favourites. His needs as a South African freedom fighter in solitary confinement were unique and unimaginable, but the answers he found in these pages were universal. Mandela himself is reported to have observed, 'Shakespeare always seems to have something to say to us.'

From the solitary prisoner to the unfettered world audience, Shakespeare's appeal mirrors the playwright's addiction to dramatic opposites: he is at once global and local, the object of universal veneration; as well as 'the man from Stratford', a provincial English town; both timeless and Elizabethan. It is said that not a day goes by without a book on Shakespeare being published somewhere in the world. Simultaneously, there's no respite from the obsessive arguments surrounding the multifaceted conundrum of his biography and his bibliography. In this double guise, he is both omnipresent (a brand, a logo and a household name) and strangely absent (mysterious, enigmatic and elusive). All or nothing; everywhere and nowhere; mythic and mundane: he might like that, too.

4.

Elsewhere in Britain and America, devotion to the poet's memory finds various kinds of expression, from the cult TV comedy *Upstart Crow* to Kenneth Branagh's gloomy quatercentenary tribute, *All Is True* (2018). At the turn of the millennium, for example, a BBC hit parade of 'Great Britons' made Shakespeare its fifth choice (ahead of Queen Elizabeth I, Isaac Newton and Diana, Princess of Wales, but behind Sir Winston Churchill, who eventually topped the poll). Simultaneously, another unlikely survey declared *Hamlet* superior to Beethoven's Ninth Symphony, Michelangelo's Sistine Chapel, the King James Bible – and the Taj Mahal.

Such twenty-first-century accolades provoke some hoary arguments about Shakespeare's fame and influence. Does that, some ask, correlate to the qualities of his work itself, or is it just another example of high-cultural hype, the perpetuation of a myth by swivel-eyed bardolators with an axe to grind – the Stratford tourist board, actors, directors, schoolteachers, publishers, and even Prince Charles? In November 2018, on his seventieth birthday, the Prince of Wales provoked a flutter of Shakespearean comment when describing his ambitions as a future king: 'You can't be the same as the sovereign if you're the Prince of Wales or the heir,' Charles told the BBC. 'You only have to look at Shakespeare plays,' he went on, '*Henry V* or *Henry IV Parts I* and *II*, to see the change that can take place.' Sometimes, writes the critic Peter Conrad, it can seem 'as if Shakespeare created us all'.

Occasionally, the liberated voltage of a Shakespearean narrative creates a surge of rhetorical power that can invert reason, defy logic, and transcend meaning. In 2012, the opening of the London Olympics became, for the *New York Times*, 'A five-ring opening circus, weirdly and unabashedly British', where millions of television viewers from across the world were transported through a mad carousel of sentimental and post-imperial English symbolism – cricketers at the wicket; massed choirs singing 'Jerusalem'; James Bond parachuting in, with Her Majesty, Queen Elizabeth II as a kind of stoic accomplice – into a weird new world. This production, declared the *New York Times*, giddy with the moment, 'somehow managed to feature a flock of sheep, the Sex Pistols, Lord Voldemort, the engineer Isambard Kingdom Brunel . . . and, in a paean to the National Health Service, a zany bunch of dancing nurses and bouncing sick children on huge hospital beds, a bold vision of a brave new future.' At some point in the proceedings, the bridge-builder Brunel (played by Kenneth Branagh, in a stove-pipe hat) stepped forward to deliver lines from *The Tempest*:

Be not afeard. The isle is full of noises,
Sounds, and sweet airs, that give delight and hurt not.
[3.2.138–9]

Improbably, those words belong to the magician's slave Caliban, whose hateful dividend from the English language, he bitterly observes, is that he should 'know how to curse'. This did not trouble the Olympic committee, perhaps because, through Shakespeare's dramatic poetry in *The Tempest*, Caliban is given a rare and poignant kind of music:

> Sometimes a thousand twangling instruments
> Will hum about mine ears, and sometime voices
> That if I then had waked after long sleep
> Will make me sleep again; and then in dreaming
> The clouds methought would open and show riches
> Ready to drop upon me, that when I waked
> I cried to dream again.
> [3.2.140–46]

For this inaugural Olympic mash-up, Caliban's weird, unearthly torment was no longer to do with the terrible cost of empire but – through Shakespearean alchemy – had become a strangely uplifting celebration of Englishness for an English-speaking world.

Many British readers and theatregoers might want to identify with such a sentiment, and claim it as a national treasure. They might even go further to assert that, as Britons, they have a unique line of communication to Shakespeare. They will be surprised to discover that the earliest evidence of Shakespeare's uncanny command of our imaginations is more often to be found in America than in his homeland. In a twist Shakespeare himself might have relished, he has become as much America's – or even Germany's – as Britain's national poet. Here, he's an icon; there, in a crisis, his poetry and plays can become a touchstone.

On one side of some seething culture wars, the challenge

of 'Who goes there?' is also a call to arms, a question to rally anyone preoccupied with the defence of global culture understood in the broadest sense. This is possibly why, in the 'general woe' (Shakespeare's words) that broke out during and after the election of 2016, it was to Shakespeare that many Americans turned in their distress.

Four

'SOMETHING IS ROTTEN IN THE STATE'

Thus bad begins, and worse remains behind.
Hamlet, 3.4.163

1.

Shakespeare makes just one casual and ambiguous reference to 'America' in his plays. Eventually, the colonies of the New World, later the United States, would become a test bed for his art – a laboratory for the catalyst of risk and originality – in a way that's eloquent about both projects, the democratic and the dramatic. In performance, both the States and the plays become a work in progress, susceptible to endless reinterpretation. As early as 1776, an anonymous 'Parody on the Soliloquy of *Hamlet*' captured the American loyalist's political dilemma:

To sign, or not to sign? That is the question,
Whether 'twere better for an honest Man
To sign, and so be safe; or to resolve,
Betide what will, against Associations,
And by retreating, shun them.

Parody can be a weird act of homage. The first settlers seem to have acknowledged that Shakespeare, writing in their mother tongue, is also the poet of historical disruption (war, famine, social crisis and revolt), with a deep, intuitive understanding of what it means to live when 'the time is out of joint [*Hamlet*, 1.5.189]'. He was many other kinds of poet, but in late-sixteenth-century England his creativity is steeped in the kind of peril, both sexual and political, to which Americans have always responded.

Fast-forward again to 2016, and a case study of Shakespeare's polyvalent appeal to Americans as a preter-naturally modern writer engaged with the burning issues of their society. On 8 October in that tumultuous year, during the most vicious presidential campaign in living memory, Professor Stephen Greenblatt, the bestselling author of *Will in the World*, published an op-ed piece in the *New York Times*, headlined 'Shakespeare Explains the 2016 Election'.

In the early 1590s, Greenblatt began, 'Shakespeare sat down to write a play that addressed a problem: How could a great society wind up being governed by a sociopath?' After a deft and topical analysis of *Richard III*, he closed with this appeal: 'Shakespeare's words have an uncanny ability to reach out beyond their original time and place and to speak directly to us. We have long looked to him, in times of perplexity and risk, for the most fundamental human truths. So it is now. Do not think it cannot happen, and do not stay silent or waste your vote.'

Overnight, Greenblatt's piece went viral, and soon became shared more than 500,000 times. As the US election plummeted out of control, beyond almost universal expectation, 'Shakespearean' became a consoling shorthand for bewildered American democrats. This was the moment that the Shakespearean adjective acquired the status of a minor linguistic meme, rooted in an old tradition of New World veneration for the life and work of William Shakespeare.

Eight months later, for instance, on 7 June 2017, in a live blog for the *New Yorker* at a US Senate committee of investigation into the unprecedented firing of John Comey, the FBI director, John Cassidy wrote: 'The other thing I took from the [Comey] hearing was what a Shakespearean turn this story has taken.' He went on to draft an outline of what 'Shakespearean' meant to him, a sketch resonant with compelling dramatic archetypes. Cassidy continued, 'If the Russia investigation does end up destroying [his] presidency, Trump will have brought much of it upon himself. Until he leaned on Comey and then fired him, he was facing a counter-espionage investigation in which he himself wasn't a formal target . . . But, rather than sitting it out and protesting his innocence, he let hubris get to him.'

Less than a week later, Cassidy's implication – these Washington puppets are just so many helpless actors in a much greater contemporary drama driven by universal imperatives, the stock-in-trade of all Shakespeare's plays – took vivid and arresting form in New York, with the Public Theatre's 'Shakespeare in the Park' production of *Julius Caesar*. This was a show, directed by Oskar Eustis, that hit the headlines from the moment a strawberry-blond Caesar (played by Gregg Henry in an MAGA baseball cap) bounded on stage in a white shirt and long red tie, accompanied by Calpurnia as a trophy wife with a Slovenian accent.

At first, the audience revelled in many deliberate echoes from contemporary America, but when Caesar's enemies butchered the Roman tyrant on the Senate floor, no one was laughing. 'For a moment,' reported the *New York Times*, 'there was absolute silence. The conspirators onstage themselves seemed overcome. One of the assassins tried to shout a triumphant slogan, "Liberty!" or "Justice!" Blood was on Caesar's shirt, knife gashes in his blazer, blood pooling on the floor. All the rhetoric about Caesar's ambition, the danger he had posed to the republic, suddenly seemed worthless. There was only the horror of violence, the shock of it, even to the men and women who had plotted it and carried it out.'

Suddenly, 'Shakespearean' was much more than a meme, a visceral mixture of threat and promise. To conservatives, this production was a shocking and distasteful affront to American values; to democrats, it was a thrilling assertion of free speech, wired into a long-standing American dialogue with Shakespeare's plays. The opening night was interrupted by demonstrations: two members of the audience rushed the stage, shouting 'Stop the normalization of political violence against the right.'

Next day, the box office was besieged. As security at the Delacorte Theater was stepped up, a couple of corporate sponsors, Bank of America and Delta Airlines, cancelled their commitments. A Fox News chyron reported 'NYC Play Appears to Depict Assassination', maliciously (and hilariously) suggesting that a politician was being 'brutally stabbed to death by women and minorities'. Fox News failed to note until the very end of its story that the drama in question was not an outrageous new script but Shakespeare's *Julius Caesar*, a play first performed around 1599. When I attended the show two days later, on a balmy June evening, an audience of about 2,000 sat on the edge of their seats. The evening passed off without incident, but never have I experienced such a tense or dramatic performance of a Shakespeare classic: it was this that inspired *Shakespearean.*

Meanwhile, one of the president's sons shared the Fox News story on Twitter: 'I wonder how much of this "art" is funded by taxpayers? Serious question, when does "art" become political speech, and does that change things?' Possibly in response, the National Endowment for the Arts addressed visitors to its homepage with a new message: 'No taxpayer dollars support Shakespeare in the Park's production of *Julius Caesar.*' Within days, the tremors of this Central Park upheaval had crossed the Atlantic. On 22 June 2017, not long after the shock of 'Shakespeare in the Park', Johnny Depp, speaking at Glastonbury, joked about killing Donald Trump. 'When was the last time an actor assassinated a president?' he teased, in a not-too-coded reference to John Wilkes Booth, President Lincoln's assassin.

2.

Six months after these sensations, 'Shakespearean' had begun to penetrate the White House. In *Fire and Fury*, Michael Wolff's anatomy of the new presidency, the *succès fou* of new year 2018, there's a quote from Steve Bannon, the president's disgraced chief strategist, who concluded his embittered account of the bad family advice seeping into the Oval Office – the malfeasance, the feuding and conniving, the cynical collusion, the deceit and the treachery – with a single word. 'It's Shakespearean,' said Bannon, an alt-right contrarian with an appetite for melodrama.

On this reading, 'Shakespearean' reflects an instinctive

recognition of the powerful affinities between Shakespeare's world and our own, as well as the deeper and darker constants of human behaviour: the follies of mankind, its vanities, cruelties, and falsehoods. At its most basic, 'Shakespearean' keys the most extraordinary or intolerable moments of our contemporary crisis into a narrative matrix that is understood to be both larger than life, even melo-dramatic, but also touched with the grandeur of simplicity. Now 'Shakespearean' becomes a prism through which to refract the blinding glare of events, and inexorably our place within them.

As well as Greenblatt, other scholars were responding to contemporary political reverberations from the Shakespeare canon. In New York, Professor James Shapiro, bestselling author of *1599: A Year in the Life of William Shakespeare*, an adviser to the Royal Shakespeare Company, steeped in Shakespeare productions, became impelled to address the American crisis from that unique perspective. At the beginning of 2018, while Bannon was still in the headlines, Shapiro began a new book with the working title of 'Shakespeare in a Divided America', an allusion to the ongoing shouting match between the many and the few within the republic.

Before spring was out, Bannon's and Shapiro's instincts had received scholarly reinforcement from Greenblatt, who returned to his theme in May 2018 with the publi-cation of *Tyrant*, a book which asked three questions: How does a truly disastrous leader – a sociopath, a dema-gogue, a tyrant – come to power? How, and why, does such a tyrant hold on to power? And what happens in the hidden recesses of the tyrant's soul? Greenblatt's publishers were in no doubt about the obvious answer:

'For help in understanding our most urgent contemporary dilemmas, William Shakespeare has no peer.'

In America, as Shapiro has observed, this is sometimes summarized as 'Shakespeare's spell'. One explanation for this gift can be found during the years 1585 to 1593, that moment in the late sixteenth century when the twenty-something William Shakespeare, fresh from Stratford, arrived in London to seek his fortune.

PART TWO, 1585–1593:

'Shake-scene'

*Shakespeare comes to maturity as a poet
and playwright in an age of extreme peril, and
discovers the originality of risk.*

Five

'THE VERY CUNNING OF THE SCENE'

Beginning in the middle, starting thence away
To what may be digested in a play.
*Troilus and Cressida, Prologue.*28

1.

When Shakespeare was born in 1564, Elizabeth I had been
on the throne for six years, and would die when her most
gifted subject was at the peak of his powers as the acclaimed
author of *Venus and Adonis*, *Hamlet* and *Twelfth Night*.
The queen and her playwright, icons of their age, shared
a mutual admiration. He flattered her; she favoured his
work. To Shakespeare, in *A Midsummer Night's Dream*,
she was 'the imperial vot'ress' [2.1.24], a shimmering figure
of impossible majesty. To the queen, he was almost a
gentleman, the upwardly mobile author of entertainments
such as *The Merry Wives of Windsor*, bestselling poems,
and some enthralling history plays. Perhaps she recognized
the value to her dynasty of his early work: two Richards
and several Henrys transformed her bloody Tudor ancestry
into a compelling contemporary drama that helped legitimize a hollow crown. Shakespeare must also have
understood his worth. In 2 *Henry IV*, one of the king's
earls observes:

There is a history in all men's lives
Figuring the nature of the times deceased.
[3.1.75–6]

Elizabeth, the symbol of 'times deceased', never forgot her significance. 'I am Richard II,' she railed at one hapless courtier in the aftermath of yet another plot, 'know ye not that?' When the poor man began to babble about the 'wicked imaginations' of her enemies, the queen cut him short. She knew her place in Shakespeare's work. 'This tragedy,' she snapped, 'was played forty times in open streets and houses.' She also embodied the spirit of the age with her fortitude of mind. 'I thank God I am endowed with such qualities,' she once told her parliament, 'that if I were turned out of the realm in my petticoat, I were able to live in any place in Christendom.'

The reign of Elizabeth I, a woman vibrant with authority, is superabundant with the dramas of history. The dread of plague, invasion, civil dissension, plot and counterplot at court, affected the minds of every citizen. In one memorandum, William Cecil, the queen's good and faithful servant, addressing the national crisis – *plus ça change* – summarized the state of the realm, in a limpid phrase, as fraught with 'perils, many great and imminent'.

The scaffold and the stage were integral to Elizabethan life. Shakespeare learned his trade in a rough, vengeful world where the feuds of politics and religion were acted out in public – from burnings and beheadings to show trials and pitched battles – to an unprecedented degree. For Shakespeare, beginning to make his career in The Theatre at Shoreditch, such events were the stuff of everyday life. Exposure to this raw material was something he shared with the queen.

Elizabeth's own story, her birth to Anne Boleyn and Protestant upbringing, her survival against many conspiracies, and her own deep sense of divinely ordained monarchy, placed her at the heart of a relentless political drama: papal anathema; rebellion at home; war in Ireland; the threat of a French or a Spanish invasion. Moreover, there was an alternative history waiting in the wings. The Roman Catholic Mary, Queen of Scots, ominously immured in Fotheringhay Castle, was the rightful heir to the throne; Elizabeth, her bastard cousin, a usurper. Until Mary was executed in 1587, there was always a political crisis looming. Shakespeare spoke for his generation in many early lines, but never to greater effect than in 2 *Henry IV*, with the old king's bitter summary: 'Uneasy lies the head that wears a crown [3.1.31].'

The queen's court mirrored the collision of creative independence and political jeopardy. As a bystander, Shakespeare witnessed the exercise of royal power – a mix of cruelty, cunning, opportunism, hypocrisy and cynicism – unmediated. And he saw it for what it was: a shocking spectacle, but also raw, timeless, and human, with a special attraction for the kind of writer he was discovering himself to be. Motivated by a hunger for artistic innovation, he was increasingly drawn to risk and creativity.

In his novel *Prater Violet*, Christopher Isherwood makes this explicit Hollywood connection with the Tudors, in the producer Dr Bergmann's speech: 'The film studio of today is really the palace of the sixteenth century. There one sees what Shakespeare saw.' What is this Shakespearean vision? To Isherwood, it is the essence of court and corporate life:

. . . the absolute power of the tyrant, the courtiers, the flatterers, the jesters, the cunningly ambitious intriguers . . . There are great men who are suddenly disgraced. There is the most insane extravagance, and unexpected parsimony. There is enormous splendour, which is a sham; there is also horrible squalor hidden behind the scenery. There are vast schemes, abandoned because of some caprice. There are secrets which everybody knows and no one speaks of.

To this, 'Isherwood' replies, in words that would have seemed to Shakespeare the natural combustion of life and art: 'You make it sound great fun.'

2.

In this fusion of history and entertainment, it was a world that can seem surprisingly familiar, a world in the midst of an acute historic disruption. Those Elizabethans, ardent consumers of ink and paper, whose splurge of ephemeral print anticipates the explosion of the Twitter-sphere, inhabited a society that parallels our own. From two worlds in flux, words like 'jeopardy', 'despair', 'mistrust', and 'insecurity', reverberating through time, characterize both national and personal self-doubt.

Shakespeare feeds on this condition, but also nurtures his instinct for drama through the gift identified by the writer Adam Phillips as 'unofficial curiosity', a quality to which audiences always respond. Official curiosity, suggests Phillips, is a form of obedience, adding: 'In our unofficial curiosity we don't know who we want to be judged by.' We get hooked, he says, on odd things – impressions, rhythms, words – the 'grain of madness' that supplies a secret, inner coherence. In Shakespeare this grain of madness becomes devoted to finding new and persuasive ways of attracting attention. As Phillips writes, 'One of the child's fundamental questions is: what is he allowed to be interested in outside the family? The history of our attention is one of the stories of our lives.' This is the story with which Shakespeare, a poet infatuated with his origins, and immersed in his life as a player and playwright, enchants his audience.

He is Prospero, but he's also Brabantio, paterfamilias and householder. Away from the perilous professional arena of the stage, he led a bourgeois life, bought and sold goods and speculated in property, visited his family, worked hard, and provided for the future, while privately entertaining a world of transgressive conjecture. Here, Shakespeare was lucky in art as well as politics. A national sense of English isolation sponsored a new insular consciousness that was equal to those 'great and imminent' perils.

Up against it as a nation, the Elizabethans expressed a native self-confidence through language and literature. Shakespeare's plays in performance offer the acute example of an art form in urgent dialogue with itself. This constant interaction between the plays and their audience, described by Hamlet (while plotting to catch the conscience of the king) as 'the very cunning of the scene', derives from Shakespeare's fascination with risk.

From the moment he was born, Shakespeare was pitched into a society that lived with the fear and danger of violent death, but also – liberated by the new media of print, books, paper and ink – expressed its darkest anxieties and aspirations, either on the public stage in drama, or at home to private readers, through quarto and folio editions. This, in turn, motivated the writers and artists of the age.

In a rather different context, in the spring of 2019, the writer-performer Phoebe Waller-Bridge, creator of *Fleabag*, gave an interview to the BBC which articulated her ambition to connect with a public:

> I am obsessed with audiences. How to win them, why some things alienate them, how to draw them in and surprise them, what divides them. It's a theatrical sport for me and I'm hooked.

Waller-Bridge described her delight in the discovery of the 'little tricks [that] construct a satisfying story'. Her account of working with her writers is evocative of theatrical experience, from an improv workshop in the 2000s to Shoreditch in the 1590s:

> We would give briefs to writers, challenging them to elicit a specific response. One, for example, was: 'Make an audience fall in love with a character in under five minutes . . .' Whatever the experiment, the audience rarely behaved in the way we expected them to, prompting many fascinating conversations and debates about character, story and language that proved invaluable lessons in playwriting.

At the heart of these workshops was that quest for the cunning of the scene, the big questions about how to affect an audience. Why do people invest in one character over another? How do you make an audience forgive a terrible crime? How might you provoke people to love and hate? 'How,' asks Waller-Bridge, 'do you make an audience laugh in one moment, then feel something completely and profoundly different in the next?' She adds:

> If there is one thing I've learned, it's that you get a lot for free from an audience if you make them laugh. The power of comedy is astonishing to me – how it can disarm an audience and leave them wide open and vulnerable. Ultimately, for the *Fleabag* audience, I wanted the drama of this woman's story to leap into their open, laughing mouths and find its way deep into their hearts.

In the same interview, Waller-Bridge is described by a member of her *Fleabag* cast as having 'no fear', a quality that Shakespeare possessed in abundance. On stage, he typically sought the node of maximum jeopardy in scenes, drawing his creative succour from the dangerous world around him while, at the same time, expertly seducing the audiences who came to his plays. Here, he would both thrill and divert, explicate and entertain. As a poet and playwright in a strange harmony with the ructions of the age, Shakespeare was blessed with an uncanny eye for whatever would hold the playhouse spellbound. This is an instinct possessed by writers with the greatest command of their narrative line. Graham Greene, for instance, always expressed a preference for what the poet Robert Browning identifies as the 'dangerous edge of things'. Waller-Bridge, who understands risk in performance, does not allude to Shakespeare, even though he seems to lurk in the wings of her imagination.

In cultivating the cunning of the scene, Shakespeare's appetite for danger was at once detached, ironical, and ruthless. In the third act of *Richard III*, after the sudden and brutal humiliation of Hastings, an anonymous Scrivener comes on stage bringing with him 'the indictment of the good lord Hastings', who is about to be executed. Shakespeare is a playwright who knows what it's like to be an actor. It is part of his 'unofficial curiosity' that he always inhabits the lives of even his most minor characters. Here, in this tiny scene, he surpasses himself in the Scrivener's commentary on the speed of Hastings' fall:

And mark how well the sequel hangs together:
Eleven hours I have spent to write it over,
For yesternight by Catesby was it sent me;
The precedent was full as long a-doing;
And yet, within these five hours, Hastings lived,
Untainted, unexamined, free, at liberty.
Here's a good world the while!
[3.6.4–10]

This cameo shows Shakespeare at his most Shakespearean, juxtaposing the Scrivener's mundane experience with the fate of the doomed Hastings: the episode is rooted in the here and now ('eleven hours I have spent'); it is steeped in dramatic irony ('within these five hours, Hastings lived'); it speaks to the whole audience, from high ('untainted, unexamined') to low ('free, at liberty'). Finally, it signs off with a tangible English shrug ('Here's a good world the while!'), before closing with a sly challenge to the audience, breaking the 'fourth wall', in the manner of *Fleabag*:

Who is so gross
That cannot see this palpable device?
Yet who so bold but says he sees it not?
[3.6.4–12]

A scene that's barely the length of the Scrivener's speech
does what Shakespeare always does: it puts the audience
on stage, and in the room, even as things unfold. This
fascination with 'the very cunning of the scene', and the
interaction of the mundane and the theatrical, is something
to which the Shakespeare Club is addicted.

That's what we call it – sometimes, casually 'the Club'
– which might suggest oak panelling, library chairs, a dress
code and a discreet entryphone somewhere in the West
End, an association that might turn out to be either furtive
or seedy. Actually, it's neither; we are natural herbivores.
If you spotted us in the theatre bar of the Donmar or the
National, you might decide we were civil servants in mufti,
or off-duty English teachers from the shires, or possibly
journalists, which is approximately half right. Three of the
seven (or are we eight?) who make up the Shakespeare
Club – now guzzling peanuts and cheap red wine – have
worked for newspapers. And yes – oh dear, yes – we are,
until quite recently, an all-male English fraternity. We
conform to the national type characterized by the American
journalist Sarah Lyall as: 'an indecipherable millefeuille of
politeness, awkwardness, embarrassment, irony, self-
deprecation, arrogance, defensiveness and deflective
humour'. As middle-class metropolitans, we occupy a
variety of roles: Novelist, Journalist, Academic, Publisher,
Actor, Scriptwriter, and finally our Archivist.

This club was established through the persistence of a

former venture capitalist who used to go to Shakespeare plays with his college friends. When it became the tradition to have a pizza dinner afterwards to hash over what they'd just seen, the 'Shakespeare Club' began. Today, we are a quintessentially English mix of stage-struck, self-improving playgoers with Eng. Lit. degrees.

Occasionally, rash intruders who should know better will ask about our 'favourite Shakespeare'. For the Club, this is an absurdly intimate inquiry. Any one of these plays, in a great production, can find a special place in our affections. Yes, we love *Lear*, *Much Ado*, and *The Tempest*, but we also cherish an independence of taste that delights in *Love's Labour's Lost*, any of the *Henry* plays, or *Measure for Measure*. Indeed, the only Shakespeare we've never seen, because it's so rarely staged, is *The Two Noble Kinsmen*.

If there's one unspoken club rule, it's that when we meet, we only discuss the play in question: no gossip; no politics; no families; and no football. You could attend a meeting of the Club having murdered your wife, and no one would even allude to the blood on your shirt. As an association, we demonstrate near-Olympic sangfroid. As I write, the gods are smiling upon us, but in the past decade – not to mince words – two of our number have got divorced, one of us checked into rehab, and all of us have had distressful troubles with teenage kids. But did any of us ever so much as mention, or even allude to, these torments? Did we hell! No, we are here to see the show. It might sound dull, but it's surprisingly addictive. We argue, we quote, we tease, admonish, reminisce, and protest (too much); on a good night, we might even get swept away by what we see. We are, no doubt, typical of English audiences through the ages, *hommes moyens sensuels*.

3.

Not only does Shakespeare put his audience 'in the room', he also peoples the stage with many kinds of character to whom we can relate, sometimes against our will, a response that has its own allure. Who will not be moved to respond to Macbeth when, in a thrilling mix of dread and excitement, the Scottish tyrant invokes the darkness that will seal Banquo's fate?

Good things of day begin to droop and drowse;
Whiles night's black agents to their preys do rouse.
[3.2.53–4]

Sometimes, the cunning of the scene flows from something more mundane: everyday life. Scan Shakespeare's cast lists and you find the common man and woman in countless civilian guises: stewards, clowns, pages, sentries, shepherdesses, messengers, citizens, grooms, musicians, priests, falconers, apprentices, vergers, scribes, porters, pirates, fishermen, knights, curates, gardeners, watchmen, prisoners, torchbearers, serving men, carriers, heralds, and even common-or-garden murderers. Each has his or her distinct identity (no one seems beneath the poet's interest), often captured in a single phrase. Many other anonymous Shakespearean characters are just as familiar as those who are named in the Dramatis Personae. Thus we remember the Fool, the Porter, the Nurse, the Apothecary, the Constable, the Old Man and the Gravedigger.

At other moments, Shakespeare's narrative grip derives from his inexplicable plot points, a tantalizing absence of backstory. By classical standards, he is an arrant rule-breaker. Why, in *Macbeth*, does Macduff abandon his family? In

Hamlet, why does the prince of Denmark, who is already of age, not inherit his late father's crown? In a famous critique of *Othello*, Coleridge singles out the 'motiveless malignity' of Iago. And why, in *King Lear*, does the old man, who has already divided his kingdom, stage that pointless – and disastrous – love test in front of the court?

Shakespeare never answers these questions, but each generation still makes intense contemporary connections with his plays. Juxtaposed with Shakespeare's opacity, there's also his gift for the shock of the real: those arresting observations of detail, expressed in unforgettable language, such as Othello's reproof to Brabantio's men: 'Keep up your bright swords, for the dew will rust 'em [1.2.59].'

Once he reached London, Shakespeare's unofficial curiosity was on fire. From around 1587/8, he would spend ten years becoming 'Shakespeare'. He would rewrite English history in the three parts of *Henry VI*, as well as in *Richard II* and *Richard III*, *Henry IV* Parts One and Two, and in *Henry V*. Already steeped in the life of the age, it's in this crucible of poetry, the playhouse and power politics, that his work begins finally to become Shakespearean. The playwright David Mamet writes about the 'feelings of wonder and reverence, the sense of truth' that animates and revitalizes the theatre. In Shakespeare, this became an expression of profound simplicity, anchored in jeopardy.

Onstage, in late-Elizabethan London, risk and originality came in many forms. Never afraid to mix high and low culture, a declaration of artistic intent that was almost avant-garde, Shakespeare also exploited the English vernacular to galvanize the action. The shock waves of Shakespeare's stylistic innovations lingered long into the eighteenth century. One hundred and fifty years after his death, Samuel

Johnson would look back to the triumphs of Gloriana's England: 'From the authors which rose in the time of *Elizabeth*,' he once wrote, 'a speech might be formed adequate to all purposes of use and elegance.' Having paid tribute to the language of Raleigh, Spenser and Bacon, Dr Johnson then declared that if, to these greats, were added 'the diction of common life from *Shakespeare*, few ideas would be lost to mankind, for want of English words in which they might be expressed.' There's an irony in this salute. For Johnson, Shakespeare is a demotic outsider, notable for his 'diction of common life', rather than the classical periods so dear to the Augustan age.

Shakespeare's delight in the language of the street is of a piece with his comparative indifference to the printed record of his work. Towards the end of *Coriolanus*, the general Cominius describes the play's hero-in-exile among the Volscians:

They follow him
Against us brats, with no less confidence
Than boys pursuing summer butterflies,
Or butchers killing flies.
[4.6.96–9]

The poet's committed ordinariness and vernacular description of experience ('butchers killing flies') are both the qualities for which he would be scorned as a young playwright, and the things that never fail to draw contemporary audiences to his work. Marlowe had changed the way we experience the theatre, but Shakespeare would change the way in which his audiences looked at plays, and he would do that through the language of Middle England.

Six

'HOT ICE'

Well, to our work alive.
Julius Caesar, 4.2.248

1.

In his 1907 introduction to *The Tempest*, Henry James seized on the poet's origins as a key to the mystery of his tantalizing absence. 'The man everywhere, in Shakespeare's work,' he wrote, 'is so effectively locked up and imprisoned in the artist that we but hover at the base of thick walls for a sense of him . . .' Part of that fortification is fashioned from words apparently dug from the earth itself, from the life and language of the land. As a country boy, born in the heart of Warwickshire, and growing up in Stratford, a town of some 1,500 souls, Shakespeare lived at eye level with fish and fowl, amid field and stream, his mind and self-expression nourished equally by the dialect of a settled rural society, memorably described by George Eliot as 'the speech of the landscape'.

Shakespeare's dialogue conceals many scraps of vocabulary that betray his Warwickshire youth. Scattered through his work are words such as *ballow*, a North-Midlands term for 'cudgel'; *batlet*, a local term, still in use until the last century, for the bat used to beat clothes in the wash; *gallow*, meaning to 'frighten'; *geck*, a word for a 'fool';

mobled, for 'muffled'; *pash,* meaning to 'smash'; *potch,* to 'thrust'; and *tarre,* to 'provoke' or 'incite'. In *Cymbeline,* a famous song ('Fear no more the heat o' th' sun') conjures memories of country life, using 'chimney-sweeper', a Warwickshire dialect word for a dandelion [4.2.259–64].

When, in *Macbeth,* the murdered Banquo is described as 'blood-bolter'd' (having his hair matted with blood), Shakespeare was recalling that snow, in Warwickshire, is said to *balter* on horses' feet. The poet Ted Hughes identified this intimacy with dialect as another key to the playwright's perennial greatness: 'Shakespeare's language,' he wrote, 'is somehow nearer to the vital life of English, still, than anything written down since.' For Hughes, this was simply 'a virtuoso development of the poetic instincts of English dialect'.

This vitality derives partly from the vigour of a semi-literate society, shaped by an oral tradition, in which folklore and feelings, speech, memory and language were one. When Shakespeare refers to this ephemeral vitality of speech, he reflects the Renaissance belief that expressions of thought were the divine gift which separates humanity from the bestial world. In *Troilus and Cressida,* when the proud Ajax becomes puffed up at the prospect of fighting Hector in single combat, Thersites describes him as inarticulate and inhuman: 'He's grown a very land-fish, languageless, a monster . . . he'll answer nobody [3.3.255–60].'

Once established in London, galvanized by the verbal traffic on the street, Shakespeare's life and work became all about language. In a freewheeling, metropolitan society, Shakespeare's experience of quotidian danger revolved around the sex and violence of the city, the habitual topic of his plays. The vernacular with which Shakespeare had grown up would be seasoned with urban slang, but, within his imagination, never lost from view. To maximize the cunning of the scene, Shakespeare instinctively dramatized his meaning in the most popular way imaginable, drawing on ordinary experience (and extra-ordinary fantasy) and 'the diction of common life'.

2.

Shakespeare's lingo – slang, banter, gossip, and protest – pops up at the most surprising moments, as if he wants to ambush his audience with the earthy cadences of the everyday world even as they watch, for instance, the carriers' scene in *1 Henry IV*. Writing in 2010, the director Adrian Noble argued that this moment reproduces 'English speech in a way that communicates across the centuries far better than any recording . . . It offers an open doorway into a different world.'

At face value, the backchat of these first and second carriers is just the whingeing of harassed FedEx drivers running behind schedule: 'Charles's Wain is over the new chimney, and yet our horse not packed. What, ostler! [2.1.2–3]' But buried in these lines are the themes of mortality and progress, plus a wealth of reportage, from the problem of fleas breeding in chimneys where men have been pissing, to pickpockets' argot, to the 'borrowing' of valuable lanterns. Gadshill, one of Falstaff's posse, also articulates an Englishman's expression of self-worth:

I am joined with no foot-landrakers, no long-staff sixpenny strikers, none of these mad mustachio purple-hued maltworms, but with nobility and tranquillity, burgomasters and great 'oyez'-ers; such as can hold in,

such as will strike sooner than speak, and speak sooner than drink, and drink sooner than pray.
[2.1.73–8]

Shakespeare's ear for the brawling energy and bravado of the mother tongue in the street or inn yard exploits the vernacular as a shortcut to the sympathies of his audience in the pit. This facility with the commonest turns of phrase – partly lifted, partly made up – yields the additional dividend of Shakespeare's intense quotability.

It's sometimes said that Shakespeare's language is like 'the air we breathe', an observation that the journalist Bernard Levin once took seriously in the composition of a paragraph stitched together from the scrappy clichés of Shakespearean dialogue that still pepper contemporary conversation.*

---

* If you cannot understand my argument, and declare 'It's Greek to me,' you are quoting Shakespeare; if you claim to be more sinned against than sinning, you are quoting Shakespeare; if you recall your salad days, you are quoting Shakespeare; if you act more in sorrow than in anger, if your wish is father to the thought, if your lost property has vanished into thin air, you are quoting Shakespeare; if you have ever refused to budge an inch or suffered from green-eyed jealousy, if you have played fast and loose, if you have been tongue-tied, a tower of strength, hood-winked or in a pickle; if you have knitted your brows, made a virtue of necessity, insisted on fair play, slept not one wink, stood on ceremony, danced attendance (on your lord and master), laughed yourself into stitches, had short shrift, cold comfort or too much of a good thing, if you have seen better days, or lived in a fool's paradise – why, be that as it may, the more fool you, for it is a foregone conclusion that you are (as luck would have it) quoting Shakespeare; if you think it is early days and clear out bag and baggage, if you think it is high time, and that that is the long and short of it, if you believe that the game is up and that truth will out, even if it involves your own flesh and blood; if you lie low till the crack of doom because you suspect foul play, if you

Although Shakespeare's mobilization of the vernacular is often dense with wordplay, allusion and double meanings, it can also be startling in its Anglo-Saxon simplicity. Prince Hal will reject Falstaff with 'I know thee not, old man.' More basic still, reaching out to the audience with a terrible confession, there's Macbeth's horror-struck 'I am in blood.'

Shakespeare also has the scriptwriter's gift for the pithy phrase: 'the marriage of true minds', or 'the chronicle of wasted time'. Some of these zingers, seeded into popular speech, have also become classic book titles such as *Remembrance of Things Past* (Proust); *Brave New World* (Huxley); and *The Sound and the Fury* (Faulkner). These, in turn, connect to the heady shorthand of the playwright's gift for unforgettable and universal theatrical scenes: Lear on the heath; Romeo on Juliet's balcony; the English army advancing on Dunsinane; Hamlet addressing Yorick's skull; Prospero casting aside his magic staff; Bottom in his ass's head; and so on.

This gift seems to have grown out of his formative years in Stratford-upon-Avon, a community that prided itself on its quintessential Englishness, an independence of spirit and thought. In this society, it was perfectly natural for him to put language and ideas to work, as a ploughman

---

have your teeth set on edge (at one fell swoop) without rhyme or reason, then – to give the devil his due – if the truth were known (for surely you have a tongue in your head) you are quoting Shakespeare; even if you bid me good riddance and send me packing, if you wish I was as dead as a door-nail, if you think I am an eyesore, a laughing-stock, the devil incarnate, a stony-hearted villain, bloody-minded or a blinking idiot, then – by Jove! O Lord! Tut tut! For goodness' sake! What the dickens! But me no buts – it is all one to me, for you are quoting Shakespeare.

might open up a new furrow. For Shakespeare, no part of speech is exempt from call-up for front-line service.

In rendering 'the diction of common speech', Shakespeare was also alert to the gap between the high-flown language of the court and the vernacular speech of the countryside. From his travels to and from Stratford, a three-, perhaps four-day journey via Banbury or Oxford, he well understood the meaning of the gulf between city and shire.

I treasure that delicious moment of comedy in *The Winter's Tale*, when the thief Autolycus comes into the company of a clown and an uneducated shepherd, and falls into conversation with these hopeless rubes. When the shepherd boasts of his business with the king, Autolycus challenges the floundering rustic to justify his representation at court with the declaration that 'I am a courtier . . . I command thee to open thy affair.' The poor shepherd, who smells a rat, is having none of this. Resisting Autolycus, he boasts:

> SHEPHERD: My business, sir, is to the King.
> AUTOLYCUS: What advocate has thou to him?
> SHEPHERD: I know not, an't like you.
> [4.4.739–41]

Now there's an impasse. Seeing that the shepherd is at a loss to answer further, the clown takes him aside with some advice: 'Advocate's the court word for a pheasant,' he whispers. 'Say you have none.' Whereupon, the shepherd turns to Autolycus, with comical and super-confident grandeur: 'None, sir. I have no pheasant, cock, nor hen.' To this, Autolycus murmurs, 'How blessed are we that are not simple men! [4.4. 742–5]', a joke that Shakespeare the player/playwright shares with his audience in the gallery.

Beyond the world of 'simple men', a booming book trade stimulated the spread of English. Shakespeare himself used to haunt the print shops in the St Paul's neighbourhood, especially the premises of his Stratford contemporary Richard Field. The appetite for books in English – 'this new world of English words' – was addictive: contemporary reading was a cutting-edge pursuit. Just as we can reduce our digital revolution to these three words – Amazon, Google, and Kindle – so the new age of reading in the late sixteenth century can be summarized in 'quire', 'quarto', and 'broadsheet'.

2.

Ever since Caxton set up his printing press in the precincts of Westminster Abbey in 1476, there had been a communications revolution in England unmatched until the present digital age. The movable type of the printing press transformed society as completely as the microchip. Before 1500, the total number of books printed throughout Europe numbered about 35,000, most of them in Latin. Between 1500 and 1640, in England alone, from squibs, pamphlets and broadsheets to folio editions and Bibles, there's an imperfect catalogue of some 20,000 items printed in English. How many other countless scraps of ephemera have been lost we will never know, any more than we can ever fathom the dark web. By 1599–1600, the year of *Hamlet*, nearly half the population of England had some kind of minimal literacy.

As he grew up, Shakespeare had been free to browse

an exotic literary menu. At school in Stratford, he had been drilled in the classical greats such as Ovid, Virgil, Horace, Catullus, and Plautus. These ancient models were now in collision with some vigorous native English invention; scholar-writers like Sir Thomas More had begun to enhance the vernacular with borrowings from Greece and Rome. Shakespeare, who contributes vocabulary such as *barefaced, impartial, lacklustre, amazement, hobnob, unreal* and *bandit,* is contemporary with a linguistic revolution, and the innovative temper of those times.

The first stirrings of mass society had already begun to oppose the many against the few. 'Culture', a word uncommon to Shakespeare and his contemporaries, was not part of contemporary debate, but the issue of high 'inkhorn terms' versus low, demotic self-expression, the difference between written and spoken English, was real and present enough, and Shakespeare was never afraid to exploit it. When he first arrived in London he encountered the full meaning of cultural ferment: a vigorous debate about the nature of the language in all media that echoed the battles between England and Europe. The young Shakespeare, floating above the fray, summarized this controversy with insouciant ease. When Berowne finally declares his love for Rosaline in *Love's Labour's Lost,* he declares he will shun 'taffeta phrases, silken terms precise'. Instead, says Berowne, 'my wooing mind shall be expressed / In russet yeas and honest kersey noes [5.2.412–13].'

It's here that Shakespeare makes a coded acknowledgement of his outsider status. In modern parlance, to prefer these 'honest kersey noes' to more elegant 'silken terms' was to privilege the vitality of social media. Plot and character will be integral to the power of Shakespeare's plays, but it's his language that must first enthral. Ben Jonson would later claim that his rival had 'small Latin, and less Greek', but Shakespeare – accommodating conflict – exploited every nuance of language, either Anglo-Saxon, or Romance.

Print was one thing, speech something else, an issue that brought Elizabethans face to face with a rhetorical dilemma. For Shakespeare and his contemporaries, the native tongue was a rough-and-ready vehicle, a cart not a carriage, outclassed by the highway grandeur of French or Latin. In the 1590s, as an island surrounded by enemies, this was a belligerent society that wanted to punch above its weight, and flex some international muscle, with everything to play for. English had not yet acquired a literary reputation, but there was no lack of ambition. According to Sir Philip Sidney, 'For the uttering sweetly and properly the conceite of the minde, English hath it equally with any other tongue in the world.' Shakespeare shares this self-confidence; his characters delight in their loquacity, and give the articulate tongue a sexual significance. Valentine in *The Two Gentlemen of Verona* is quite explicit:

That man that hath a tongue I say is no man
If with his tongue he cannot win a woman.
[3.1.104–5]

Contrariwise, for Benedick in *Much Ado About Nothing*, Beatrice is simply 'My lady tongue'. To some Shakespeare characters, any loss of language is intolerable. When Mowbray is banished in *Richard II*, he unloads a bitter lament:

The language I have learnt these forty years,
My native English, now I must forgo,
And now my tongue's use is to me no more
Than an unstringed viol, or a harp.
[1.3.153–6]

In *Titus Andronicus*, when Lavinia's tongue is torn out, this violation leaves 'a crimson river of warm blood, Like to a bubbling fountain stirred with wind [2.4.22–4]'. Lucius, unaware of what has befallen his sister, asks for an explanation. Titus' brother Marcus intervenes:

O, that delightful engine of her thoughts,
That blabbed them with such pleasing eloquence,
Is torn from forth that pretty hollow cage
Where, like a sweet melodious bird, it sung
Sweet varied notes, enchanting every ear.
[3.1.82–6]

It was this 'pleasing eloquence', together with the classics of Greek and Latin, in which the young William Shakespeare had been schooled. For a would-be writer, this was to be in the right place at the right time. In hindsight, the gift from history that Shakespeare enjoyed was to have reached maturity at a moment of unprecedented social change. In turn, this was the direct result of a unique confluence of three historical flood tides: the English Reformation, a resurgent English nationalism, and finally the English Renaissance, which added between 10,000 and 12,000 new words to the dictionary, another modern literary artefact symbolic of changing times.

3.

Estimates vary – some scholars suggest an extended vocabulary of about 30,000 words – but there's now a consensus that in his plays, sonnets and narrative poems, Shakespeare regularly used about 18,000 words. Of these, he is said to have invented about 10 per cent, some 1,700 new words, and achieved this by changing the parts of speech, adding prefixes and suffixes, connecting words together, borrowing from abroad, or by simply inventing, the way a rapper like Snoop Dogg does today, filching from, and adapting, the vernacular. Not only does Shakespeare sponsor linguistic novelty, he will always delight in thrilling dramatic antitheses:

'Hot ice and wondrous strange snow' –
A Midsummer Night's Dream.

'In time we hate that which we often fear' – *Antony and Cleopatra.*

'My only love sprung from my only hate' – *Romeo and Juliet.*

In *Love's Labour's Lost*, the 'braggart' Don Armado, intoxicated with the exuberance of his own verbosity, is described by Berowne, with some irony, as 'a man of fire-new words, fashion's own knight [1.1.176]'.

The urge to elucidate the chemistry of Shakespeare's fire-new words has the unintended consequence of keeping his plays perennially modern. Lately, exploiting neuroscience at Liverpool University, Professor Philip Davis, using EEG and fMRI scanning techniques to investigate the effect on the brain of his unconventional sentences, has found that Shakespeare's magic with words and phrases has a measurable cerebral outcome. This ungrammatical and highly energized compression evokes a powerful neurological response in that Shakespearean concept, 'the mind's eye'.

Davis and his team have demonstrated how Shakespeare's creative mistakes, as they put it, 'shift mental pathways and open possibilities' for what the brain can do. How, then, is Shakespeare's language different from normal language? Here are just some of the ways in which Shakespeare grammatically shifts the function of words:

Albany, making a verb into an adjective: 'A father, and a gracious aged man . . . have you madded' – *King Lear*.

An adjective made into a verb: 'thick my blood' – *The Winter's Tale*.

A pronoun becoming a noun: 'the cruellest she alive' – *Twelfth Night*.

Such lines, says Professor Davis, are 'a way of upping the audience's attention level, what we might call the "wow factor".' The cerebral dividend of Shakespeare's language, a mash-up of Stratford and Shoreditch, is never less than a marriage of bling and barnyard. There would always be an 'honest, kersey' side to his writing, as steady and settled as a quiet conversation in a country pub.

Sometimes, too, his speeches track the dramatist's Stratford mind from phrase to phrase. Early in his career as an actor and playwright, Shakespeare grasped that the play of speech most dazzles the human imagination when it paints pictures in the mind, and expresses the actual, not the abstract. In *Antony and Cleopatra*, describing Antony's disastrous defeat at the battle of Actium, one of his followers compares Cleopatra to 'a cow in June' who, when 'the breeze' is upon her, 'hoists sails and flies [3.10.13–14]'. Enobarbus intervenes to confess that he 'did sicken at the sight'. Seven lines later, Antony is described fleeing 'the fight in height' to chase after his lover, 'like a doting mallard [3.10.19]'.

Such images have the limpid, haunting beauty of water-fowl at dawn. In *Much Ado About Nothing*, Hero pictures Beatrice sneaking up on her conversation in terms only a country boy such as Shakespeare could have imagined:

> For look where Beatrice like a lapwing runs
> Close by the ground to hear our conference.
> [3.1.24–5]

It's the detail of these observations from the Forest of Arden that pique our curiosity. Sometimes, we can glimpse Shakespeare exulting in the vernacular of his origins, as when Tranio, in *The Taming of the Shrew*, quizzes Petruchio's servant about the future bridegroom.

TRANIO: What to thine old news?
BIONDELLO: Why, Petruchio is coming, in a new hat and an old jerkin, a pair of old breeches . . . An old rusty sword . . . his horse hipped, with an old mothy saddle and stirrups of no kindred, besides, possessed with the glanders and like to mose in the chine, troubled with the lampass, infected with the fashions, full of windgalls, sped with spavins, rayed with the yellows, past cure of the fives, stark spoiled with the staggers, begnawn with the bots . . .

Biondello goes on about Petruchio's horse for the length of a long psalm, but eventually allows Tranio a question ('Who comes with him?'), which receives this answer: 'O sir, his lackey, for all the world caparisoned like the horse.' This, it turns out, means 'with a linen stock on one leg, and a kersey boot-hose on the other, gartered with a red and blue list; an old hat, and the humour of forty fancies prick'd in't for a feather: a monster . . . in apparel [3.2.42–68]'.

Shakespeare's instinctively precise observation is one of his hallmarks. In *King John*, Hubert, a citizen of Angers, conjures the distracted way in which the townspeople digest local events by recalling a blacksmith 'with open mouth swallowing a tailor's news'. In this scene, a snapshot of Stratford life, the tailor becomes so distracted, with 'his shears and measure in his hand', that he stands 'on slippers, which his nimble haste / Had falsely thrust upon contrary feet [4.2.196–9]'.

This image of a tailor in shoes worn on 'contrary feet' displays Shakespeare the dramatist working in close-up. As the son of a semi-literate, and possibly alcoholic, Stratford glover, he's at one with country life and animal skins. In *Twelfth Night*, an allusion to the family leather business becomes Feste's joke that 'A sentence is but a cheverel glove to a good wit, how quickly the wrong side may be turned outward [3.1.11–13].' More generally, in 2 *Henry IV*, Justice Shallow's servant Davy interrupts his master's meeting with Falstaff to inquire, 'Shall we sow the headland with wheat? [5.1.12]' Shallow's answer ('With red wheat, Davy') is steeped in Warwickshire farming practice. Early in *The Winter's Tale*, Polixenes describes to Hermione the innocence of his relationship with Leontes with a simile that's still warm in the poet's memory:

We were as twinned lambs that did frisk i' th' sun,
And bleat the one at th'other.
[1.2.69–70]

Shakespeare's mother tongue would become seasoned with urban slang, but once he arrived in London the young playwright was a man of his moment, immersed in the life and times of ordinary city-dwellers, obsessing over his audience, their servant as much as their master. To become 'Shakespeare', he would anatomize a new world, for all time, in poetry such as no audience had ever known, by reminding them who they were, and where they had come from.

Seven

'THE DEATH OF KINGS'

Let's talk of graves, of worms and epitaphs,
Make dust our paper and with rainy eyes
Write sorrow on the bosom of the earth.
Let's choose executors and talk of wills.
Richard II, 3.2.140

1.

Elizabethan England was all too familiar with many kinds of drama: savage violence, superstition, sudden death, sorcery and the supernatural. Shakespeare's early work puts all of this on stage in a theatrical tapestry woven together by the poet's fascination with mother tongue and countryside – the English language and its landscape. Still more fundamental, the spell cast by Shakespeare's plays begins with history. In a kingdom ruled by a queen, hallowed patriarchal traditions sponsored archetypal narratives to which the actor-playwright seems to have been preternaturally attuned.

The cult success of *Game of Thrones*, inspired by the Wars of the Roses, indicates the kind of voltage history can bring to a screenplay. Tudor Shakespeare morphs into contemporary Shakespeare, because his plays, provoked by the dramas of his age, reflect the all-time dramas of history, brought to life by the sheer power of his characterization: Prince Hal ('the imp of fame'); Falstaff ('the fat knight'); Richard III (a 'poisonous, bunch-backed toad'); and many more.

Shakespeare's early histories swiftly connect him to a dedicated metropolitan English audience. Perhaps as early as 1589, it was the first part (or possibly the second part) of *Henry VI* that put him on the map. These dynastic dramas, as commercial a genre as any boxed set of *Succession*, come down to us as both humane and yet historical. The playwright's fundamental insight is the omnivore's, that history is written in blood: violent, nihilistic, terrifying, grim, comic, treacherous and seductive. Yet, through Shakespeare's 'unofficial curiosity', the histories are always vibrant and tender with surprise, sympathy and excitement. These plays are also, in the interstices of sometimes astonishing violence, suffused with the humanity of men and women coming to terms with terror.

In *Richard II*, this throwaway conversational exchange between Exton and his servants both advances the plot and humanizes the grandee:

EXTON: Didst thou not mark the King, what words he
   spake?
'Have I no friend will rid me of this living fear?'
Was it not so ?
FIRST MAN: Those were his very words.
[5.4.1–4]

Elsewhere, Shakespeare's rendering of 'the times deceased' comes with a relentless parade of violence, a bloody flux whose language speaks of spiders and scorpions, bleeding heifers, slaughtered calves, innocent lambs threatened by wolves, butchers with axes and headless bodies heaped on piles of dung.

Here, the brightest dawn can be interrupted by the most casual, meaningless death, and the most passionate embrace broken by a sword. Kisses will be snatched in the shadow of the gallows, lovers' fingers might touch at a fatal rendezvous, while children are murdered in front of their mothers. Jewelled goblets can be spiked with belladonna, a cask of wine becomes a coffin, or a basket of strawberries preface a bloody execution. Shakespeare's terror, moreover, is egalitarian: even the psychopath Macbeth is not immune to 'saucy doubts and fears'. Shakespeare's violence in many different plays is like almost no other: enemies choking on their own blood (*Julius Caesar*); opponents skewered (*Hamlet, Romeo and Juliet*); heads lopped off (*Macbeth, Henry VI*); tongues torn out (*Titus Andronicus*); eyes gouged (*King Lear*); conspirators butchered (*Richard II*) and prisoners massacred (*Henry V*).

After sunset, there is no respite. Spies will be racked in darkness, and sleepers roused by soldiers in the small hours. Murderers will be confronted by the ghosts of their guilt in the still of the night, and when the blue dawn breaks, there will be only another cycle of dread to contend with: daggers or betrayal; torture or the noose; and either the edge of the axe or the agony of loss. Above all, throughout the histories, Shakespeare's characters, in Montaigne's insight, will 'laugh and cry for the same thing'. They might smile at horrific villainy, or shed tears for a clown. They can banter at the edge of a cemetery, or howl with mad laughter over a corpse. History in these plays has its own inexorable gravity, and remains unrelenting, repetitive, banal, implacable, merciless, tragic, inscrutable, mundane, imprisoning, cruel, exhilarating – and finally supreme, the goddess named Clio.

Our Shakespearean past is often found stitched into everyday experience. In 2013, for example, a box of broken bones unearthed from a municipal car park in Leicester revived memories of that archetypal Shakespearean villain, Richard III: a monster of sadism, cruelty and cunning, less fit than any Plantagenet or Tudor monarch for the English throne. If Richard III ('the king in the car park') is possibly the most disputed entry in a catalogue of sovereigns not renowned for their grace, humanity, or statesmanship, this must be owed to Shakespeare, for whom the king was a self-declared freak 'rudely stamped . . . deformed, unfinished [1.1.20]'.

On the London stage, one contemporary British director was quick to seize the initiative, and make a twenty-first-century connection. Not long after the Leicester bones had passed an official DNA test, the Almeida Theatre staged a new production of *Richard III*, directed by Rupert Goold, and starring Ralph Fiennes. As the audience took their seats, on stage a group of workmen in fluorescent jackets was excavating a hole in the ground, invoking the discovery of Richard's skeleton. Much stress was laid on his curved spine, which inspired Fiennes's performance. As the lights went down, the deformed king emerged from his grave to deliver that character-shaping declaration of intent:

> Now is the winter of our discontent
> Made glorious summer by this son of York;
> And all the clouds that loured upon our house
> In the deep bosom of the ocean buried.
> [1.1.1–4]

2.

The first characters Shakespeare ever wrote for the stage are among his most particular and individual: Richard III, Henry VI and King John, who all appear before 1595, are real people rooted in the historical record, personalities his genius animates with intuitions about the hazards of kingship. There are, however, other sources for his stage-craft. From Christopher Marlowe he had learned about the performance potential of history, and how the drama of a reign could morph into the tragedy of history itself. This is also a sleight of hand. Shakespeare's histories (seemingly so vivid and particular) are far from mere documentary versions, and articulate a highly theatrical exposition of Tudor myth. Later, in the 1600s, in *Macbeth*, *King Lear*, and *Cymbeline*, he would translate shadowy Celtic kings from a semi-mythical island past into characters who are more vivid than history, in plays that are, in a deep sense, all about England. For now, his purpose was to bring the past into the present in the most arresting way he could devise. Audiences crave excitement. What better subject for an expectant metropolitan playhouse than 'sad stories of the death of kings [*Richard II*, 3.2.152]', the national saga?

The reason to perform these plays, writes Nicholas Hytner, 'is always to discover them as if for the first time, and to confront the competing claims of then and now.' Hytner concedes a moving target. In 2005, he had thought that the histories were driven by a specifically Tudor terror of a return to the bloody chaos of the Wars of the Roses. 'Now, in 2016,' he continues, 'that terror feels much closer. Town and country are divided, and so are . . . Scotland and England. There is nothing remote about Hotspur's rage on behalf of the neglected North, at "the jeering and disdained contempt" of the proud king. Falstaff, milking Gloucestershire for money and "continual laughter", is the incarnation of London's contempt for Middle England.'

Far back in the 1590s, working off his sources like a Hollywood scriptwriter, Shakespeare was dramatizing the pages of Holinshed and Thomas More, and his subject was explicitly monumental: a century of struggle for the English throne, the Tudor drama in which the young playwright found some of his best plots and most potent theatrical metaphors. From *Richard III* (1592/3) to *Henry V* (1599), his uncanny way with the English past sealed his grip on the hearts and minds of English audiences.

He became a master of fusing character with events, and of reflecting personality in the mirror of politics. It was More's *History of King Richard the Third* that first caught Shakespeare's eye. But, as he characterized the 'poisonous bunch-backed toad [1.3.244]', he also humanized his protagonist. In Thomas More's account, Richard is accursed, a parricide who broke all ties of kinship, like the figure of Vice in a morality play. As a loyal Tudor servant, More had no interest in an impartial history. He wanted to present a narrative of evil with the hunchback king as a secular Satan.

The young Shakespeare, however, seizing a dramatic opportunity, translated an ordinary chronicle play into a star vehicle for a great actor, initially Richard Burbage, the player with whom he loved to collaborate, unlocking the twisted humanity of a tragic reign. It was Shakespeare's inspiration to transform the king into a sinister comic performer, a character audiences will both love and loathe.

Shakespeare's independence of imagination is rarely

compromised, and his narrative method is always oblique: to fuse past and present into a continuous dramatic scene, with many strategic omissions. Each of these tragedies describes the wheel of history turning, to come full circle. A vision that's timeless becomes rich in unforgettable moments of astonishing intimacy.

In the histories, Shakespeare's kings and queens suffer the ebb and flow of power in the most heart-stopping, personal way. In *Richard III*, for instance, Shakespeare's language is often plain, blunt and devastating. Queen Margaret, 'the she-wolf', becomes one of his greatest historical characters:

I had an Edward, till a Richard killed him;
I had a husband, till a Richard killed him.
[*To Elizabeth*] Thou hadst an Edward, till a Richard
    killed him;
Thou hadst a Richard, till a Richard killed him.
[4.4.40–44]

Nor does the playwright mince words when describing Richard of Gloucester as an 'elvish-marked, abortive, rooting hog [1.3.225]'. Among his admirers at court, Shakespeare would soon become renowned as the high-flown poet of *Venus and Adonis*. Writing for the playhouse, he must find new ways into the hearts and minds of the groundlings. For instance, at an unforgettable moment – in Act Three of *Richard III* – when Shakespeare's monstrous protagonist plays with his subjects in cat-and-mouse suspense.

It's four in the morning. Peremptorily roused from sleep, Richard's council has been summoned to the Tower. None of those present – Hastings, Stanley, Buckingham, Norfolk, and the Bishop of Ely – has any idea what's happening or, a worse dread, any inkling of Richard's intentions. Their conversation is edgy and distracted:

> BUCKINGHAM: Who knows the Lord Protector's mind
>   herein?
> Who is most inward with the noble Duke?
> ELY: Your grace, we think, should soonest know his
>   mind.
> [3.4.7–9]

Whereupon Richard, the Lord Protector, Shakespeare's 'bottled spider', enters, saying nothing. The onstage tension is already at breaking point. What does Richard intend? In this terror-struck and breathless atmosphere, Richard turns to the Bishop of Ely. Borrowing from Thomas More, Shakespeare introduces a note of sinister geniality:

> RICHARD GLOUCESTER: My lord of Ely, when I was
>   last in Holborn
> I saw good strawberries in your garden there.
> I do beseech you send for some of them.
> [3.4.31–3]

From this mundane exchange ('I saw good straw-berries . . .'), the destruction of Hastings unfolds with relentless ferocity. And we, the audience, are in the room, with stageside seats. However grandly elevated the themes of the histories, Shakespeare never forgets that his plays are being enacted in front of ordinary Londoners on an afternoon's outing to the theatre, and that they must enlist the sympathies and anxieties of his audience: you and me.

3.

The records of the Shakespeare Club, maintained by our Archivist since 1999, are, he says, a record of 'every production the Club has seen, noting director, company and cast'. The Archivist interprets his role in his own way. If members of the Club go off-piste to attend a production outside the Club, he does not catalogue these attendances, though he might make 'a cursory note'. How best to explain the Club? We are creatures of our age, gender and class, no doubt; and clannish about our rituals. When my plans for *Shakespearean* were first announced, the Club's reaction was to form a confidential subcommittee to address the problem posed by this book. (I never heard a word of this until much later, when one of our number, teasing, suggested that a better title might be: *The Club*.)

As a collective, we are associates more than friends, and rarely meet beyond the shadows of the stalls or the hubbub of the bar. But we like each other and are harmonious as members of a group in which each of us has a role. First, there's our Novelist, the sole representative of the opposite sex, who functions as a mix of nanny, fairy godmother and muse, supplying vital insights into the feminine psyche. Next, there's our resident 'snapper-up of unconsidered trifles', the Journalist, on the alert for his next column. The Academic is our founder and show-runner, who likes to bring a copy of the play in question to study during the interval. Fourth, there's the Publisher, who provides warmth and good humour, and approaches the plays as a connoisseur, with a remarkable memory for cast lists and venues. Fifthly, the Scriptwriter, part West End, part Hollywood, contributes a frisson of theatrical savvy. Sixth, there's the faithful Archivist, on whom I have gratefully relied for the data recorded here. Finally, there's the Actor, who actually trained for the theatre but is no longer stage-struck. He follows our movements by email, and joins us intermittently, usually unimpressed by what he finds. His attitude to the Club hovers between despair and disbelief. I believe he thinks we are a comically inadequate group of middle-aged wannabes, and who's to say he's wrong?

The Club's dedication to Shakespeare has yielded many strange dividends. We must be among an eccentric minority who have attended a production of *Sir Thomas More*, the collaboration of the early 1590s to which Shakespeare probably contributed just one speech, lines about the rights of refugees that stand out from a heavily revised script with characteristic authority:

As but to banish you – whither would you go?
What country, by the nature of your error,
Should give you harbour? Go you to France or
    Flanders,
To any German prince, or Spain or Portugal,
Nay, anywhere that not adheres to England,
Why, you must needs be strangers.
[Lines 140–45]

Despite the obvious gulf between Tudor and twenty-first-century society, there are some curious but telling parallels between Elizabeth I's England and the Brexit Britain of Elizabeth II. With Walter Raleigh and the first colonizers, we share an appetite for global trade and adventure. We are also familiar with visceral and bloody clashes of religion. The barbarism of war between Protestants and Catholics may be over, but there's the same savage conflict of bitterly opposed faiths in the assault of Islamic fundamentalism on the West. Like Shakespeare's contemporaries, some of us live in an atmosphere of disabling anxiety.

Shakespeare's world connects with our world through commensurate emotions. The young Shakespeare may have been fascinated by kings and their courts, but he also began to address popular politics. It was here, exploring the 'mind' of the common people, that he began to become Shakespearean, testing another kind of modern hazard: popular passions, and the power of the mob.

As an Elizabethan, he was familiar with the fragility of the state, and its vulnerability to external threat or internal dissension. His contemporaries feared the Wars of the Roses as much as the Armada. In 1589–91 (the dates are disputed), soon after his arrival in London, a metropolis buzzing with obstreperous, polyglot energy, he began to address 'the nature of the times deceased' from the commoners' point of view. His first history play, *Henry VI*, seethes with the transgressive thrill of popular revolt, as well as the Machiavellian, psychopathic frenzy of Richard Gloucester:

I that have neither pity, love, nor fear.
Indeed, 'tis true that Henry told me of . . .
I have no brother, I am like no brother;
And this word, 'love', which greybeards call divine,
Be resident in men like one another

And not in me – I am myself alone.
[3 *Henry VI*, 5.5.69–84]

The threat of Richard's demonic ambition is one thing.
The frenzy of the mob is something else, but Shakespeare
treats it with a mix of laughter and dread. The grammar-
school boy from Stratford is nervous of popular disorder
among the illiterate classes, and uneasy about street protest,
but he seasons his account of Jack Cade's uprising with
flourishes of demotic humour.

In 2 *Henry VI*, his rebels are Anglo-Saxon yahoos to
their marrow. They want to trash metropolitan society and
terrorize the toffs (scrap learning, liberate the gaols, burn
books, and let the city conduits 'run nothing but wine').
'The first thing we do', declares an anonymous butcher,
in a famous line, 'let's kill all the lawyers [4.2.78].'

In Shakespeare, English protest becomes second cousin
to football hooliganism, some distance in ideology and
rhetoric from the barricades. The rabble-rouser in chief,
John ('Jack') Cade, a rebellious clothier, is less a pocket
Trotsky than a pub bore:

There shall be in England seven halfpenny loaves sold
for a penny, the three-hooped pot shall have ten hoops,
and I will make it felony to drink small beer. All the
realm shall be in common . . . and I will apparel them
all in one livery, that they may agree like brothers, and
worship me their lord.
[4.2.67–77]

Cade's followers are all too familiar – butchers, tanners,
weavers and brewers – from trades that Shakespeare lived

amongst in London. Two class-conscious rebels (Bevis and Holland) enter the scene whingeing about the 'threadbare' state of the commonwealth. Holland declares, 'Well, I say it was never merry world in England since gentlemen came up.' The two men spy some 'hard hands'.

> HOLLAND: I see them! I see them! There's Best's son, the tanner of Wingham—
> BEVIS: He shall have the skins of our enemies to make dog's leather of.
> HOLLAND: And Dick the butcher.
> [4.2.23–7]

At this moment, Shakespeare is not so far from a rowdy Saturday night on an English high street. His account of Cade's rebellion has an immediacy we recognize: it is philistine, anti-clerical, vicious, vulgar, and bullying. 'Dost thou use to write thy name?' demands Cade, interrogating Emmanuel, a hapless clerk cornered by the mob. 'Or hast thou a mark to thyself, like an honest plain-dealing man?' Fatally, the clerk answers, 'I thank God I have been so well brought up that I can write my name.'

> ALL: He hath confessed – away with him! He's a villain and a traitor.
> CADE: Away with him, I say, hang him with his pen and inkhorn about his neck.
> [4.2.101–9]

From such casual brutality, which will put the audience into the antechamber of their worst nightmares, it's a short step to a full-throated assault on those traitors who 'speak French'. Cade's vicious xenophobia strikes a deep chord of chauvinism among his Kentish followers. If 'the Frenchmen are our enemies' there can be only one logical conclusion:

CADE: Can he that speaks with the tongue of an enemy
    be a good counsellor, or no?
ALL: No, no – and therefore we'll have his head!
[4.2.168–72]

This crowd is different from the politically motivated plebeians of *Julius Caesar* (1599) or *Coriolanus* (1607–8). Cade's men are a 'rascal people, thirsting after prey [4.4.50]'; their motivation is a weird mix of the mercenary and the mindless; his followers have a peasant hatred of ink and paper. When their class enemy, Lord Saye, is finally cornered, Cade denounces him as 'filth' in resonant and topical abuse:

CADE: Thou hast most traitorously corrupted the youth
    of the realm in erecting a grammar school . . .
    appointed justices of the peace to call poor men
    before them about matters they were not able to
    answer.
[4.7.30–40]

When the doomed Lord Saye tries to defend himself with a desperate quip – ''tis *bona terra, mala gens*' – Cade's furious response is 'Away with him! Away with him! He speaks Latin [4.7.55].'

Later, in *Coriolanus*, Shakespeare would return in middle-age to the clash of the people with the state. For the moment, in these early histories, he connects the bleakest tragedy to the experience of humanity: the sub-ordination of ideology to human appetites becomes his Shakespearean message. By the time 3 *Henry VI* was packing audiences into the playhouse during 1591–2 (the dates are unclear), he was manipulating the narrative of history to his dramatic purposes, cutting and transposing sequences, revising and reimagining old scenes, but also coining speeches that went straight into the bloodstream of contemporary conversation. Shakespeare always had a great line in great lines. When Richard, Duke of York upbraids the indomitable Queen Margaret, he never spoke to better effect:

> O tiger's heart wrapped in a woman's hide!
> How couldst thou drain the life-blood of the child
> To bid the father wipe his eyes withal,
> And yet be seen to bear a woman's face?
> [1.4.138–41]

These were phrases that would haunt Shakespeare throughout the next decade of his London literary career, his polemical first appearance in the literary record as 'Shake-scene'.

Eight

'UPSTART CROW'

It was alway yet the trick of our English nation, if they
have a good thing, to make it too common.
2 Henry IV, 1.2.215

1.

Shakespeare's early life and work is replete with the many
mysteries that become an essential part of his provocation.
How, and when, as a young man, he first came to London,
and what exactly his relationship was with his fellow
playwrights, no one knows for certain. There's a blank
page in his curriculum vitae from 1585 to 1592 known
to scholars as the 'lost years'. Biographical guesswork only
kindles the fires of conspiracy theory. Was he, for instance,
a Catholic? The clues to any answer are ambiguous, and
leave a huge literature arguing the question both ways.

Setting aside speculations about his life as a young
player, the record shows the presence in Stratford of a
certain 'William Shakeshafte' in August 1581, followed on
27 November 1582 by his wedding to an older woman,
Anne Hathaway (mistakenly recorded as 'Anne Whateley').
After this marriage, there are two christenings: the baptism
of his first-born Susanna on 26 May 1583, and the baptism
of his twins Hamnet and Judith on 2 February 1585, when
he was still just twenty-one. Thereafter comes silence, until

1592, when he bursts onto the record as 'Shake-scene', the object of envious theatrical gossip. Where such intermittent dates are tangible evidence, much else depends on hints such as the shepherd's speech in *The Winter's Tale*:

> I would there were no age between ten and three-and-twenty, or that youth would sleep out the rest; for there is nothing in the between but getting wenches with child, wronging the ancientry, stealing, fighting. [3.3.58–62]

These teasing correlations between the life and the work have romanticized his Stratford years, blurring hearsay into myth. In *Nothing Like the Sun*, the novelist Anthony Burgess riffs on the poet's love life and the secret history of his desires:

> It was all a matter of a goddess – dark, hidden, deadly, horribly desirable . . . WS, stripling, in worn tight doublet, patched cloak, but gloves very new. Beardless, the down on his cheek gold in the sun, the hair auburn, the eyes a spaniel's eyes.

Shakespeare's youthful mind was also conditioned by the special circumstances in which he found himself as he moved away to London. At first, he was an ambitious provincial moving from the drowsy lullaby of the countryside to the mercenary uproar of the city. By the mid-1590s, as he made his way in the world, Shakespeare was living a bachelor life with lodgings in Bishopsgate, in the heart of the city, a short walk from the Curtain Theatre, close to the Clink, and next to St Helen's, a medieval church that now stands in the shadow of the Gherkin on St Mary Axe.

In this corner of Bishopsgate, Shakespeare's former neighbourhood is bounded by Leadenhall Street, and also by the A10, the old Cambridge road. Step into St Helen's, as I've done with the Shakespeare scholar-detective Geoff Marsh, and you pass through the looking-glass of many centuries into a hushed, tranquil world of cold stone floors, disembodied footfalls, echoing recesses, and mullioned windows, where sunlight filters through the faint greenish opacity of old church glass. It's very quiet here in what survives of the nave. Among the memorials to the dead, the hurly-burly of the city seems remote, and almost inaudible. Here, it's not difficult to imagine Shakespeare in a timeless setting, perhaps thumbing through a new translation from the classics, conversing with a lawyer, or scanning the proofs of a quarto edition of his latest play. (His Stratford contemporary, the printer Richard Field, had his press nearby in St Paul's Churchyard.)

To imagine Shakespeare here now, speaking a dialect of English we'd understand, a Warwickshire accent with burred 'r's, seems both natural and satisfying: in performance, his best lines come off the page as if uttered in passing conversation; his characters step from the stage to the street like men and women we could almost imagine meeting. Shakespeare himself wears the burden of his poetical and dramatic mind without fuss. Rarely in English literature has such a great writer seemed so approachable.

The tranquillity of St Helen's is another illusion. Beyond the echoing shadows of this parish lurked every sort of danger: drunken punch-ups, sword fights, stabbings, and the sinister imminence of plague. In this metropolitan milieu, Shakespeare's experience revolved around urban jeopardy, a universal theme. Opposition to the theatre, indeed, focused on its capacity to sponsor sex and violence. The pit was seen by its many Puritan enemies as little better than a shortcut to the brothel; backstage, the habitat of harlots and courtesans. Actors were considered to be debauched, hot-headed, impetuous and dangerous. As play-wrights, the young Marlowe, Jonson and Kyd (all caught up in street-fighting) were classed with vagabonds, pimps, and thieves.

Crime inspired a roguish vocabulary: varlet, cutpurse, ragamuffin, knave, hood, crook, ruffian, rascal, boor, lout, yob, rustic, larrikin, hooligan, scoundrel, hoodlum, villain, felon, thief, malefactor, thug, rowdy, brute, savage, outlaw, fiend, hellhound, butcher, desperado, etc. Shakespeare himself riffs on such lowlife synonyms in *Macbeth* when the tyrant commissions Banquo's murderers:

Ay, in the catalogue ye go for men,
As hounds and greyhounds, mongrels, spaniels, curs,
Shoughs, water-rugs, and demi-wolves are clept
All by the name of dogs.
[3.1.93–6]

Sex, and its traffic, inspired an equal vocabulary evoc-ative of universal desires: wench, squall, moll, dame, harlot, hackney, gown, vaulter, wagtail, hobbyhorse, flax-wench, squirrel, hussy, strumpet, tart, drab, stale, nun, trollop, trull, trot, punk, quean, doll, and so on. When Petruchio woos Kate in *The Taming of the Shrew*, Shakespeare marries country cadences with the sex of the city:

PETRUCHIO: Good morrow, Kate, for that's your name,
    I hear.
KATHERINE: They call me Katherine that do talk of
    me.
PETRUCHIO: You lie, in faith, for you are call'd plain
    Kate,
And bonny Kate, and sometimes Kate the curst;
But Kate, the prettiest Kate in Christendom,
Kate of Kate Hall, my super-dainty Kate –
For dainties are all cates, and therefore 'Kate' –
Take this of me, Kate of my consolation . . .
Myself am moved to woo thee for my wife.

Having traded insults such as 'ass' and 'wasp', their
intoxicating crosstalk slips towards bawdy backchat, a
favourite register:

PETRUCHIO: Who knows not where a wasp does wear
    his sting?
In his tail.
KATHERINE: In his tongue.
PETRUCHIO: Whose tongue?
KATHERINE: Yours, if you talk of tales, and so farewell.
PETRUCHIO: What, with my tongue in your tail? Nay,
    come again,
Good Kate, I am a gentleman.
KATHERINE: That I'll try.
[2.1.213–18]

Here, terminating their strange flirtation, she slaps him,
like any sensible Stratford girl.

2.

Whenever it was that Shakespeare first came to London, he would have stood apart from his contemporaries in the theatre. This glover's son from the Midlands, who had not been to college, was always an outsider. He sounded different, too. In his life of Christopher Marlowe, the biographer Park Honan notes that Shakespeare's voice was described (by Robert Greene) as 'nothing gratious', a sour comment on his Midlands accent. Marlowe, by contrast, had grown up with the clipped vowels of Kent, which contracted 'Medways Towne' to 'Maidstone'. While there's no record of any particular meeting, Marlowe would have recognized that this Will Shakespeare was something else: his imagination on fire, and possessed with a ruthless eye for a theatrical metaphor and a dramatic plot.

From the few surviving contemporary sightings, the new arrival seems to have been a pleasant, hard-working, modest fellow – 'sweet Will'. Contemporary directors such as Trevor Nunn and Nicholas Hytner report their sense of a man sitting at the back of the room, or to one side of a tavern, intently observing and listening. (Adrian Noble also wonders if he might have been a heavy drinker.) He certainly never sought to attract attention, preferred to avoid the limelight, and seems to have made only modest efforts to publish clean texts of his plays.

Compared to Ben Jonson, who launched his own complete works in 1616, Shakespeare was negligent in the administration of his *oeuvre*, and indifferent to the spelling of his name (which was rendered, variously, as 'Shakespere', 'Shaxberd' and 'Shagsper'). In the end, seven years after his death, it was two fellow actors who collected his play-scripts into a single volume. Every surviving detail of his early career only confirms his discreet singularity, his fanatical privacy, and his shadowy lack of ego.

In one crucial respect, however, he was at one with the metropolitan London that rattled through the streets around Bishopsgate and Shoreditch. He was an ambitious young man who had joined an extraordinarily vigorous, competitive and brilliant circle of playwrights, almost all of whom had been educated at Oxford or Cambridge. As well as enjoying the rare privilege of a classical education, Shakespeare's contemporaries were of an age: John Lyly (born 1554); Thomas Watson (1556); George Peele (1556); Thomas Kyd (1558); Christopher Marlowe (1564); Thomas Nashe (1567); and Robert Greene (1558), who graduated from Cambridge in 1583. By 1606, every one of these young men – an extraordinarily gifted generation of poets and playwrights – would be dead, some of them violently, with Shakespeare the outstanding survivor.

Among these university wits, the grammar-school boy from Stratford was, in Puck's words from *A Midsummer Night's Dream*, a 'hempen homespun [3.1.70]'. Where Shakespeare might recall 'Pillicock sat on Pillicock Hill' from childhood, the mind of a playwright such as Marlowe, educated in Cambridge, would more likely default in *Doctor Faustus* to 'Ha! *Stipendium peccati mors est.* The reward of sin is death: that's hard [5.2.66–8].' But Shakespeare was a quick study, and seems never to have been afraid to display his newly acquired learning. With Peele, he collaborated on *Titus Andronicus*, one of the most popular shows of its day, replete with the sickening horror relished by Elizabethan audiences. Later, he would exploit Thomas Lodge's romantic tale *Rosalynde* as the inspiration for *As You Like It*. Before that, when he sat down in 1593 to write *Venus and Adonis* he adopted the stanza used by Lodge in *Scylla's Metamorphosis*. Always competitive, with magpie instincts, he became, like the rogue Autolycus in *The Winter's Tale*, 'a snapper-up of unconsidered trifles [4.3.24]'.

Who knows, precisely, what these university men thought of Shakespeare and his light-fingered ways? Authorship was less sacrosanct and more collaborative. The concept of 'plagiarism' did not come into English usage until the 1620s, but unattributed borrowing is never popular, and in 1592 there was that explosion of malice – the first 'Shakespeare' reference in print – hinting at an undercurrent of resentment towards the clever young man from nowhere.

Robert Greene, author of *Pandosto* (1588), a leading light of the 1580s, had dominated literary London as a roistering egomaniac. In the face of fierce competition, however, he sank into obscurity, bitterness and ill health. By the age of thirty-two, he was dying in penury and squalor. At his death, Greene left some miscellaneous papers which, to the eye of the printer and minor contrarian Henry Chettle, contained some distinctly commercial jibes against some of his rivals, including the newcomer from Stratford-upon-Avon.

Chettle rushed these into print as *Greene's Groatsworth of Wit, Bought with a Million of Repentance*. The dying man's words were full of accusations: against himself (for neglecting his wife and son); against Marlowe (for his atheism); against some other actors (for competing with poets); and, most notoriously, against the anonymous player with the Midlands vowels who'd had the temerity to try his hand at playwriting:

There is an upstart Crow, beautified with our feathers, that with his *Tygers hart wrapt in a Players hyde*, supposes he is as well able to bombast out a blanke verse as the best of you: and being an absolute *Johannes factotum*, is in his owne conceit the onely Shake-scene in a countrey.

There could be little doubt whom Greene had in mind. His reference to 'his tiger's heart wrapped in a player's hide' is a jocular echo of that line from *3 Henry VI.* 'Jack of all trades' (*Johannes factotum*) was a typical sneer at a presumptuous provincial. But 'Shake-scene' nailed it. The toxic words of a dying man, resonating from beyond the grave, pierced Shakespeare like a malediction. Greene's barb went deep. When, in *Hamlet*, written nearly a decade later, Polonius reads out the prince's love letter to his daughter Ophelia, '"To the celestial and my soul's idol, the most beautified Ophelia",' he interrupts himself with a tetchy critique: 'That's an ill phrase, a vile phrase, "beautified" is a vile phrase [2.2.109–12].'

3.

In the short term, the wounded 'Shake-scene' had only one recourse. Exactly how or when is not known, but by the end of 1592 he had acquired a wealthy new patron, the Earl of Essex's protégé, Henry Wriothesley, Earl of Southampton, one of the richest young men in England, from whom he accepted a lucrative commission to write a long narrative poem based on the myth of Venus and Adonis in Ovid's *Metamorphoses*. At this juncture, with the playhouses closed by the plague, it was poetry, not plays, that would engage Shakespeare's imagination to capture another audience.

There was a further reason for Shakespeare to sequester himself from city life. Politics and the theatre were becoming more perilously intertwined than ever. His associate Christopher Marlowe, in particular, had become seriously mixed up with Elizabethan espionage. In a paranoid age of plotting, Shakespeare was familiar with this dangerous world, and makes his own coded commentary on Walsingham, the queen's spymaster, in *Troilus and Cressida*, through the pregnant words of Ulysses, the chilliest of political pragmatists:

> The providence that's in a watchful state
> Knows almost every grain of Pluto's gold,
> Finds bottom in th'uncomprehensive deeps,
> Keeps place with aught, and almost like the gods
> Do infant thoughts unveil in their dumb cradles.
> There is a mystery, with whom relation
> Durst never meddle, in the soul of state,
> Which hath an operation more divine
> Than breath or pen can give expressure to.
> [3.3.189–97]

Shakespeare is always notable for his intuitions about our covert selves. These edgy lines indicate something equally remarkable: a familiarity with the operation of the secret state. But from whom did he acquire this? From his contemporary, the playwright who was also a government agent? The speculation that Shakespeare heard about espionage from Christopher Marlowe opens another door into the shadowy interior of their puzzling relationship.

In the new year of 1592, Marlowe had been operating out of the Dutch seaport of Vlissingen (Flushing). Towards the end of January he was arrested, but seems to have escaped significant retribution. By the early summer of 1592, he was back on the streets of Shoreditch. Little is known of Marlowe's activities for the rest of that year. In 1593, in the company of another poet – both of them, according to one historian, 'bit-players in the same complex and rather pointless intelligence game' – he appears to have joined some 'men of quality' on a mission to visit James VI of Scotland, apparently meddling in the highly sensitive area of the royal succession. According to the playwright Thomas Kyd, with whom Marlowe had shared lodgings, he was now mixed up with a certain Robert Poley, another Elizabethan spy.

Nine

'DEAD SHEPHERD'

> When a man's verses cannot be understood, nor a
> man's good wit seconded with the forward child,
> understanding, it strikes a man more dead than a
> great reckoning in a little room.
> *As You Like It, 3.3.9*

1.

The haunting, strange, and tragic tale of Marlowe and
Shakespeare, which animates and darkens *Shakespeare in
Love* (1999), introduces yet another dimension to the
fascination of their beginnings as poets and playwrights
who shared provincial origins, the one from Canterbury,
the other from Stratford. Marlowe occupied a place in
Shakespeare's life that was a mix of mentor, contemporary,
sometime collaborator, and competitor. For T. S. Eliot,
centuries later, they were the only game in town. Comparing
their gifts, he wrote:

> The whole of Shakespeare's work is *one* poem; and it
> is the poetry of it in this sense, not the poetry of isolated
> lines and passages or the poetry of the single figures
> which he created, that matters most. A man might,
> hypothetically, compose any number of fine passages
> or even of whole poems which would each give

satisfaction, and yet not be a great poet, unless we felt them to be united by one significant, consistent, and developing personality. Shakespeare is the one, among all his contemporaries, who fulfils these conditions; and the nearest to him is Marlowe.

Despite a frustrating absence of hard evidence, there's no doubt that, in their mid- to late-twenties, the two men would have known each other as associates of the Lord Strange's Men. Each, in his own way, was drawn to varieties of risk – Shakespeare in theatre; Marlowe in politics. Their early years were never less than dramatic. One would survive and prosper; the other became a figure of immediate renown, the subject of awestruck thespian gossip, especially in Cambridge where a student satire, the *Parnassus Plays*, describes him as a writer with 'wit sent from heaven, but vices sent from hell'.

Christopher ('Kit') Marlowe had grown up as the son of a shoemaker, attending the local school, much as Shakespeare had done. But Canterbury was a different kind of provincial town. Ever since the murder of Thomas à Becket in its great cathedral, it had become one of the most famous shrines in Christendom, a city of massacre and miracles. This was Marlowe's creative inheritance.

A young man of ambition, he had made his way with a scholarship to Corpus Christi College, Cambridge, where he received his bachelor's degree in 1584. By the age of twenty-one, where Shakespeare was married with a family, Marlowe had embarked on a dangerous, high-flying career in Cambridge and London. In 1587, the Privy Council noted with approval that 'in all his actions [Marlowe] had behaved him selfe orderlie and discreetelie wherebie he had done her majestie good service'. In other words, he had become a government agent.

The outstanding difference between these two young writers was in reputation. While Shakespeare was putting 'upstart crow' behind him, Marlowe was recklessly smoking, drinking and uttering risky thoughts ('only fools like not boys and tobacco'), or blaspheming dangerously (Christ was a pervert who enjoyed acts of sodomy with his beloved disciple John). Some of these provocations may have been inspired by the 'School of Night', a clandestine coterie centred on Sir Walter Raleigh. Despite, or perhaps because of, these transgressive instincts, by 1588, the year of the Armada, Marlowe had become the metropolitan star.

Tamburlaine the Great (1587) swept Elizabethan audiences off their feet, and set English tragedy on a new path that inspired a generation. Marlowe seems to have known what he was doing. From his first line, he assertively separates himself from the 'clownage' of the herd:

> From jigging veins of rhyming mother-wits
> And such conceits as clownage keeps in pay,
> We'll lead you to the stately tent of war,
> Where you shall hear the Scythian Tamburlaine
> Threatening the world with high astounding terms,
> And scourging kingdoms with his conquering sword.
> [*Tamburlaine the Great, Part 1*, Prologue.1–6]

The first performances of *Tamburlaine* transformed English theatre, and introduced a stage-struck audience to the rhetorical protagonist whose 'mighty line' would dominate the playhouses for a decade and more:

Nature that framed us of four elements,
Warring within our breasts for regiment,
Doth teach us all to have aspiring minds . . .
Until we reach the ripest fruit of all, . . .
That perfect bliss and sole felicity,
The sweet fruition of an earthly crown.
[*Part 1*, 2.7.18–29]

The majestic beat of Marlowe's blank verse – its variations of pace and rhythm; its splendid colour and movement; its infectious command of classical imagery – had a sonorous energy that was something quite new:

Awake, ye men of Memphis! Hear the clang
Of Scythian trumpets; hear the basilisks,
That, roaring, shake Damascus' turrets down!
[*Part 1*, 4.1.1–3]

It was not all bombast. In retrospect, Marlowe stands out as a rhetorical more than a dramatic genius: his thunderous stage poetry gave his heirs a wonderful vehicle of expression:

Holla, ye pampered jades of Asia!
What, can ye draw but twenty miles a day,
And have so proud a chariot at your heels,
And such a coachman as great Tamburlaine.
[*Tamburlaine the Great, Part 2*, 4.3.1–4]

No writer competing for a popular London audience could ignore this kind of verse. There were passages in *Tamburlaine* and, most especially, *Doctor Faustus* (1592), that would pass into literary folklore:

'Dead Shepherd'

Was this the face that launched a thousand ships
And burnt the topless towers of Ilium?
Sweet Helen, make me immortal with a kiss.
Her lips suck forth my soul: see where it flies.
Come, Helen, come, give me my soul again.
[*Doctor Faustus*, 5.1.97–101]

Marlowe, the greatest playwright of the Elizabethan stage; Marlowe, the sophisticated, university-educated poet, well-versed in classical mythology with an easy command of Latin and Greek; and Marlowe the brawling free-thinker, approached the challenge of drama as if it was a kind of opera, detached from reality. In *Tamburlaine the Great*, his tragic hero is a narcissistic, dominant, loquacious figure brimming with gorgeous poetry but rather deficient in humanity.

On stage, Marlowe's puppets do not readily relate to the other characters around them. Their speeches are what Covent Garden knows as 'park and bark': static arias of great power and beauty somewhat tenuously related to the action. *Tamburlaine* is highly episodic. Even when the 'Scythian shepherd' utters his most famous lines, he does not evoke much sympathy:

What is beauty, saith my sufferings, then?
If all the pens that ever poets held
Had fed the feeling of their masters' thoughts,
And every sweetness that inspired their hearts,
Their minds, and muses on admired themes . . .
[*Tamburlaine the Great, Part 1*, 5.2.97–110]

Scene for scene, a Marlowe script is quite unlike
Shakespeare's more humane grasp of theatrical reality, and
always subordinates stagecraft to soaring flights of poetry:

> Now walk the angels on the walls of heaven,
> As sentinels to warn the immortal souls
> To entertain divine Zenocrate.
> [*Tamburlaine the Great, Part 2*, 2.4.15–17]

Nonetheless, during 1591–3, Marlowe was the greater
star. In the words of the Shakespeare scholar Stanley Wells,
'If Shakespeare had died when Marlowe did, we should
now regard Marlowe as the greater writer.'

2.

Eventually, the whirligig of time would transform the
balance of power. In the early 1590s, however, Shakespeare
was the late starter. In his early years – as Greene's jibe
implied – Shakespeare had paid Marlowe the sincere flat-
tery of imitation. After Marlowe wrote *The Jew of Malta*
(in 1589), his rival would follow in 1596 with *The
Merchant of Venice*. When Marlowe embarked on a new
and highly original history play, *Edward II*, in 1592,
Shakespeare answered with *Richard II* in 1595. There's
also the strong suggestion that Marlowe collaborated with
Shakespeare on part of his first history play, *Henry VI*.

So far as we know, Marlowe and Shakespeare seem to
have nurtured a mutual respect through their association
with London's playhouses. In the summer of 1592, however,
Shakespeare was up against it, and perilously close to the
dangerous edge. There was an outbreak of mob violence
in Southwark that alarmed the government. Lord Burghley,

the queen's first minister, took this opportunity to impose new restrictions on London's theatres, an immediate blow to Shakespeare's livelihood. Soon after this, the 'ragingest fury' of bubonic plague struck the city, and the death toll began to rise. The authorities shut down every place of public assembly, including all the playhouses.

Just as Shakespeare faced financial exigency, he received that heaven-sent commission from the Earl of Southampton. From 1592–3, he was at liberty to live away from London. With *Venus and Adonis* (1593), followed by *The Rape of Lucrece* (1594), he began to strike out on his own. The dedication of *Lucrece* suggests an intimacy with his young patron that possibly explains this new pitch of creativity: 'The love I dedicate to your lordship is without end; whereof this pamphlet without beginning is but a superfluous moiety . . . What I have done is yours; what I have to do is yours; being part in all I have, devoted yours . . .' Soon after this, he secured Southampton's commission to compose some sonnets that would bring life and art together, placing Shakespeare the poet at the heart of his own creative endeavours, perhaps for the first time.

Marlowe's career was also reaching its fateful climax. In May 1593, a sequence of events began to unfold that drove his short life to extinction. The former Cambridge scholar was arrested on suspicion of dangerous religious opinions (his fellow dramatist Thomas Kyd, already in prison, had informed against him), but was not charged. He was, however, required to report daily to the Privy Council. Whatever the circumstances, we know that on 30 May Marlowe travelled down to Deptford to meet Robert Poley and two other men, at the home of Mistress Eleanor Bull, a widow. At the end of the day, an argument broke out, and there was a fight in which the playwright was stabbed in the eye. Now – whatever their cause – the plots, the sinister interrogations, and the government machinations no longer mattered. Christopher Marlowe was dead.

For two days his body lay in the local church awaiting an inquest, which was held on 1 June. It's an irony that, whereas so much about Shakespeare and his circle has been lost in the fog of the past, and whereas so many mysteries surround the life and work of Marlowe (even the dates in the stained glass of his memorial window in Westminster Abbey are qualified with a ?), the official account of his death is detailed and, apparently, beyond dispute, 'one of the best recorded episodes in English literary history'.

The inquest reports that four men – Marlowe and Poley, Ingram Frizer and Nicholas Skeres – had met at Mistress Bull's house on Deptford Strand. They'd spent the morning in conversation, then had lunch, smoked pipes, and afterwards taken a walk, before relaxing in the garden. At six o'clock – the spring day cooling – they had come indoors to have supper, after which an argument broke out about the 'sum of pence owed' for the day's expenses. This row about what the inquest called the 'recknynge' (the reckoning, or the bill) got out of hand. Marlowe, 'moved with anger', was said to have struck one of his fellows, who in self-defence stabbed his assailant with a dagger above the right eye, piercing the skull of the playwright, who 'then and there instantly died'. The coroner and his jurors visited the scene of the crime, viewed the body, and swiftly decided that Ingram Frizer had killed Marlowe 'in the defence and saving of his own life'. Who will ever know what darkness this opaque, bland phrase conceals?

Where and when Shakespeare heard the news is not known either. But it set off a complicated chain of reflections, a confusion of horror, grief, excitement, dismay, and ambition. It is hard to overestimate the significance of this moment. Marlowe was the outstanding English poet and playwright of the age. Shakespeare had grown up in his shadow, though perhaps the balance of creative power was beginning to shift in his favour. At his death, Marlowe left his uncompleted masterpiece *Hero and Leander*, a posthumous tribute to *Venus and Adonis*. If he had lived, who can say where this rivalry might not have taken these two young poets? After May 1593, however, one thing was beyond question: Shakespeare stood alone. Now he was free to become himself, fulfil his gifts, and become Shakespearean.

3.

The shock of Marlowe's violent death shuddered through the literary world. Tributes to the dead man resounded within a close-knit community. No one was quicker into print than Thomas Nashe, the author of *Isle of Dogs*, another Cambridge 'scholar', younger than Marlowe, but in awe of his reputation. In *The Unfortunate Traveller*, his latest fable, he saluted the news of Marlowe's killing with an epitaph to 'one of the wittiest knaves that ever God made'. Nashe was not only sure of Marlowe's greatness – it was his gift, he wrote, 'to set on fire all his readers'. In words later echoed by Ben Jonson to describe Shakespeare's genius, Nashe declared that Marlowe's mind and pen were as one: 'what they thought they would confidently utter'. For Nashe, it was this independence of mind that made him the greatest of English writers:

'His life he contemned in comparison of the liberty of speech.'

But now that voice was silent, and this irruption of violence haunted Shakespeare, who would obsess on the loss of his rival for years after. In *Richard II*, the king confronts himself in a mirror while repeating one of Marlowe's most celebrated lines in a cadenza of homage:

Was this face the face
That every day under his household roof
Did keep ten thousand men? Was this the face
That like the sun did make beholders wink?
Was this the face which faced so many follies,
That was at last outfaced by Bolingbroke?
[4.1.271–6]

Both *Romeo and Juliet* and *A Midsummer Night's Dream*, written soon after Marlowe's death, have passages with oblique echoes of the dead man's style. Some have even seen Prospero in *The Tempest* as a bookish magus inspired by the memory of Marlowe. At the turn of the century, when Shakespeare sat down to write *As You Like It*, the figure of Marlowe infiltrated his lines like a spectre. His work had echoed Marlowe before (notably in *2 Henry IV*, where Pistol reminds the audience of *Tamburlaine the Great* with his mangled 'hollow pampered jades of Asia') but now Shakespeare, addressing him directly, made an explicit nod to *Hero and Leander*, and Marlowe's memory, during a scene in the Forest of Arden. 'Dead shepherd,' says Phoebe, the haughty shepherdess, 'now I find thy saw of might: "Who ever loved, that loved not at first sight?" [3.5.82–3]' For Shakespeare, this pastoral expression of raw sorrow is the only occasion throughout his plays when, as Charles Nicholl observes, 'he quotes and acknowledges – rather than quietly borrowing – a line by a contemporary author'.

Shakespeare had not quite finished with coded tributes to the memory of his 'dead shepherd', planting another valedictory allusion deep in the Forest of Arden, the green-wood where men and women can be free and true to themselves. Expressing his feelings in a double code, at once oblique and classical, he puts his most elegiac words into the mouth of Touchstone, the exiled duke's court jester. Competing with Jacques, the sad-eyed satirist of human vanity, for whom 'all the world's a stage', Touchstone, clownishly comparing himself to Ovid, starts to ramble about the poet's exile among the barbarians of Tomis on the Black Sea:

> When a man's verses cannot be understood, nor a man's good wit seconded with the forward child, understanding, it strikes a man more dead than a great reckoning in a little room. [3.3.9–12]

Marlowe's violent end was a shocking and tragic loss, but it yielded a creative dividend: among his circle, this 'great reckoning' sponsored a sharpened awareness of fate, youth and mortality, the transience of fame, and the primacy of poetry. The well-springs of the human imagin-ation and the source of new ideas must always be mysterious, but it was now that Shakespeare began to become more like himself, with a new maturity that also derived from his appointment as a shareholder, a 'joint payee', of the Lord Chamberlain's Men in March 1595.

A stage is one thing, a library something else. The actor's spoken word is truant, and free; the playwright's script a loaded weapon. The 1590s became the decade in which Shakespeare explored his bisexual self in poetry and his dramatic self on the stage, revelling in the cross-fertilization of character, ideas, and images. A succession of youthful masterpieces – a hot streak without parallel on the English stage – followed Marlowe's murder: *Love's Labour's Lost* (1594–5); *Romeo and Juliet* (1595); *A Midsummer Night's Dream* (1595/6); *Richard II* (1595/6); *The Merchant of Venice* (1596–7); the two parts of *Henry IV* (1596–8); *Julius Caesar* (1599); culminating in *As You Like It* (1599). Remarkably, Shakespeare seemed to be able to switch from genre to genre, becoming 'historical', 'pastoral' or 'comical' as it suited. These are plays that become the groundwork for what would follow in the coming century. They embody the cultural, emotional and intellectual history of the nation, but their afterlife as modern plays has little to do with that national story. They survive and flourish as archetypal human dramas – Oedipal, cathartic, primal and theatrical.

With so much of his writing expressed in performance, the urgent dichotomy of speech and paper became an obsession with Shakespeare in a way that resounds through our modern imagination. After Marlowe's death, Shakespeare turned to the sonnet as a form in which he could both express and disguise himself.

4.

In hindsight, 1593 – Shakespeare's thirtieth year – was a career milestone to match 1599, his more celebrated *annus mirabilis*. Politically and socially, these were uneasy times, a decade in which the Elizabethan state fell into a profound mood of institutional paranoia directed towards English Catholics. These apprehensions, and an associated air of danger, began at court. Elizabeth was old and increasingly impossible; the vexed succession question was still unresolved; and the Earl of Essex a constant threat. Walsingham's agents were everywhere. The weather was terrible, and the economy was afflicted by rampant inflation. To cap it all, the threat of plague became a full-blown terror, sweeping through London in 1592–3, and again in 1603, when more than one-quarter of London's population was wiped out. In the spring of 2020, traumatized by Covid-19, modern Shakespeare audiences began, for the first time, to make a contemporary connection with the Elizabethan experience of plague.

Thomas Dekker, a Shakespeare collaborator, and author of *The Wonderful Year*, describes the 'unmatchable torment' of the plague victim, incarcerated at home ('a vast silent charnel-house') to prevent the spread of infection, with lamps 'burning in hollow and glimmering corners . . . About him a thousand corpses . . . filling his nostrils with noisome stench . . .' A terror he compares to 'an infernal prison'.

In Bishopsgate, the young Shakespeare, in the thick of such quotidian danger, was writing about matters of love and hate, or life and death. There was also, as an additional spur to his imagination, a new company of players setting up at the Theatre on Curtain Road in Shoreditch. These soon became the Lord Chamberlain's Men (eventually the King's Men). Shakespeare was responding to their patronage, too. With that 'shepherd', his theatrical sparring partner, lost to senseless violence, Shakespeare was no longer the 'upstart crow', and would

soon become singled out for greatness, compared with
the classical masters. At a personal level, there's every
indication that he mourned Kit Marlowe with a sadness
that lingered out the century. In *Shakespeare in Love*,
another rendering of a 'Shakespearean' sensibility, Tom
Stoppard extracts both comic and serious entertainment
from his cinematic version of Marlowe and Shakespeare's
creative rivalry. In the film, 'Will' is portrayed as
distraught, guilt-stricken and finally contrite.

Just before Marlowe's death, Shakespeare had seen
Venus and Adonis off the press in an edition published by
the printer Richard Field. In English poetry, this was something new and original, a radical reimagining of classical
myth. Rather than simply retelling a page from the
Metamorphoses in conventional verse, Shakespeare extends
Ovid's thirty-odd lines to an exquisite 1,194 lines, simultaneously dramatizing the story and composing long
passages in dialogue, which treated a poetic subject *as if
it were a play*, where Venus and her lover are exposed to
dramatic confrontations expressed in sustained, almost
operatic similes:

> Now was she just before him as he sat,
> And like a lowly lover down she kneels;
> With one fair hand she heaveth up his hat;
> Her other tender hand his fair cheek feels.
> His tend'rer cheek receives her soft hand's print
> As apt as new fall'n snow takes any dint.
> [*Venus and Adonis*, 349–54]

Shakespeare's readers can see at once that he has found
fresh artistic satisfaction in an exclusively lyrical kind of

self-expression. This poem becomes less a traditional story of violation (Ovid's version), more a playful and highly modern study of sexual frustration, the transience of youthful beauty, and the anguish of erotic obsession. This, 'the first heir of my invention', published in 1593, was reprinted in 1594, 1595, 1596, 1599, 1602 (three times), and 1617.

By some margin Shakespeare's most successful work in print, *Venus and Adonis* was a comprehensive and persuasive riposte to Greene's accusations of plagiarism. Many late-Elizabethan readers were dazzled. Field's edition rapidly became a word-of-mouth sensation, a bestseller. Perhaps it was the success of *Venus and Adonis*, combined with the Earl of Southampton's patronage, and the need to escape the oppressive dangers of the city, that took Shakespeare back to the country. Here, he could work alone and undisturbed. For the next few years, he was writing and circulating many of the verses that would eventually become collected into the single most famous and influential volume of poetry in the English language.

PART THREE, 1594–1599:

'Words, Words, Words'

How Shakespeare became 'Shake-speare' after Marlowe's death: the dialogue of history, art and life in his poetry and plays.

Ten

'SIN OF SELF-LOVE'

Adieu, valour; rust, rapier; be still, drum: for your
manager is in love; yea, he loveth. Assist me, some
extemporal god of rhyme, for I am sure I shall turn
sonnet. Devise wit: write pen, for I am for whole
volumes, in folio.

Love's Labour's Lost, 1.2.173

1.

Shakespeare is the greatest writer in the English language,
possibly in any language – to most a genius; to some a
god – yet the trajectory of his life and work follows the
path of many less exalted literary artists: implausible as
this might sound, after a career in the world of print – at
the publishers Faber & Faber, and then at *The Observer*,
there's a pattern I can relate to here. In the first instance,
there's that tipping point of creativity, the moment when
the alchemy of risk and originality begins to catch on with
audiences. After an intimacy with book publishing, I know
how, like hearing a great new melody for the first time,
the unique timbre of an original voice – the thrill of the
new – is always a moment of magic.

Similarly, for the Shakespeare Club, the frisson of some
new productions is not always found in the staging, but
rather in hearing familiar lines as if for the first time. Ian

McKellen's *King Lear* of 2007, for instance, electrified the opening scene with sinister majesty in his delivery of 'Give me the map there [1.1.37].' From those first five mono-syllables, the audience knew we were heading into an abyss of madness.

King Lear comes late in Shakespeare's work. It helps to recognize the precise nature of his achievement during those crucial years before 1599. The seeds of a dramatic, even a cultural revolution had been planted from 1587, partly by Marlowe. With hindsight, what happened as Shakespeare became increasingly Shakespearean was not simply a biographical transit, more a social and cultural paradigm shift. The playwright was blazing new trails, mapping new frontiers of drama, and making discoveries of immense significance.

After this came artistic consolidation: here, too, he takes a route that would be followed by many subsequent English, American, and Irish literary masters, from Pope, Swift, Melville and Twain, to Conrad, Eliot, Beckett, Joyce, and Lawrence. In a very English way, he became a play-wright for his people.

Shakespeare's theatre was raucous, bawdy, and above all, popular. The playhouse was sweaty, noisy, crowded, and, as Peter Brook puts it, 'rough', an essential part of his apprenticeship. Shakespeare had seen mystery plays enacted on carts and trestles in the open air. From instinct and experience, he understood those audiences who knew little about theatre, but who, when they attended one of his plays, liked what they found. He articulated a concept of existence, rooted in humanity, that embraced values we live with today. After Shakespeare, as barriers between high art and the low culture were swept away, the world of drama became progressively more modern, accessible and popular. It's a short step from *Hamlet* and *King Lear* to Samuel Beckett. When Hamlet falls into crosstalk with Polonius, it becomes an out-take from *Godot*.

'Do you see yonder cloud,' asks the prince, teasing the self-important courtier, 'that's almost in shape of a camel?' Polonius has to agree: ''Tis: like a camel, indeed.' Hamlet, tormenting him, contradicts: 'Methinks it is like a weasel.'

> POLONIUS: It is backed like a weasel.
> HAMLET: Or like a whale.
> [*Hamlet*, 3.2.365–70]

Polonius, outwitted, concedes: 'Very like a whale,' a line that conscripts the king's counsellor to the madhouse.

Momentous change was in the air. Within a decade, culture and society would never be the same. After the 1590s, the Western world was about to enter a period of convulsion, from the European crisis of the Thirty Years War (1618–48) to the English Civil War and the subsequent Commonwealth. Analysing such changes in contemporary art, the critic Arthur Danto has described the interpretative concept of 'mandate and breakthrough'. For Shakespeare, the mandate was: 'tell us who we are', followed by the breakthrough: 'give us insights into what we think and feel'.

During these breakthrough years, Shakespeare seized on every aspect of contemporary drama, to challenge and inter-rogate it. Where Marlowe's plays had become a vehicle for high-flown speeches, Shakespeare mobilized the vernacular. Where Elizabethan works of dramatic tragedy were often a series of tableaux, Shakespeare's plays were mobile and fluid. Where once they had been all about kings and queens,

Shakespeare democratized the action. Conversely, when drama was seen as inferior to poetry, Shakespeare put poetry into his plays, while also transforming a poem like *Venus and Adonis* into a thrilling kind of dramatic experience. Finally – most radical of all – a play was supposed to observe 'the unities' (of time and place) with an intelligible, coherent plot. But Shakespeare would turn such considerations on their head. And he did this without the 'Look, Mum, I'm dancing' of literary celebrities like Ben Jonson. Indeed, Shakespeare, the outsider from Stratford, was almost wilfully discreet. While his country sank deeper into the darkness of state terror, he celebrated creative renewal through the consolations of his art, and its fascinating opacity.

By the end of the sixteenth century, Shakespeare was fully immersed in a parallel universe: the London stage. His mid-season life as a poet and playwright is one of 'self' interleaved with 'words, words, words' – a line of Hamlet's he varied, just once, in *Troilus and Cressida* [5.3.111], with 'words, words, mere words'. In this, he was following every writer's first impulse: placing himself at the heart of his creative energy. His life now was one of unremitting hard work punctuated with interludes of tranquillity, a pattern attributable to the plague.

The plays written soon after the death of Marlowe have an infectious energy, alive with passionate and exuberant characters – Romeo, Mercutio, Juliet, Rosalind, and Prince Hal – who mirror the playwright's youth. At the same time, they exhibit a growing maturity. In the case of a king such as Richard II, the assassin Brutus, or even a buffoon such as Falstaff, these individuals begin to acquire the deeper qualities of introspection, conscience, and self-doubt that make them so appealing to modern audiences. In the

1590s, this was avant-garde. Richard II's soliloquies are partly inspired by Marlowe's *Edward II* (1592), but they also represent something absolutely new in the playhouse, an internalized dramatic narrative:

> My brain I'll prove the female to my soul,
> My soul the father, and these two beget
> A generation of still-breeding thoughts;
> And these same thoughts people this little world
> In humours like the people of this world,
> For no thought is contented.
> [*Richard II*, 5.5.6–11]

Such introspection will become the hallmark of the great roles in Shakespeare's Jacobean tragedies, during those breakthrough years of artistic consolidation: *Othello* (1604); *King Lear* (1605); *Macbeth* (1606); and *Coriolanus* (1608).

After the 1590s, Shakespeare's art matures at speed. He discovered that, in the marriage of risk and creativity, language comes under pressure to provide tempting and deniable ambiguities. Such subtleties, the currency of the age, still provoke the curiosity of modern audiences. In 'How we weep and laugh for the same thing', Shakespeare's contemporary, the essayist Montaigne, who had such an important influence on his imagination, was exploring an insight that speaks directly to the playwright's obsessions. To understand the complex contradictions of emotion, says Montaigne, helps us avoid trivial interpretations of humanity: 'we ought to consider when judging such events how our souls are often shaken by conflicting emotions. Even as there is said to be a variety of humours assembled in our bodies . . . so too in our souls.'

Shakespeare's mature 'self', which seems always to have been ambiguously divided between 'a variety of humours', exemplifies F. Scott Fitzgerald's modern definition of a first-rate intelligence: an ability 'to hold two opposed ideas in the mind at the same time, and still retain the ability to function'. As a successful playwright, Shakespeare now exploited his binary nature to find new meaning in the poetry he wrote for his aristocratic patron, as well as the local, but lower, esteem of theatrical fame.

Possibly during 1592–4, with London at the mercy of the latest epidemic, and the playhouses closed, Shakespeare may have begun seriously to engage with writing sonnets. But first, as a kind of warm-up, he completed *The Rape of Lucrece*. In this long poem, twinned with *Venus and Adonis*, but darker in subject and tone, Shakespeare explores themes that would come to fruition in *Measure for Measure*. The poem interrogates the consciousness of Tarquin, the sexual predator, but it also identifies with Lucrece, the victim, who commits suicide after failing, in a 'helpless smoke of words', to come to terms with her anguish. Here again, Shakespeare was focusing on the 'inward mind'.

2.

While *Venus and Adonis* and *The Rape of Lucrece* made Shakespeare respectable in a way that renown as a play-wright never could, it was the sonnets that set him apart from the competition. If, after their publication in 1609, Shakespeare had never written another line, these sonnets would have guaranteed his immortality as the finest lyric poet of his generation. Well-informed readers sometimes ask of great writers: who first recognized their genius? No one discovered Shakespeare; Shakespeare discovered himself.

'The Sonnets', writes the poet and critic Don Paterson in his tour de force, *Reading Shakespeare's Sonnets*, 'have been awarded the ultimate accolade human culture can bestow: proverbialism.' Nothing that he ever wrote thereafter, including *Hamlet*, has been so bedevilled by so much passionate, at times demented, exegesis. Once 'a Shakespeare sonnet' became synonymous in the public mind with 'a love poem', it was a short step for his work as a whole to become 'Shakespearean'.

In the beginning, these verses were a well-kept secret, to be shared with his patron and an inner circle that included the Earl of Essex. When the cleric Francis Meres refers to them in 1598, in his commonplace book *Palladis Tamia* – 'The sweet, witty soul of Ovid lives in mellifluous and honey-tongued Shakespeare, witness his *Venus & Adonis* . . . his sugared Sonnets among his private friends, etc.' – they are still a word-of-mouth phenomenon for elite literary circles. At this moment, as best he was able, Shakespeare kept his sonnets to himself. A few years later, they would become pirated.

From the first, Shakespeare set out to transform the sonnet into something hitherto unknown. At number 18, having found his voice, Shakespeare the poet appears to be in love with a young man. For the next one hundred sonnets, approximately, the reader follows the up-and-down progress of this love affair. After that, there's a shift. Sonnets 126–52 are addressed to the poet's mistress, the 'dark lady'. Aside from this fashionable sexual ambivalence, what's notable here is something new and original: Shakespeare's daring discovery of 'the self'. Among his first sonnets, numbers 3, 4, 6, 7, 10, 13, 14, and 16 make specific allusions to some version of the 'self' (number 10 does this twice, in fact). Shakespeare was exploring a new kind of identity, hinting at autobiography in the deniable way he prefers. There is something teasing and theatrical about his love triangles:

Take all my loves, my love, yea, take them all:
What hast thou then more than thou hadst before?
No love, my love, that thou mayst true love call –
All mine was thine before thou hadst this more.
[Sonnet 40, 1–4]

The slippery 'Will' of the sonnets perfectly captures Shakespeare's instincts as an artist. Even the form itself, both coded and stagey, with its frisson of self-exposure, mirrored his preference for a visible invisibility. And throughout, there's no respite from this Will's delirious punning:

Whoever hath her wish, thou hast thy Will,
And Will to boot, and Will in overplus . . .
So thou, being rich in Will, add to thy Will
One will of thine, to make thy large Will more.
[Sonnet 135]

Is he, or is he not, the poet of these sonnets? Is he homo- or hetero- or bisexual? We will never know for sure: ambiguity is his strikingly modern default position. Besides, he is finding, in the 'self', fertile territory for a covert drama of identity. Shakespeare's engagement with his 'self' in the sonnets was risky and innovative, but that was his first instinct. It would only be a matter of time before this celebration of inwardness found its way before the popular mass audience that was the polar opposite of Southampton and his friends.

The delicious, secret intimacy of the sonnet lacked the gratification of the public utterance. The mature Shakespeare's connection to his audience would focus on the articulate voice. For now, Southampton's patronage was fulfilment enough, but he could never shake off the tug of the theatre. It was in performance that his actors gave meaning to those 'fire-new words'. Once the playhouses reopened, Shakespeare was released from sequestration (what we know as 'lockdown') as Southampton's house poet to embark on a succession of youthful masterpieces, culminating in *As You Like It* and *Hamlet*.

3.

While Shakespeare worked on his sonnets, and in an equally intimate but less contemplative mode, he was also exploring the dramatic potential of sex and violence in an archetypal love story. Actually, *Romeo and Juliet* is one of the Shakespeare Club's disappointments. We have often noticed that it's the tragedy of this tragedy that it's rare to find the roles of Romeo and Juliet matched with young actors equal to the challenge. (Perhaps a new show, *& Juliet*, the #MeToo musical, can defy this jinx.) Nonetheless, this was the first of Shakespeare's plays to hit a universal nerve. Hereafter, the world's lovers will picture themselves on a balcony under Italian starlight. This stirring paean to adolescent rebellion is both deeply Italian (based on a fifteenth-century Italian source), and strikingly Anglo-Elizabethan. The Montagues and Capulets step from the pages of Renaissance romance; but their brawling households take inspiration from the streets of London; while

Juliet's Nurse and many of Verona's servants seem to have migrated from Stratford.

A uniquely intense combination of character, plot, and location moves with a speed and ferocity that can leave audiences gasping. This headlong lovers' tragedy never draws breath from one scene to the next. In just over two hours, Shakespeare sweeps spectators through five remorseless nights and days, from the first clash of swordplay in the streets of Verona to the 'glooming peace' of the Capulet tomb.

The shock effect of *Romeo and Juliet* is linguistic as much as emotional. After Marlowe, as from a lesson well learned, love and language become Shakespeare's dominant themes. All the play's hot-headed principals indulge in feverish wordplay – puns, paradoxes and literary provocations – calculated to inflame the senses. In Act Two, at the scene of their ecstatic first meeting, there's a moment of physical attraction that demonstrates the playwright's utter mastery: the shy touching of Romeo and Juliet's hands, and Romeo's cheeky first line (to which Juliet has an outrageous riposte), as if the lovers have been raised on readings from the sonnets:

ROMEO: [*touching her hand*] If I profane with my
    unworthiest hand
This holy shrine, the gentler sin is this:
My lips, two blushing pilgrims, ready stand
To smooth that rough touch with a tender kiss.
JULIET: Good pilgrim, you do wrong your hand too much,
Which mannerly devotion shows in this.
For saints have hands that pilgrims' hands do touch,
And palm to palm is holy palmers' kiss.
[1.5.92–9]

Next, it's Juliet, rather more sophisticated than her thirteen years, who responds to Romeo's flirtatious 'dear saint':

> JULIET: Saints do not move, though grant for prayers'
>   sake.
> ROMEO: Then move not while my prayer's effect I
>   take.
> [*He kisses her*]
> Thus from my lips, by thine my sin is purged.
> JULIET: Then have my lips the sin that they have took.
> ROMEO: Sin from my lips? O trespass sweetly urged!
> Give me my sin again.
> [*He kisses her*]
> [1.5.104–9]

To which Juliet replies, with saucy allusiveness: 'You kiss by the book.'

Soon after, when they meet again, Juliet will need only the slightest encouragement (from Romeo's teasing question 'What shall I swear by?') to plunge into the swooning and self-conscious depths of erotic self-love:

> ROMEO: What shall I swear by?
> JULIET: Do not swear at all,
> Or if thou wilt, swear by thy gracious self,
> Which is the god of my idolatry,
> And I'll believe thee.
> [2.1.153–7]

The 'self' – that 'self' we know so well today – is all: deliciously carnal, articulate and divine. Romeo and Juliet, with hearts stitched onto their sleeves, are the most perfectly passionate and tragic of lovers. They allow the playwright to enact and articulate their unfulfilled desires in language that smoulders with sexual and sensual anticipation:

> ROMEO: O, wilt thou leave me so unsatisfied?
> JULIET: What satisfaction canst thou have tonight?
> ROMEO: Th'exchange of thy love's faithful vow for
> mine.
> JULIET: I gave thee mine before thou didst request it,
> And yet I would it were to give again.
> ROMEO: Wouldst thou withdraw it? For what purpose,
> love?
> JULIET: But to be frank and give it thee again.
> And yet I wish but for the thing I have.
> My bounty is as boundless as the sea,
> My love as deep: The more I give to thee
> The more I have, for both are infinite.
> [2.1.167–77]

The Elizabethan 'die' conceals a secondary sense of 'orgasm'. Here are two doomed adolescents who are going to die for love, in the thrill of lust, with some of the most heart-stopping lines in the First Folio. Juliet's anticipation of her longed-for 'death', and of having 'bought the mansion of a love, But not possessed it [3.2.26–7]', morphs into one of Shakespeare's great tragic speeches:

> Come, gentle night; come, loving, black-browed night,
> Give me my Romeo, and when I shall die
> Take him and cut him out in little stars,

And he will make the face of heaven so fine
That all the world will be in love with night
And pay no worship to the garish sun.
[3.2.20–25]

Full of passion and risk, *Romeo and Juliet* also has its
own original poetic brilliance. Within the first half of the
play, there's one speech where Shakespeare freezes the
action to conjure up a fairy world in language replete with
nods to Warwickshire, a virtuoso display of style spun
from his provincial experience. For Mercutio's Queen Mab
speech, an entrancing, lyrical cadenza firmly rooted in the
here and now, Shakespeare's headline to a scene within a
scene comes out of nowhere.

'O, then,' begins Romeo's bosom buddy, after a two-page
prelude of bawdy adolescent banter, 'I see Queen Mab
hath been with you [1.4.53].' And off he goes, for almost
fifty lines. Following this aria, Mercutio's death after a
headlong sword fight with Tybalt ('A plague on both your
houses!') will humanize the action in the hectic middle of
the play with the dying man's ominous joke ('Ask for me
tomorrow, and you shall find me a grave man'), and drive
it towards a cathartic conclusion. After 'Queen Mab',
Mercutio becomes a character we care about. The unforgettable poetry of this speech brings the long first act to
a climax, the curtain-raiser to Juliet's first entry.

Never static, this show-stopper unspools in a restless
montage of movement, imagined in vivid close-up: Queen
Mab is 'no bigger than an agate stone / On the forefinger'
– an intimate Stratford reference – 'of an alderman'. The
queen's 'chariot is an empty hazelnut'; its wheels have
spider's legs for 'wagon spokes'; her coachman is 'a small

grey-coated gnat', and her nocturnal transport also comes from nature – 'cricket's bone'; 'wings of grasshoppers'; and 'the smallest spider's web'.

Hectic as passion itself, Queen Mab 'gallops night by night' through the dreams of courtiers. Now Shakespeare leaves the countryside and returns to court, among lawyers, soldiers, hangers-on and priests, all of whom find the queen disturbing their nightly dreams. Mercutio's stream of consciousness recalls young girls ('maids') lying on their backs, being instructed in the arts of sex by a diva, who has now morphed into a 'hag' . . .

'Peace, peace,' protests Romeo. 'Thou talk'st of nothing.' Still, these lines have served their purpose, connecting Romeo's friend to an imminent country world of mystery, nightmare and magic. The star-crossed love story of *The Most Excellent and Lamentable Tragedy of Romeo and Juliet* would soon become twinned with *A Midsummer Night's Dream*. At about the same time – the precise dates are unclear – possibly as a release from the wild darkness of the one and the madcap comedy of the other – Shakespeare wrote a linguistic light opera, set in France, his word-struck celebration of 'a bawdy planet', *Love's Labour's Lost*.

4.

A marriage of whimsy and will-fulness, this virtually plot-free play about love, language and levity marshals the 'huge army of the world's desires [1.1.10]', in a cornucopia of bombast, rhodomontade and comic grand-iloquence. Its premise is absurd: the king of Navarre is insisting his circle devote themselves to three years' study, untroubled by sexual desire, during which the company (and conversation) of women shall be excluded from court. The king's opening speech is also haunted by the shade of Christopher Marlowe: a meditation on the price of fame becomes a reflective passage which, with its play on scythe/Scythian, hovers on the brink of an elegy to the 'dead shepherd'.

> Let fame, that all hunt after in their lives
> Live registered upon our brazen tombs . . .
> Th' endeavour of this present breath may buy
> That honour which shall bate his scythe's keen edge
> And make us heirs of all eternity.
> [1.1.1–7]

Navarre's remedy for the ravenous threats of time is the calculated rejection of society, a quest for some abstract quality of existential 'meaning', in which, resisting 'the huge army of the world's desires . . . Navarre shall be the wonder of the world [1.1.10–12].'

The king's plans for a celibate graduate utopia fall apart, however, when the princess of France and her sexy retinue arrive on official business, and his project disintegrates into a battle of wits:

> KING: Fair Princess, welcome to the court of Navarre.
> PRINCESS: 'Fair' I give you back again, and welcome I
>   have not yet. The roof of this court is too high to
>   be yours, and welcome to the wide fields too base
>   to be mine.
> [2.1.90–94]

As a play, *Love's Labour's Lost* is nothing if not playful. The king's men (Berowne, Longaville, Dumaine and the

'Spanish braggart' Don Armado) rapidly subvert their isolation: at least their tongues are free, and full of mischief. What matters to these principals and their hangers-on, a motley crew of loquacious reprobates, is the quality that Shakespeare and the Elizabethans prized above all else – to wit: wit, the most reliable means of keeping oblivion at bay, symbolized by the black-clad figure of Marcady, the messenger who punctures the climax of the play's levity with his sombre brief tale of mortality. Shakespeare's introduction of Marcady in Act Five inserts a brilliant irruption of menace; in just seven lines, a masterpiece of compression:

MARCADY: God save you, madam.
PRINCESS: Welcome, Marcady,
But that thou interrupt'st our merriment.
MARCADY: I am sorry, madam, for the news I bring
Is heavy in my tongue. The king your father—
PRINCESS: Dead, for my life.
MARCADY: Even so. My tale is told.
[5.2.709–15]

Love's Labour's Lost, while nodding to Marlowe's memory, also looks back to Verona, and the sonnets. Berowne, who has followed Navarre into self-isolation, will fall in love with his beautiful Rosaline. Thus Berowne and Rosaline become prototypes for the sparring couples in *Much Ado About Nothing* (Beatrice and Benedick) and *As You like It* (Rosalind and Orlando). But Berowne is not in their league as a lover; his role in the frivolities of Navarre is to be a Marlovian wit. Meanwhile, the king's ambitions for a great intellectual experiment fizzle out in a kind of flirtatious filibuster. Shakespeare is more addicted to Berowne's maverick posse: the show-off, Don Armado; Moth, his page; the policeman, Dull; Holofernes, a schoolmaster; and finally Costard, the clown, who, describing his fellows, observes that 'they have been at a great feast of languages and stolen some of the scraps [5.1.36]'. In putting down Moth, Costard articulates a ludicrous Latinate portmanteau word, *honorificabilitudinitatibus* ('the state of being loaded with honours'), in which Shakespeare executes the definitive parody of 'inkhorn terms':

> I marvel thy master hath not eaten thee for a word, for thou are not so long by the head as *honorificabil-itudinitatibus*; thou art easier swallowed than a flapdragon.
> [5.1.39–42]

Love's Labour's Lost marks an important transition, with Shakespeare limbering up for the future. Among the characters gorging on the excesses of language, Don Armado with his 'fire-new words' is a character who promises much from a playwright who has 'drunk ink' [4.2.25], and who finds himself perfectly situated in:

> . . . the place where – where, I mean, I did encounter that obscene and most preposterous event that draweth from my snow-white pen the ebon-coloured ink which here thou viewest, beholdest, surveyest, or seest.
> [1.1.235–9]

Eventually, the ink-dipped playwright mobilizes the king of Navarre to bring these revels to a close:

KING: Come, sir, it wants a twelvemonth an' a day,
And then 'twill end.
BEROWNE: That's too long for a play.
[5.2.863–4]

Shakespeare's instincts about plays in performance are never far from the surface of his work. *Love's Labour's Lost* is set in France, but its emotional fulcrum is firmly located within English language and culture; its comic characters celebrate a polyglot kind of Englishness that London audiences would recognize. It was here during 1593–9 that Shakespeare completed his conquest of the Elizabethan play-going audience, through his instinctive grasp of their deepest emotions, and his delight in the two things that were possibly most dear to them as free men and women, English citizens: the 'diction of common life', and a profound nostalgia for the greenwood of Merrie England, a place that probably never existed but which continues to animate our imagination:

When daisies pied and violets blue,
And lady-smocks, all silver-white,
And cuckoo-buds of yellow hue
Do paint the meadows with delight.
[5.2.879–82]

This pastoral Eden is peopled with everyday folk: girls bleaching their 'summer smocks'; shepherds blowing on frozen fingers; church congregations coughing through the parson's sermon; and 'greasy Joan' keeling her pots and pans.

Love's Labour's Lost possibly mirrors an absence from

London during some plague years. When Shakespeare returned to the city after 1594, it was to unite country and metropolis, drama and language, landscape and comedy in *A Midsummer Night's Dream*, a work of art inspired by the landscape of his country youth. As Berowne sets off during 'Spring' and 'Winter', the closing songs of *Love's Labour's Lost*, with Armado's 'You that way: we this way,' Shakespeare releases his audience from a Continental spell, to return them home to England:

Change not your offer made in heat of blood;
If frosts and fasts, hard lodging and thin weeds
Nip not the gaudy blossoms of your love,
But that it bear this trial and last love,
Then, at the expiration of the year,
Come challenge me.
[5.2.792–7]

It is in this congenial society of 'rude mechanicals', 'hempen homespuns', and 'the fairy world' of Oberon and Titania, that Shakespeare will return to his roots to 'paint the meadows' in a play that's a kind of satire on *Romeo and Juliet*.

Eleven

'WOOD'

And as imagination bodies forth
The forms of things unknown, the poet's pen
Turns them to shapes, and gives to airy nothing
A local habitation and a name.
A Midsummer Night's Dream, 5.1.14

1.

In *A Midsummer Night's Dream*, Shakespeare's 'wood', with its archaic secondary meaning of 'mad', from Old English 'wode', became a new arena of risk and originality, an otherworldly outdoor 'plot' of playhouse fantasies in which to bewitch an audience. To many Elizabethans, the 'imagination' was a danger zone; the word never lost its sinister connotations of treasonous plotting. In *A Midsummer Night's Dream*, when Theseus declares that 'the lunatic, the lover, and the poet' are 'of imagination all compact [5.1.7–8]', Shakespeare is making an oblique nod to the perils implicit in his art, and the risks of the unfettered mind in a society unaccustomed to the kind of freedoms later generations would take for granted. It is in this sense that Antonio in *The Tempest*, scheming against Alonso, tempts Sebastian:

My strong imagination sees a crown
Dropping upon thy head.
[2.1.212–13]

Nevertheless, the 'imagination' would be territory to which Shakespeare returned again and again, with ever-present risk, within varieties of 'wood', from the groves of Athens to the Forest of Arden. The novelist and am-dram devotee Bernard Cornwell, describing his summer work at the Monomoy Theatre in Chatham, Massachusetts, conveys the evergreen qualities of this comedy. 'The theatre was full,' he writes, 'and all I could hear was laughing, yet the jokes had been written over four hundred years before.' From beyond the footlights, Cornwell captures the potency of Shakespeare in perform-ance: 'Playing his words on stage fascinates me. There is no better way to discover his plays than to be part of them . . . to realise his lasting genius as you stand in the lights listening to an audience gasp, laugh, or break into applause.'

It's here, alas, that our Shakespeare Club's experience morphs into memories of school plays, that gruesome parade of ruffs and codpieces and those absurd sword fights on noisy, overlit stages in front of gawping parents. The pulse of blank verse – the iambic pentameter – is supposed to mimic the steady beat of the heart. Mangled in performance by stuttering or gabbling adolescents, it becomes at best a subject for comedy . . .

Over hill, over dale,
Thorough bush, thorough brier,
Over park, over pale,

Thorough flood, thorough fire:
I do wander everywhere . . .
[2.1.2–6]

It is the summer of 1967 – the summer of love – and I am fourteen years old, playing first fairy in the Sherborne School production of *A Midsummer Night's Dream*. This anonymous fairy – as any fule kno – is the crucial cameo at the beginning of the act that introduces the audience to Shakespeare's mischievous hobgoblin Robin Goodfellow, a.k.a. Puck, the quintessential Shakespearean spirit of misrule. Such rustic versifying, in green tights, my first experience of Shakespeare in performance, tethers my teenage self somewhere between a dream and a nightmare.

Dream visions, from Chaucer's *Legend of Good Women* to Spenser's *Faerie Queen*, have a special hold on the English mind, but it's typical of the playwright's mash-up mentality in the woods of his maturity that he wove them into rustic folklore and country rituals to make a wholly new kind of English setting. At this point in his career, Shakespeare's landscapes dazzle as vividly as his language. Never reluctant to plunder his Stratford origins, but with a sharp eye on court life, his youthful comedies celebrate the experience of the shires, while also hooking a Middle-England audience into the poetic dramas of his imagination. As Shakespeare finds his voice as a dramatist, the vigorous metropolitan vernacular gets relocated in the English countryside.

From *Love's Labour's Lost* to *A Midsummer Night's Dream*, this traffic between language and landscape holds the key to Shakespeare's work in the years before the end of the Tudor dynasty. Such a dialogue between poetry and place becomes a vital thread in the English literary tradition, a conversation that Shakespeare might be said to have invented. During a broadcast made in 1973, Seamus Heaney, who also grew up on the land, far from the city, confessed that the spirit of the countryside was one key to his life as a poet: 'my words – the words for me – seem to have more nervous energy when they are touching territory that I know, that I live with.' Heaney continued, 'I can lay my hands on [a place] and know it. And the words come alive and get a kind of personality when they are involved with it for me. It's almost an element to work with, as much as it is an object of admiration.'

A Midsummer Night's Dream brings all Shakespeare's natural poetic and dramatic gifts into a perfect, at times thrilling, harmony. *Landscape plus poetry equals comedy* is a fundamental Shakespearean equation, in which the ferment of language becomes a vital catalyst. In simple terms, language makes humanity human, at home and in the world. Without 'words, words, words', there can be no expressions of thought or sympathy. Thought inspires ideas, and ideas nourish the inward mind, Shakespeare's obsession. All of this comes more vividly into play when, having moved to London, Shakespeare the provincial becomes Shakespeare the city-dweller.

A Midsummer Night's Dream becomes the mirror to this experience, a heady, pastoral romp riffing outrageously on the torments of young love, a play about a society in transition, exploring the interaction of country and city: airy metropolitans versus rude mechanicals. This manic comedy, ostensibly set outside Athens, could only have been written by a Midlands country boy. The fairy king Oberon's complaint about the weather, for instance, is sublimely English.

The fold stands empty in the drowned field,
And crows are fatted with the murrain flock.
The nine men's morris is filled up with mud,
And the quaint mazes in the wanton green
For lack of tread are undistinguishable.
[2.1.96–100]

These lines express a countryman's nostalgia and longing, from a mind nourished by the dialect of a settled landscape. When Puck describes to Oberon the frenzy of Bottom the weaver's fellow actors after his 'translation' as an ass, the image that fills the playwright's imagination is one that Shakespeare has witnessed intimately for himself:

As wild geese that the creeping fowler eye,
Or russet-pated choughs, many in sort,
Rising and cawing at the gun's report,
Sever themselves, and madly sweep the sky –
So, at his sight, away his fellows fly.
[3.2.20–24]

Planted in this English landscape, and peopled with characters you might expect to meet on Henley Street in the bustling heart of Stratford, the play also has a cast of woodland elves, a hobgoblin, a mythical duke, his Amazon trophy-wife-to-be, together with a fairy king and queen spun from 'airy nothing'. Shakespeare is conjuring up dramatic comedy, but one that's also 'a rare vision', a world buzzing with supernatural energy and supersonic movement (Puck will boast to Oberon about circling the globe 'in forty minutes'), a place located between heaven and earth that's somehow strangely neither of heaven nor earth, to which the playwright will give 'a local habitation and a name'.

To animate this magic, Shakespeare supercharges every line of his poetry with dramatic tension, as if conducting a masterclass in open-air performance. When Peter Quince salutes 'a marvellous convenient place for our rehearsal', he adds, with a nice double-entendre, that 'this green plot' shall be their stage. Once Puck has been introduced, the audience learns about Oberon's dispute with the fairy queen, Titania, and her 'little changeling boy'. The launching of this new theme (a lovers' quarrel) comes with lines of inexplicable beauty as Oberon recalls his former sighting of the love god Cupid:

My gentle Puck, come hither. Thou rememb'rest
Since once I sat upon a promontory
And heard a mermaid on a dolphin's back,
Uttering such dulcet and harmonious breath
That the rude sea grew civil at her song,
And certain stars shot madly from their spheres
To hear the sea-maid's music?
[2.1.148–54]

Elsewhere, *A Midsummer Night's Dream* displays all the contrasts that appeal to Shakespeare. It is at once mundane and fantastic, funny and sad, real and dreamy, rustic and high-flown, insular and exotic. Woven together, these opposites suggest another definition of 'Shakespearean': a shape-shifting drama that's susceptible to infinite contemporary reinterpretation.

In the post-war years, for instance, this play was rediscovered first in 1965 by Jan Kott (in *Shakespeare Our*

Contemporary) as a drama rich in the 'latent content' of Freudian psychoanalytic theory, and then again, in 1970, with a celebrated production by the director Peter Brook, for whom the heart of the play is about Oberon's feud with Titania, 'a man taking his wife whom he loves totally and having her fucked by the crudest sex machine he can find'. In 2019, Nicholas Hytner's magical gender-fluid revival turned this insight on its head by flipping the roles (and speeches) of the fairy king and queen.

Such inversions are in the spirit of a play whose script becomes an intoxicating hybrid of classics and folklore. Probably written around 1595, with references to the notoriously bad summer of 1594, it is rare among Shakespeare's plays in having no explicit model. Shakespeare's *Dream* is also rooted in his own time and place, despite its 'Athenian' opening. Shakespeare had an uncanny eye for psychological case studies of erotic obsession. An entertainment linking darkness with imagination with sexual desire is also a young man's play (he wrote it aged about thirty), revelling in language and dramatic licence, while mixing comedy and tragedy, classical myth and provincial folklore, reason and fantasy, night and day, life and love.

2.

On this occasion, without an earlier source, he knits together an overwrought pastoral comedy from Chaucer's Theseus ('The Knight's Tale'), *The Golden Ass* of Apuleius, Ovid's 'Pyramus and Thisbe' (*Metamorphoses*), and from childhood memories of folklore, a world of maypoles and misrule, mummers' plays and morris dancing, teeming country customs rooted in the Midlands and fused into a comedy for the one night of the year which celebrated country folk's right to make love out of doors.

Into this mad matrix, the playwright transmutes the lives of four metropolitan lovers (Lysander and Hermia; Demetrius and Helena) and an am-dram company of artisans (Bottom, the weaver; Peter Quince, a carpenter; Francis Flute, a bellows-mender; Tom Snout, a tinker; Snug, a joiner; and Robin Starveling, a tailor). Shakespeare, still better known as a poet, is plainly stage-struck. The harmless fun he pokes at the absurdities of Bottom and his 'rude mechanicals', an artisan cast of would-be thespians, rehearsing in 'a wood near Athens', is the work of a young writer dazzled by play-acting and -writing. Early in the unfolding lovers' plot, Demetrius defines the fix he's in with a perfectly equivocal, punning protest to Helena:

Where is Lysander, and fair Hermia?
The one I'll slay, the other slayeth me.
Thou told'st me they were stol'n unto this wood,
And here am I, and wood within this wood.
[2.1.189–92]

Demetrius is being driven mad in a place that sponsors nothing but wonderful insanity. His 'wood' also inspires, in its helpless, love-struck characters, some magical poetry steeped in country imagery. The mischievous and sinister Robin Goodfellow, a.k.a. Puck, is a figure from the darker parts of the forest, a home to bears, bats, and snakes, but Titania the fairy queen, in love with Bottom, has a ridiculous, rustic sweetness that's winning. She instructs her elves, in pastoral lines reminiscent of Mercutio's Queen Mab:

Be kind and courteous to this gentleman.
Hop in his walks, and gambol in his eyes.
Feed him with apricots and dewberries,
With purple grapes, green figs and mulberries;
The honeybags steal from the humble-bees,
And for night tapers crop their waxen thighs
And light them at the fiery glow-worms' eyes
To have my love to bed, and to arise;
And pluck the wings from painted butterflies
To fan the moonbeams from his sleeping eyes.
[3.1.156–65]

Even the frazzled metropolitan lovers get intoxicated by the countryside. Helena, numbering the intimacies of her childhood with Hermia, recalls that it was 'as if our hands, our sides, voices and minds had been incorporate':

So we grew together
Like to a double cherry: seeming parted,
But yet an union in partition,
Two lovely berries moulded on one stem.
So, with two seeming bodies but one heart.
[3.2.209–13]

Are we dreaming or awake? Is this Greece or Warwickshire? Is Oberon Theseus' double? Is it a matter of life and death, or love and laughter? (Both interpretations have been made.)

The director Richard Eyre writes persuasively that 'The life of a theatre should always be in the present tense.' As vivid as an hallucination, *A Midsummer Night's Dream* is a present-tense play rife with contemporary confusion.

Bottom says: 'I have had a dream past the wit of man to say what dream it was [4.1.102–3].' But it's also premonitory. At the end of Act Five, in the glimmering candlelight of the closing lines, Puck's valedictory speech becomes a spooky kind of incantation from the heart of Merrie England:

> Now the hungry lion roars,
> And the wolf behowls the moon,
> Whilst the heavy ploughman snores,
> All with weary task foredone.
> [5.2.1–4]

As Puck paints a picture of a world far removed from the rites of May, Shakespeare's audience would experience a frisson of dread, a reminder of the skull beneath the skin.

Bubonic plague stalked Elizabethan London throughout Shakespeare's career, striking most mercilessly in 1603, when as much as one-quarter of the population perished. Usually, there was little respite. When the symptoms struck – feverish headaches, vomiting, buboes (swollen lymph nodes) – the victim knew that he or she was doomed, often within hours. Everyone understood the meaning of the plague. All classes were affected; few survived a brush with infection. Shakespeare will allude to these conditions in *King Lear*, the old man's denunciation of Goneril:

> Thou art a boil,
> A plague-sore or embossèd carbuncle
> In my corrupted blood.
> [2.2.396–8]

Actors, at work in the playhouses, and mixing with crowds, were especially at risk. The plague bacillus would lurk in heavy woollen clothing, passing from carrier to carrier with fearsome speed. Thomas Dekker, one of Shakespeare's co-writers, described 'the loud groans of raving sick men . . . in every house grief striking up an alarum'. How often, he continues, 'hath the amazed husband, waking, found the comfort of his bed lying breathless by his side, his children in the same instant gasping for life . . .' Puck connects this plague-wracked society, tormented by famine and disease, to the dark side of the English landscape:

Now the wasted brands do glow
Whilst the screech-owl, screeching loud,
Puts the wretch that lies in woe
In remembrance of a shroud.
[5.1.5–8]

His closing lines of incantation are an ominous reminder that, as a 'pooka', he remains a medieval spirit of mischief and mayhem, sweeping up the 'dust' of humanity, uttering syllables (though not sentiments) you'll hear in *EastEnders*, or *Coronation Street*:

I am sent with broom before,
To sweep the dust behind the door.
[5.1.19–20]

If *A Midsummer Night's Dream* was written during 1595, as many scholars believe, it makes a bridge between the amorous, pastoral society of the poet's youth, and the much more sinister England of the 1590s, a society in the grip of near-universal jeopardy. In response to such dread, it was one of Shakespeare's most typical artistic decisions to explore yet more comedy. *As You Like It* (1599) recapitulates the lessons Shakespeare had learned since the death of Marlowe, but in the more sombre key that speaks of his maturity. Once again, there's the flight of the principals to the liberating greenwood. A young woman named Rosalind (not Rosaline) is again a love-object for an infatuated young man, Orlando, not Berowne or Romeo. When she adopts the disguise of 'Ganymede' Shakespeare savours an intensely modern flirtation with sexual identity partly derived from the sonnets.

The erotic fever of *Romeo and Juliet*, the linguistic arpeggios of *Love's Labour's Lost*, and the literary landscapes of *A Midsummer Night's Dream*, woven together, become sober, richer and more reflective. Jacques is a deeper character than Berowne, and it's here that Phoebe, a shepherdess, pays her heartfelt tribute to the memory of Christopher Marlowe, the 'dead shepherd'.

For Shakespeare, the sole survivor, there's also a new self-confidence in the title of the play which reflects an explicit awareness of a Shakespearean audience. In 'As You Like It' he was addressing his audience, using the breezy, most colloquial terms of the second person plural. That 'You' speaks of a successful playwright who can confidently say that his next comedy will be a trifle, 'much ado about nothing', a throwaway title suggesting that 'Mr Shakespeare' had more important matters in mind.

'As You Like It' finds the playwright fully in command of his medium and his gifts, at once engaged but also detached, as if saying, 'This is yours as much as mine. Take it, or leave it.' This antithetical formula is simultaneously ambitious (to succeed) and negligent (towards the outcome). He is at once professional, and amateur, both a great English artist and also an inveterate crowd-pleaser.

By the turn of the century, Shakespeare had become discreetly celebrated. Now known at court, he was recognized as a writer of uncommon gifts and sophistication. His experience around the perilous caprices of the queen, the necessity of expressing deniable convictions next to evasive half-truths, inspired lines in *As You Like It* that open a window onto the poet's evolution as a more public figure. Touchstone's speech 'upon a lie seven times removed' speaks of the playwright's fascination with the etiquette of hypocrisy:

> I did dislike the cut of a certain courtier's beard. He sent me word if I said his beard was not cut well, he was in the mind it was. This is called the Retort Courteous. If I sent him word again it was not well cut, he would send me word he cut it to please himself. This is called the Quip Modest. If again it was not well cut, he disabled my judgement. This is called the Reply Churlish. If again it was not well cut, he would answer I spake not true. This is called the Reproof Valiant. If again it was not well cut, he would say I lie. This is called the Countercheck Quarrelsome. And so to the Lie Circumstantial, and the Lie Direct. [5.4.68–80]

These are the insights of a survivor and subtle equivocator, a literary politician. Shakespeare was mastering the skills of artistic dissimulation to shelter his creative privacy.

As the author of bestselling poetry, he had begun to inspire a lot of speculation about exactly what he was up to. After close on a decade of self-expression as first a poet and then a playwright, Shakespeare had perfected his gift for being simultaneously present and absent as a writer, for reconciling opposites, and for fusing life and art in a way that was personal but unaccountable and explicit yet inexplicable: at once risky and addictive.

At this point in his life, William Shakespeare is ready for yet another challenge. Once more, he was lucky. At the turn of the century, in art and politics, he would find himself confronted with that opportunity. With a new drama of politics distracting the old queen, there would also be a new stage on which to construct another theatrical kingdom. Soon he would get his own playhouse, the cockpit of his fame as a writer.

Twelve

'W. SHAKE-SPEARE'

Or shall I live your epitaph to make,
Or you survive, when I in earth am rotten.
Sonnet 81, 1

1.

The poet Byron once boasted, on the publication of *Childe Harold*, that he 'woke up to find himself famous'. Such fantasies are strangely persistent; bookish commentators often talk about 'overnight success'. The truth is that behind every literary breakthrough lie hours and hours, probably years, of hard graft, late nights and early-rising.

'Shake-speare', the literary phenomenon, was hardly an overnight sensation. For much of the 1590s, according to the written record, the author of 1594's box-office smash *Titus Andronicus*, or successful plays like *Richard II*, *Richard III* and *Romeo and Juliet* (published in quarto editions during 1597), was semi-invisible. The title pages of these first printings identify the Lord Chamberlain's Men as the company that performed the script, but make no reference to any scriptwriter.

In 1598 things change. 'Shake-speare' and his fortunes begin to look up. Word-of-mouth and the circulation of his 'sugared Sonnets' in court circles, brought his reputation to a tipping point. The poet Richard Barnfield became one of the first to celebrate a fellow poet's genius, in the language conventional to literary praise:

> And Shakespeare, thou whose honey-flowing vein,
> Pleasing the world, thy praises doth continue,
> Whose *Venus* and whose *Lucrece* (sweet and chaste)
> Thy name in fame's immortal book have placed.
> Live ever you, at least in fame live ever:
> Well may thy body die, but fame dies never.

In the same year, reprints of *Richard II*, *Richard III* and *Love's Labour's Lost* advertised 'W. Shake-speare' as the author on the title page for the first time. Before the introduction of copyright in the eighteenth century, a playwright who sold a play script to a theatre company retained no subsidiary rights in his material. There are, however, a number of tiny clues that Shakespeare was growing confident in his authorship, and moreover that his audiences had an appetite for the work of this 'W. Shake-speare'. (It was not until the 1608 quarto edition of *King Lear* that he would receive top billing as playwright.)

Just before Barnfield's encomium, Shakespeare had enjoyed such a great success with his new play, *The History of Henry IV*, that the production became swiftly divided into two crowd-pleasing parts. The royal protagonist of both plays was the 'Prince Hal' who became Henry V of English legend, but the star of the show was that first Shakespearean hero, 'the fat knight' who was making such an instant hit with London audiences.

Two years earlier, in 1595, by accident or design, Shakespeare had set up this moment of theatrical history in a closing scene of *Richard II*. Bolingbroke the usurper, who has just become Henry IV, falls into conversation about Hal, his heir, with Harry Percy and some attendant lords. He describes the 'young wanton' who, he regrets, has become renowned for hanging out in London's 'taverns' with some disreputable lowlife. These 'unrestrainèd loose companions [5.3.7]' have names like Poins, Peto and Bardolph, Pistol, and Corporal Nym, the soldier-thief. In the company of their leader, a disreputable old knight with a penchant for sherry-sack and fast women, they have been roaming at large throughout the East End, the kind of men who beat up nightwatchmen and perpetrate petty theft against unsuspecting wayfarers.

Possibly to mark his return to the playhouse after months writing poetry, this became the moment when Shakespeare let the common man, poet of the vernacular, monopolize the stage in all his drunken, lecherous, stinking, sweaty, and amoral grossness. At this juncture, that popular excrescence is not an anonymous 'Third Citizen', but carries a name (and several dozen pounds of excess body weight) which is uniquely Shakespearean: Sir John Falstaff (formerly Oldcastle).

2.

The Bankside audience could not get enough of either the fat knight, or his posse. There are many components to the secret of this attraction, not least the transgressive thrill of being in bad company. More formally, the Hal–Falstaff scenes in both parts of *Henry IV* conform to the principle of dramatic antagonism, make a suggestive commentary on the resilient fluidity of English society, and achieve a brilliant reconciliation between the two dominant themes in the life and work of the young playwright: politics and the English language.

Falstaff is never Jack Cade, but he is merrily at one with the common people of East Cheap. He is – as every commentator points out – wired into the English tradition as the figure of Vice, the Lord of Misrule. In 2019, some newspaper columnists mistakenly compared the UK's new prime minister Boris Johnson to Bertie Wooster. A darker, and more persuasive, comparison is Falstaff. A master of the revels, the fat knight sees himself, with typical modesty, as 'not only witty in myself, but the cause that wit is in other men [2 *Henry IV*, 1.2.9–10]'. Above all – and it's here that Shakespeare's imagination catches fire – he is a lord of language, a kind of manic, dissolute prose-poet whose every line is entrancing:

> But to say I know more harm in him than in myself were to say more than I know . . . If sack and sugar be a fault, God help the wicked. If to be old and merry be a sin, then many an old host that I know is damned . . . No, my good lord, banish Peto, banish Bardolph, banish Poins, but for sweet Jack Falstaff, kind Jack Falstaff, true Jack Falstaff, valiant Jack Falstaff, and therefore more valiant, being as he is, old Jack Falstaff,
> Banish not him thy Harry's company . . .
> [*1 Henry IV*, 2.5.471–83]

'Banish plump Jack, and banish all the world.' In his majestic quotability, Falstaff enters the pantheon as the first fully Shakespearean character, the co-equal of Lear and Prospero, Macbeth and Rosalind. According to the critic Harold Bloom, one of Hegel's best insights is the way Shakespeare always empowers his finest creations to be 'free artists of themselves'. Falstaff is one such free artist. As the principal attraction of *Henry IV*, he unites language and history, Shakespeare's twin obsessions, sousing his lines in so much alcohol as to intoxicate a generation of playgoers:

A good sherry-sack hath a two-fold operation in it. It ascends me into the brain, dries me there all the foolish and dull and crudy vapours which environ it, makes it apprehensive, quick, forgetive, full of nimble, fiery, and delectable shapes, which, deliver'd o'er to the voice, the tongue, which is the birth, becomes excellent wit. The second property of your excellent sherry is the warming of the blood, which, before cold and settled, left the liver white and pale, which is the badge of pusillanimity and cowardice.

In a modern film script, this might be the limit of such a speech, but this is the playhouse: Shakespeare, with an audience before him in the pit, lets his star extract maximum exposure from his moment centre stage:

But the sherry warms it, and makes it course from the inwards to the parts' extremes; it illuminateth the face, which, as a beacon, gives warning to all the rest of this little kingdom, man, to arm; and then the vital commoners and inland petty spirits muster me all to their captain, the heart; who, great and puffed up with his retinue, doth any deed of courage. And this valour comes of sherry.
[2 *Henry IV*, 4.2.93–109]

The sententious Falstaff, like Ulysses in *Troilus and Cressida*, or Menenius in *Coriolanus*, also smuggles in a subversive commentary on the mayhem implicit in the histories, engaging the cultural, intellectual and emotional mood of the times. At the battle of Shrewsbury, standing over the body of Sir Walter Blount, our cowardly rogue launches into a self-conscious and ironical meditation on the absurdity of heroism, the old *dulce et decorum* lie:

What need I be so forward with him that calls not on me? Well, 'tis no matter, honour pricks me on. Yea, but how if honour prick me off when I come on, how then? Can honour set-to a leg? No. Or an arm? No. Or take away the grief of a wound? No. Honour hath no skill in surgery, then? No. What is honour? A word. What is in that word 'honour'? What is that 'honour'? Air. A trim reckoning! . . . Therefore I'll none of it. Honour is a mere scutcheon. And so ends my catechism.
[*1 Henry IV*, 5.1.127–41]

Falstaff may be dissolute, immoral, cowardly, deceitful, dishonourable, and incorrigible, but his merry pragmatism (and his love for Prince Hal) elevates his character out of such baseness, while his addiction to irony makes him a profoundly English hero, a natural reprobate, crowd-pleaser, and prince-charmer:

FALSTAFF: And yet there is a virtuous man whom I have often noted in thy company, but I know not his name.

PRINCE HARRY: What manner of man, an it like your majesty?

FALSTAFF: A goodly, portly man, i'faith, and a
corpulent; of a cheerful look, a pleasing eye, and a
most noble carriage; and, as I think, his age some
fifty, or, by'r Lady, inclining to threescore. And now
I remember me, his name is Falstaff.
[*1 Henry IV*, 2.5.420–28]

In the Shakespeare Club, we have enjoyed many
Falstaffs, notably Anthony Sher in Greg Doran's 2014
production. Almost as memorable, for the wrong reasons,
was Michael Gambon's performance in 2 *Henry IV* at the
National Theatre in 2005. Those who saw John Wood, as
Justice Shallow, steal the scene from Falstaff (with Gambon
suffering memory problems) will never forget a great classical actor bringing some of Shakespeare's most casual and
insubstantial lines [3.2.1–295] vividly to life.

The playscript is one thing, notes towards a show; the
play in performance something else, a multi-dimensional
spree: always provocative, sometimes boring, occasionally
thrilling, typically an enthralling mix of many sensations.
If our Shakespeare Club has any wisdom to impart here,
it will be derived from our long experience of watching
his plays being brought to life on stage by some great
English actors who are immersed in Shakespeare's lines,
good, mediocre, bad, entrancing, or indifferent. Among the
almost one million words of the First Folio, there are some
well-known duds. Ben Jonson is not alone in wishing that
this hard-pressed man of the theatre had 'blotted a thousand' drafts. On the other hand, when our greatest actors
are on fire with their passion for his work, the results can
be extraordinary. We have seen some of the finest contemporary stage moments imaginable. In more than twenty

years of theatre-going, several starry highlights live on in my memory: Derek Jacobi's Lear, Harriet Walter's Brutus, Andrew Scott's Hamlet, Vanessa Redgrave's Volumnia, Adrian Scarborough's Ariel, Tom Hiddleston's Coriolanus, Glenda Jackson's Lear, and Simon Russell Beale's Iago all come to mind. Moreover, it's not just the marquee names that remain in theatrical memory, it's also the attendant lords, the fools and rustics, the chambermaids and grooms, murderers and messengers, spear-carriers and porters who take their lines to generate a moment of magic on stage. A Shakespeare line that gets well-turned in performance can become a revelation about a scene or a character that can also sponsor a new interpretation.

After scenes such as these, so engrossing to his audience, it's at this juncture that 'Shake-speare' steps up to address the playhouse. In the Epilogue to 2 *Henry IV*, the author's explicit promise of Falstaff's return in a forthcoming new play, *Henry V*, is a rare and precious moment of Elizabethan showbiz history:

> One word more, I beseech you. If you be not too much cloyed with fat meat, our humble author will continue the story with Sir John in it, and make you merry with fair Catharine of France; where, for anything I know, Falstaff shall die of a sweat – unless already a be killed with your hard opinions. For Oldcastle died a martyr, and this is not the man. My tongue is weary; when my legs are too, I will bid you good night.
> [5.4.Epilogue.24–32]

'Shake-speare', having broken cover as 'our humble author', would go on to oblige his audience and (theatrical legend insists) Queen Elizabeth herself with further episodes in the life and loves of the fat knight. *The Merry Wives of Windsor*, much of whose fun is at the expense of foreigners, notably the French, is Shakespeare's most contemporary English comedy.

Ever since W. H. Auden dismissed *The Merry Wives* as 'a very dull play indeed', it has been fashionable to prefer *Falstaff*, Verdi's version. How, apart from its cast, does this out-and-out English comedy, roistering through Windsor Great Park, connect with the history dramatized in *Henry IV* and *Henry V*? As well as celebrating Falstaff and his delightful linguistic chicanery, this Elizabethan romcom signals the high-water mark of Shakespeare's youthful English playwriting.

Ostensibly the slapstick of Falstaff's humiliation by the 'merry wives', Page, Ford and Quickly, the play is another comedy of the English language, boldly located in the 'burbs – actually, in one recent RSC production, in suburban Essex. Mistress Quickly sets the tone, complaining of the Welsh parson, Dr Caius, 'Here will be an old abusing of God's patience and the King's English [1.4.4–5]'. In the same spirit, Mistress Page's husband describes Corporal Nym as a fellow who 'frights English out of his wits [2.1.131]'. And Falstaff gets the last word when he protests Dr Caius' teasing: 'Have I lived to stand at the taunts of one that makes fritters of English? [5.5.141–2]'

Amid the prevailing mood of hectic improvised hilarity, there's no formal source for the plot, which Shakespeare pulled together from folk tales of jealous husbands and witty wives. According to Friedrich Engels, writing to Karl Marx, 'the first act alone contains more life and reality than all German literature.' This farcical 'reality' is partly borrowed from *Henry IV* and features the loud-mouth Pistol, Justice Shallow and Corporal Nym, on the razzle. Falstaff, who has just arrived in Windsor with Pistol and Nym, is hatching a plan to seduce two married women – the Mistresses Page and Ford.

The first comic climax of the play occurs when Falstaff, exposed as a preposterous Don Juan, flees one enraged husband in a laundry basket and is dumped in a dirty backwater of the Thames near Datchet. The bloated philanderer finally gets his come-uppance at midnight in Windsor Great Park. Here, disguised as Herne the Hunter, he is outed as a #MeToo villain, and the good people of Windsor celebrate the triumph of true love in the wedding of young Fenton to his adoring Anne. As in classic romcom, all live happily ever after, but Shakespeare seems to have recognized that Falstaff can have no place amid the gritty patriotism of his next history play, *Henry V*. Such an immortal character must be sent into eternity with Mistress Quickly's blessing, her account of Falstaff's demise:

> A parted just between twelve and one, ev'n at the turning o' th' tide – for after I saw him fumble with the sheets, and play with flowers, and smile upon his finger's end, I knew there was but one way. For his nose was as sharp as a pen, and a babbled of green fields. 'How now, Sir John?' quoth I. 'What, man! Be o' good cheer. So a cried out, 'God, God, God', three or four times.

Mistress Quickly, a doughty Englishwoman of robust temperament, has no time for the consolations of faith;

besides, she loves Sir John: 'Now I, to comfort him, bid him a should not think of God . . . [*Henry V*, 2.3.11–23]'

Shakespeare had a tangible personal investment in these scenes, and with good reason. Falstaff recalls the playwright's first years in London when, as an impressionable young man from Stratford, he had fallen into the company of roistering Robert Greene, Thomas Kyd, Christopher Marlowe, and the rest. When, during 1597–9, he came to write his *Henry* plays, he had many reasons to look back to 1593, the year when his career had been at a crossroads, and Kit Marlowe in his prime.

3.

'Sweet Will' had come a long way, and Shakespeare's creative 'mandate' now began to yield its unique dividend. The 'Shake-speare' who begins to appear on the title pages of quarto editions after 1598 was becoming part of the national conversation, and there was money to be made from the reading public, a new constituency. Just as in the last years of the twentieth century, there was a new book culture in the making: a series of small but significant insurrections had placed the jargon and habits of the market at the centre of every literary transaction. At some point in 1598 or 1599, the wily publisher William Jaggard, having somehow obtained manuscript copies of two Shakespeare sonnets, proceeded to pirate them in a slender quarto volume opportunistically entitled *The Passionate Pilgrim*, a publication that is said to have 'much offended' the poet.

This became one of the fastest-selling books of the day, nine editions in as many years. Exploiting Shakespeare's fame, the publisher of *The Passionate Pilgrim* simply lifted three sonnets from *Love's Labour's Lost*, adding two Shakespeare sonnets already in private circulation. To bulk up this slender edition, Jaggard also interpolated fifteen other verses from other hands, including poems by Bartholomew Griffin and Richard Barnfield. For good measure, Jaggard included an abbreviated, unattributed version of 'Come live with me and be my love'. Six years after his death, Christopher Marlowe still haunted Shakespeare's public life.

Rumours about the 'English Ovid' and his manuscript sequence of sonnets continued to swirl through literary London. Some of his best theatrical lines – notably Falstaff's sally against 'honour' in *1 Henry IV* – also seeped into those conversations near the throne, where Shakespearean references had become a kind of knowing shorthand among a court which favoured theatrical savoir-faire.

This came from the top. Through her role as queen – in her costume, utterances and demeanour – Gloriana, the 'imperial vot'ress', had always exhibited a deep, intuitive sense of the theatrical. Now, in these final years of Elizabeth I's reign, domestic political events would once again become as dramatic as ever. At precisely the moment when Shakespeare was beginning to enjoy professional security, the theatre world and the players with whom he associated were about to be perilously implicated in the lethal politics surrounding the Earl of Essex, the fallen former favourite.

4.

The rise and fall of Robert Devereux, Earl of Essex, at the court of Elizabeth I provides a strange, unnerving coda to the history of the reign, at once a political subplot and a romantic tragedy, with an almost intolerable (in some instances fatal) risk-quotient. In 1587, aged fifty-three, the queen had become infatuated with a young man more than thirty years her junior. Success, power, youth, royal favour, popular glory, exclaims Lytton Strachey in *Elizabeth and Essex*. 'What was lacking in the good fortune of the marvellous Earl?' In Elizabethan society, Essex was a celebrity; his relationship with the queen went far beyond politics. It was ecstatic, obsessive and turbulent, with both parties blowing hot and cold. When Essex addressed letters to his queen, it was almost as if the 'marvellous Earl' was a character at the playhouse. 'I was never one day, nor one hour, free from hope and jealousy,' he wrote. 'As long as you do me right, they are the inseparable companions of my life. If your Majesty do in the sweetness of your own heart nourish the one, and in the justice of love free me from the tyranny of the other, you shall ever make me happy . . . I humbly kiss your fair hands.'

This kind of fever could not last. By the mid-1590s, the moody Earl's fall from grace had begun. In 1598, things came to a head with a typical display of petulance, an Achilles-in-his-tent sulk familiar to Essex-watchers. The queen in her turn, wearying of such scenes, let it be known that her 'temerarious' former lover 'hath played long enough upon me, and now I mean to play a while upon him'. She informed the Earl that 'I value *my* self at as great a price as *he* values *him*self.' When, in one scene at court, Elizabeth boxed his ears and 'bade him be gone with a vengeance', Essex rashly responded with 'a great oath that he neither would nor could swallow so great an indignity'.

Into this combustible mix of sex and politics came the shocking news of a military disaster in Ulster, the slaughter of an English contingent by the Earl of Tyrone's forces at

Blackwater. Ireland's capacity to enrage and perplex the English state is a long-standing feature of our history. This, the most serious military reverse in the whole of Elizabeth's reign, left Dublin vulnerable to the Irish. In response to this outrage, boastful Essex put himself forward as a leader 'strong in power, honour and wealth, in favour with the military'. After misgivings on all sides at the prospect of war in Ireland, the charismatic Earl prepared to lead the biggest English army in living memory into battle against Tyrone. In Shakespeare's theatre, art and life were once again united. By new year 1599 – with Essex's expedition on everyone's mind – the loyal playwright was at work on a new play about another risky English overseas adventure.

Thirteen

'A KINGDOM FOR A STAGE'

> Now entertain conjecture of a time.
> *Henry V, 4.Chorus.1*

1.

After 1599, as an acclaimed poet, Shakespeare spoke to an Elizabethan elite. As a popular playwright – at a moment when perhaps as many as one in ten Londoners went to the playhouses on a regular basis – he commanded a significant public following. In the final days of the Tudor century, this high/low audience for his work would shortly reward him with 'a kingdom for a stage'. Aged thirty-five, the playwright stood at the head of his profession. A year earlier, in his *Palladis Tamia*, Francis Meres had singled out '*Shakespeare* among the English' for comedy and tragedy:

> the most excellent in both kinds for the stage: for Comedy, witness his *Gentlemen of Verona*, his *Errors*, his *Loves Labours Lost* . . . his *Midsummers Night Dream* . . . ; for Tragedy his *Richard the 2*, *Richard the 3*, *Henry 4* . . . and his *Romeo and Juliet*.

Soon, the events of 1599 would put Shakespeare 'among the English' in ways that no one could possibly have foreseen: Will 'Shake-speare' was becoming Shakespearean.

Meanwhile, the Earl of Essex, feasting on the prospect of glory, had intemperately declared, 'By God, I will beat Tyrone in the field,' adding in a terrible hostage to fortune that 'nothing worthy Her Majesty's honour hath yet been achieved' in Ireland. Led by Essex, the English army prepared to set sail for Dublin during the spring of 1599. While Queen Elizabeth grappled with rebellion, and the Earl worried about the likely outcome of this poisoned chalice, the continued threats of the Essex faction troubled the court. Shakespeare, whose patron the Earl of Southampton was part of Essex's circle, found himself on the periphery of some exceedingly dangerous politics. As part of Southampton's retinue, Shakespeare would have followed the Earl of Essex's preparations for war in Ireland with a particular interest. In London, recruiting officers enacted scenes reminiscent of Falstaff's meeting with Justice Shallow in 2 *Henry IV.* In the course of a satire on corrupt recruiting practice, the conscript Feeble utters these memorably ominous words: 'By my troth I care not, a man can die but once. We owe God a death . . . he that dies this year is quit for the next [3.2.232–6].'

In these disrupted months Shakespeare's art, life and times formed a distinctive unity. Politics and plays, history and drama, had become fused into a single metaphor, that 'we are all players' (*totus mundus agit histrionem*), a popular observation derived from Petronius. In the vernacular, Shakespeare expressed this thought as 'All the world's a stage' [*As You Like It*, 3.1.139], renewing it in *Hamlet*, when the prince describes the players as 'the abstract and brief chronicles of the time [2.2.527]'.

With this interplay of kingdom and stage, the symbiosis between Shakespeare and his audience now reaches a dramatic climax. The Shakespeare who had appealed to his audience as 'gentle creditors' in the epilogue to 2 *Henry IV* was about to become the prime mover in a complex cultural and political transaction between players and playgoers.

As much as Shakespeare styled himself the 'humble author', this was a conventional expression of theatrical modesty. As a player, a playwright, and a poet, he was renowned among a competitive field. Shakespearean characters began to infiltrate the private correspondence of the chattering classes. In 1599, the wife of his patron the Earl of Southampton can be found exchanging gossip with her husband about the sex lives of their circle through coded allusions: 'All the news I can send you,' she writes, 'that I think will make you merry is that I read in a letter from London that Sir John Falstaff is by his Mrs Dame Pintpot made father of a goodly miller's thumb, a boy that is all head and very little body.' Contemporary recognition of Shakespeare's gifts, in a society that took little interest in the lives of its artists, crops up in some odd places and celebrates the poetry of 'sweet' Will Shakespeare as much as his plays. To the poet John Weever, echoing Meres, he is 'honey-tongued', but chiefly by reputation.

Meanwhile, during some difficult days at court, Shakespeare was paying fierce attention to the anxieties of his public, and their appetite for something fresh. On this occasion, there was a real incentive, and – mixed up with contemporary politics – some very high stakes. That new theatre was in the offing.

2.

Among London's rival stage companies – the Admiral's Men, Pembroke's Men, and Lord Strange's Men – who performed in a variety of playhouses such as the Rose, the Curtain, the Theatre, and the Swan, it was the Lord Chamberlain's Men, led by the actor-manager James Burbage, father of the great actor, who represented the elite. They had the queen's favourite clown (Will Kempe), the biggest star (Richard Burbage), and the leading play-wright (William Shakespeare). What they lacked – and it was something that threatened their livelihood – was a secure venue.

The impresario James Burbage's lease on the Theatre, a popular playhouse built in 1576 and his company's long-standing Shoreditch home, had expired in April 1597. When Burbage fell out with Giles Allen, the absentee landlord, he made an irreconcilable situation worse by investing in plans for an indoor theatre at the derelict Blackfriars monastery. The Lord Chamberlain's Men were on the point of occupying this new performance space when the well-heeled residents of Blackfriars protested to the Privy Council about the 'riffe-raffe' the new theatre would attract to their neighbourhood, and the project foundered, with worse to follow.

Amid this crisis, old James Burbage died unexpectedly, leaving his sons Cuthbert and Richard with a producers' nightmare: no prospect of a stage in Blackfriars, and no possible extension of the lease in Shoreditch. Still more dire, Allen was now threatening to 'pull down' Burbage's Theatre and 'to convert the wood and timber thereof to some better use'. The only good news was the offer of another venue in Southwark, beyond the reach of repres-sive city regulations, a lease that could come into effect on Christmas Day, 1598. This new site was ideally placed on the south bank, but it had just one drawback: it lacked a playhouse. To this, the Burbage boys came up with the classic showbiz answer: the show must go on.

In the dying days of 1598, while Essex pondered the invasion of Ireland, the Lord Chamberlain's Men engaged in a new kind of Elizabethan piracy. On 28 December, during a snowstorm that muffled London's holiday streets, the Lord Chamberlain's Men, like a band of brothers, armed with 'swords, daggers, bills, axes and such like', crossed the river to Shoreditch to repossess the Theatre. With such a huge stake in his company's future, William Shakespeare was surely in their midst, joined by James Burbage's widow, Ellen, who is said to have 'looked on approvingly', according to Anthony Holden's persuasive biography.

The Burbage team had no time to lose. Giles Allen was away in the country, at his Essex estate. Once the new year came, who knew what might not happen to the Theatre's valuable timber? Besides, the Lord Chamberlain's Men were expected to perform before the queen at Whitehall on New Year's Day. Led by the master builder Peter Street, his stagehands had just four short winter days to dismantle their theatre and cart its hefty wooden frame to Street's warehouse near Bridewell Stairs on the Thames, south of Bishopsgate.

This daring coup was not unopposed; there was a nasty stand-off between Allen's men and Burbage's players. When the angry landlord brought suit three years later, he alleged that the Lord Chamberlain's Men 'did riotously assemble themselves . . . and in very riotous, outrageous and forcible manner . . . attempted to pull down the said Theatre, whereupon divers of your subjects then going about in peaceable manner to procure them to desist from their unlawful enterprise, they [resisted] with great violence . . .'

Eventually, during some bitter legal wrangling with Allen, these vital timbers would be ferried across the river to Southwark. By May, June or July 1599 (accounts differ), the Theatre had been reconstituted on the south bank as a state-of-the-art playhouse, the largest in London, with a capacity of 2,500–3,000 and boasting a confident new name: the Globe. With five fellow actors, Shakespeare was now a 'sharer' (a stakeholder) in an entertainment business popular throughout London. Before it burned down in 1613, the Globe would become the most famous theatre in European stage history.

The omens might be good, but the Lord Chamberlain's Men were taking no chances. Since the mid-1580s, the anonymous play *The Famous Victories of Henry the Fifth* had been a staple of the Elizabethan repertory. They would launch their latest season with their house playwright's new play about Henry V and his triumph over the French at Agincourt. With Essex about to take the field abroad, another glorious saga of military victory overseas might become box-office gold.

While he worked on his version of the Henry V saga, Shakespeare was now more than ever an integral part of a booming cultural economy. London's acting companies were becoming increasingly respectable. Actors, who were now part of privileged households such as the Lord Chamberlain's or the Lord Admiral's, were no longer vulnerable to arrest as vagabonds. A once-marginal profession was moving into the mainstream, symbolized by the building of the Globe. Metropolitan London, which numbered a population of between 150,000 and 250,000 was theatre-mad. Some estimates put the weekly attendance at the playhouses towards 15,000, or some 10 per cent of the local population. Shakespeare was not just addressing contemporary themes in a contemporary setting, he was engaging in a highly, even dangerously, public manner with the issues of the day. The frisson enjoyed by any citizen going to see a performance by the Lord Chamberlain's Men was essential to the thrill of being an Elizabethan playgoer.

The principal players in the Lord Chamberlain's Men seem to have enjoyed a career-long rapport, culminating in their work on the First Folio. Shakespeare played to their strengths in his scripts, especially to Richard Burbage's genius. We no longer have such long-standing repertory companies, but we do have *Monty Python's Flying Circus*. The founding cast of this immortal comic troupe (John Cleese, Eric Idle, Michael Palin, Terry Gilliam and the late Graham Chapman and Terry Jones) today occupy a place in contemporary theatre culture that's analogous to Burbage, Heminges and Condell.

At the Globe, Shakespeare, as the newly established dramatist-in-residence, was in a position of privilege and opportunity. Writing at top speed in the spring of 1599, as he completed *The Life of Henry the Fifth*, he mobilized all the qualities that experience taught would animate his scripts: surprise, jeopardy, provocation and irreverence, seasoned with seat-of-the-pants daring. With a theatre in which to workshop his plays at will, and an audience to please, a new intimacy enters his work, derived from the Globe's all-inclusive motto: *Totus Mundus Agit Histrionem*.

3.

The work that signalled a new season by the Lord Chamberlain's Men conscripted the audience into the traffic of the stage, an innovation inspired by its design. From the moment in *Henry V* the Chorus steps forward to deliver 'O for a muse of fire', Shakespeare is speaking to his players, and more especially to his audience within the 'wooden O', about the nature of the project in which they are now all involved. The Chorus's tone is conversational, even intimate:

> But pardon, gentles all,
> The flat unraisèd spirits that hath dared
> On this unworthy scaffold to bring forth
> So great an object. Can this cockpit hold
> The vasty fields of France? Or may we cram
> Within the wooden O the very casques
> That did affright the air at Agincourt? . . .
> Piece out our imperfections with your thoughts:
> Into a thousand parts divide one man,
> And make imaginary puissance.
> Think, when we talk of horses, that you see them,
> Printing their proud hoofs i' th' receiving earth.
> [1.Chorus.8–27]

Theatrical folklore says that Shakespeare himself played the Chorus. One thing is beyond question: writing in the present tense, he was addressing audiences of the future, 'gentles all'. With mature Shakespeare, time collapses; past and present become seamless; while art and politics morph into a dramatic unity, the one echoing the other.

The play became a text with a special appeal in times of crisis. In the spring of 1944, for example, with D-Day looming, a film of *Henry V,* starring Laurence Olivier, became part of the Allied war effort. Olivier had been persuaded to 'have a bash' at *Henry V,* though he was 'as nervous and uncertain as a virgin' about playing the king and conducting an unaccustomed role behind the camera as director. In the end, he decided that it seemed better 'to be riding a terrible great horse myself than pretending to trust somebody else whose riding I suspect'.

This film, dedicated to 'The Commandos and Airborne troops of Great Britain', took considerable pains to find parallels between fifteenth- and mid-twentieth-century patriotism. It was very much Olivier's show, 'Henry, Henry, Henry through an entire two hours', as he put it. His vision for the screenplay was absolute but not always workable. 'Now this is a beautiful tune I've thought of,' he told William Walton. 'Yes,' replied the composer. 'It's a lovely tune, out of *Meistersinger*.' Sometimes, the strain of being both star and director became intolerable. When his production manager asked how many horses he would need for a scene, Olivier is said to have exclaimed, 'I don't know how many fucking horses I want.'

On the eve of D-Day, *Henry V* had a special relevance for a nation and its allies preparing to invade France. Olivier's film captured the imagination of English, and especially American, audiences thousands of miles from Harfleur, unversed in early-Tudor history. The poet James Agee, film critic for *Time* magazine, established the prevailing mood when he declared that, in *Henry V*, 'the movies have produced one of their rare great works of art . . . brought to the screen with such sweetness, vigour, insight and beauty that it seemed to have been written yesterday, a play by the greatest dramatic poet who ever lived.'

It was the Chorus's famous line – 'Think, when we talk of horses' – that had suggested the film's point of entry.

The action opens in a replica of the Globe with groundlings in the pit, and actors creating an artificial period atmosphere. Once the Elizabethan context is established, the camera soars above a model of medieval London before zooming into the embarkation for France, cinematic realism evocative of the D-Day planning. Away from the period setting, Shakespeare's dialogue, reduced from 3,000 to about 1,500 lines, seems both natural and modern.

The play made the transition to film under Olivier's guidance, shooting in wartime Britain and Ireland, where local extras enacted his battle scenes in Co. Wicklow. Olivier was proud of his achievement. After its release in November 1944, the movie did especially well in America. There were screenings on college campuses across the States, and one American critic declared that it made him feel proud to be British. 'It doesn't date at all,' was Olivier's comment.

More than half a century later, the director Nicholas Hytner found his National Theatre production of the play, on the outbreak of the Iraq war, becoming doubly Shakespearean, with past and present making uncanny echoes. When Colonel Tim Collins addressed the men of the Royal Irish Regiment, he declared, 'We are going to liberate Iraq, not to conquer . . . There are some who are alive at this moment who will not be alive shortly. Those who do not wish to go on that journey we will not send . . .' Was he not channelling Henry's St Crispin's Day speech? Hytner observes, in another Shakespearean aside: 'There was no avoiding what the play had become.'

At its premiere in 1599, *Henry V* was singular for many reasons, especially for Shakespeare's confident, crowd-pleasing review of the story so far:

Now all the youth of England are on fire,
And silken dalliance in the wardrobe lies.
[2.Chorus.1–2]

These are long speeches. Act Four begins with an urgent portrait of the English army on the eve of a famous victory:

Now entertain conjecture of a time
When creeping murmur and the poring dark
Fills the wide vessel of the universe.
[4.Chorus.1–3]

This set-piece was also seasoned with such Shakespearean felicities as 'a little touch of Harry in the night', but these are not just historical soliloquies. Concealed in each chorus are several coded allusions to the condition of England. Speaking to his audience about English society was another important step towards becoming a national poet and playwright.

On stage, he continued to explore the limits of his art, especially the articulate dramatization of the 'inward' mind. After Henry's dramatic meeting with a common soldier, Shakespeare returns to the question of a 'king's repose', reflections that echoed his own queen's predicament:

'Tis not the balm, the sceptre, and the ball,
The sword, the mace, the crown imperial,
The intertissued robe of gold and pearl,
The farcèd title running fore the king,
The throne he sits on, nor the tide of pomp
That beats upon the high shore of this world . . .
[4.1.257–62]

In the spring of 1599, just before *Henry V* would go into rehearsal, the Earl of Essex staged the next episode of his tragic personal adventure, an ostentatious military departure that staked everything on his prospects in Ireland. During the afternoon of 27 March – in a pointed demonstration of military might – Essex assembled his followers in a field just north of the Tower of London to march through the city of London and maximize publicity for his cause.

To Shakespeare this scene was irresistible, and he broke all the rules in response. 'How London doth pour out her citizens,' exclaims the Chorus in the fifth act of *Henry V*, describing the king's victorious return from France, in lines coloured by Essex's departure:

> The Mayor and all his brethren, in best sort,
> Like to the senators of th'antique Rome
> With the plebeians swarming at their heels,
> Go forth and fetch their conqu'ring Caesar in –
> As, by a lower but high-loving likelihood,
> Were now the General of our gracious Empress –
> As in good time he may – from Ireland coming,
> Bringing rebellion broachèd on his sword,
> How many would the peaceful city quit
> To welcome him!
> [5.Chorus.25–34]

This unequivocal reference to contemporary politics becomes the only occasion throughout Shakespeare's plays when his mask slips and the faintest hint of anxiety peeps through the surging patriotism of his lines.

Cue: the playwright of the Globe's next new play. To

the Shakespeare who was steeped in Thomas North's translation of Plutarch, the impetuous Earl's dramatic mobilization of an army on the streets of the capital evoked 'Caesar' and 'Rome' more than 'Henry', 'Elizabeth', or 'England'. Shakespeare's decision to follow Plutarch at this moment of acute political anxiety was a master stroke, placing the dangerous subject of 'tyranny' at a double remove. This device was yet another dimension of his instinct for ambiguity. When Shakespeare sat down to write *The Tragedy of Julius Caesar* for the Globe, he was working with a subject that was encrypted twice over, by temporal as well as geographical distance.

Within London's gossipy theatre community, this new play must have been a subject of high expectation. While Peter Street's men worked round the clock to plaster the timber frame of the Globe with laths, lime and animal hair to create the durable illusion of a stone structure, Shakespeare was writing, on deadline, to complete a new script fit for the new theatre, as well as making a subtle commentary on the politics of the moment.

4.

In that tense summer of 1599, Shakespeare seems also to have been galvanized by the opportunities of the Globe. *Henry V* had been short, swift and highly charged. *Julius Caesar*, some 800 lines shorter, is even more urgent and compressed, as if, says James Shapiro, 'written without interruption in a few short weeks'. Again, in the creation of *Julius Caesar*, art and life were one: he was writing under pressure in the way he seems to have preferred, taking dramatic inspiration from a story whose lineaments had long acquired the status of myth. Julius Caesar was also a character with fabled connections to the neighbourhood in which the Globe was situated. Just across the Thames from Southwark, the Tower of London was believed to have been built by Caesar during the Roman occupation of Britain.

Shakespeare's confidence about his new play possibly derived from the materials he had to hand. The new edition of Thomas North's 1579 translation of Plutarch's *Lives of the Noble Greeks and Romans* on which he drew came from the presses of the printer-publisher Richard Field. The use of this classical source in an English version is symbolic of his mature artistic method.

It was Shakespeare's principal responsibility to fulfil the first rule of showbiz and put bums on seats. If he was going to revisit a classical theme, he would have to conduct his exploration of its meaning through the lens of contemporary politics. *Julius Caesar* may be populated with many famous Roman characters – Calpurnia, Cassius and Cinna, for instance – but they walk the streets of Stratford and London, debating food prices and holiday allowances, issues close to the hearts and minds of a late-Elizabethan audience.

This latest show was another hit. On 21 September 1599, a Swiss tourist, Thomas Platter, went down to Southwark 'after dinner, about two o'clock', an excursion he recorded in his diary, providing a snapshot of the Globe in performance during its first year:

> in the straw-thatched house we saw the tragedy of the first Emperor Julius Caesar, very pleasantly performed, with approximately fifteen characters; at the end of the play they danced together admirably and exceedingly gracefully, according to their custom, two in each group dressed in men's, and two in women's apparel.

Platter saw *Julius Caesar* in September 1599. Less than a month later there was more contemporary political drama, when the players and playwright of the Lord Chamberlain's Men were once again brushed by the wings of history.

5.

Essex's command of the queen's forces in Ireland had been a disaster from start to finish, his army weakened by desertion, malnutrition and disease. When Elizabeth ordered him to invade Ulster, Essex replied that he lacked the men, confessing that only 4,000 of the 16,000 who'd sailed with him in the spring were fit for combat. The queen raged; the Earl dithered. Obey the queen, fight the Irish with sickly troops, and risk a terrible defeat; or do nothing, and admit failure? Faced with two unthinkable outcomes, Essex hatched a new strategy, beset with risk. He would not attack Ulster; instead, he would return to England at the head of his most loyal troops, and confront his queen with a show of military might.

This reckless flirtation with civil war was fleeting, and quite silly; word soon got back to London. Essex could procrastinate no longer. Foolishly, he allowed himself to become distracted by a parley with Tyrone, one to one. The upshot of the rendezvous, after a dinner at 'a fern table' under Irish stars, was that both parties agreed to a cessation of hostilities. At the end of September 1599, emboldened by this apparent breakthrough, Essex set off for the English court at Nonsuch Palace.

In a movie moment, the headstrong Earl burst into the royal presence, travel-stained, breathless – and un-announced. Lytton Strachey dramatizes the scene: 'There was Elizabeth among her ladies, in a dressing-gown, unpainted, without her wig, her grey hair hanging in wisps about her face, and her eyes starting from her head.' The queen's response to this outrageous intrusion was to place Essex under house arrest, followed by an inconclusive Star Chamber examination. A stand-off ensued. The fallen favourite, whose health was failing, remained in captivity, while the queen debated his case with her advisers.

Eventually, he was further interrogated for eleven hours by the Star Chamber, which imposed a massive fine and ordered him to the Tower, a sentence commuted to more house-arrest. Shakespeare was following these events, but also planning his latest play. Rarely, throughout his work, is the catalyst of risk and originality so explicit. In the autumn of 1599, amid worsening domestic politics, he was gearing up for a work that would owe everything to the disruptions of the time, and most especially to the Globe, which was in severe danger of acquiring a political as well as a theatrical role.

At this decisive moment, the Lord Chamberlain's Men and their playwright found themselves dangerously implicated in the political drama that was roiling the capital. Southampton – Shakespeare's patron – was a vocal Essex supporter, who had been actively plotting the Earl's advancement. Early in February 1601 the long-anticipated showdown occurred.

The spark that set off this explosion was a letter from James VI of Scotland encouraging the Earl's cause. For Queen Elizabeth, the accession question was her Achilles' heel. As rumours of a *coup d'état* swept through London, Essex lost control of events. Fatally, one of his keenest advocates, Sir Gelly [*also Gilly or Gelli*] Meyrick took it into his head to stoke the national debate about deposing the sovereign through the use of a Shakespeare play.

On 6 February 1601, Meyrick and some of Essex's supporters arrived at the Globe with an urgent request that the Lord Chamberlain's Men stage an ad hoc performance of *Richard II*, including its notorious 'deposition' scene (the shocking overthrow of a weak English monarch), the next day. Fearful for their lives, the players tried to refuse with various excuses: the script was 'old and out of use'; they could not muster enough players at such short notice, etc. Sir Gelly, on behalf of his master, upped the ante. The Essex party would sponsor the show to the tune of forty shillings on top of the players' regular fee, plus whatever they took at the box office.

Next day, the Lord Chamberlain's Men gave their reluctant performance, to an audience of pro-Essex supporters, a rare fusion of theatre and politics. Word of the show had spread rapidly through London. Gawkers and thrill-seekers hurried to the Globe to see the highly charged, dramatic spectacle of a reigning monarch overthrown by a disaffected nobleman.

Now things began to move fast, as often happens on the political stage. On 7 February, the evening after the show, Essex was ordered to appear before the Privy Council, but refused to leave home, alleging that there was a plot to kill him led by his old enemy, Walter Raleigh. Simultaneously, some of his supporters began plotting to seize the city. The next morning, a Sunday, the queen struck. Elizabeth sent a powerful delegation of state servants, including the chief justice, the Lord Keeper and the Earl of Worcester, to Essex House with a warning against acts of treason.

The unfolding drama quickly became a crisis when the crowd, vehemently pro-Essex, took the royal party hostage. Impetuously, Essex placed himself at the head of two hundred troops in a reckless mounted assault on London. But the Ludgate was barred to him, and the further he pressed into the city, the more obvious it became that there was no popular appetite for an uprising to his cause. Seizing the opportunity, the authorities recovered their nerve. The herald proclaimed the headstrong Earl a traitor and when he tried to flee, Essex found his escape route blocked by armed men.

By nightfall, he had fought his way back to Essex House only to find his hostages freed, his headquarters under siege, and his situation desperate. When, that same evening, the Lord Admiral threatened to bombard the would-be usurper's headquarters, Essex realized he had to give himself up. By midnight he was on his way to the Tower. Within a week, he was brought to trial for treason. His co-defendant was the Earl of Southampton; and in court, Essex quoted Shakespeare. 'I am indifferent how I speed,' he told his accusers. 'I owe God a death.'

It was always a show trial; the accused were denied legal counsel and swiftly found guilty. Essex broke down and abased himself in words that could just as well have found dramatic utterance at the Globe Theatre: 'I know my sins unto Her Majesty and to my God. I must confess to you that I am the greatest, the most vilest and most unthankful traitor that has ever been in the land.'

Soon after, on the morning of 25 February, Essex was beheaded in the courtyard of the Tower, an execution witnessed by, among others, Sir Walter Raleigh. The marvellous Earl's courage amid the shambles of the scaffold was widely noted. In the words of Malcolm in *Macbeth*, he died like a man 'studied in his death', surrendering 'the dearest thing' as if it were 'a careless trifle [1.4.7–11]'.

Southampton was spared, but Meyrick and some other co-conspirators were hanged or beheaded. In other respects, the government was less vindictive than many had feared. The actor Augustine Phillips, a sharer in the Globe, was asked by the Privy Council to explain the treasonous performance of *Richard II*. After a terrifying meeting with representatives of the Elizabethan state, he, Shakespeare, and their fellows escaped with a reprimand. Future quarto editions of the play would be published with the 'deposition scene' ruthlessly excised. (None of the *Richard II* quartos published in Elizabeth's reign have the deposition scene. The Q4 of 1608 is the first.)

Shakespeare, meanwhile, was now fully committed to a new play containing scenes of popular revolt. In the writing of *Hamlet*, there are several moments when late-Elizabethan politics break into the text. The horror felt by the queen's advisers towards Essex creeps into Claudius' fear of Hamlet. 'How dangerous is it that this man goes loose,' exclaims Claudius, before expressing the real-life dilemma in which Elizabeth I had found herself:

> Yet must not we put the strong law on him.
> He's loved of the distracted multitude,
> Who like not in their judgement but their eyes,
> And where 'tis so, th'offender's scourge is weighed,
> But never the offence. To bear all smooth and even,
> This sudden sending him away must seem
> Deliberate pause. Diseases desperate grown

By desperate appliance are relieved,
Or not at all.
[4.3.2–11]

In the 1600s, it was the Globe's constant appeal to new audiences that Shakespeare would rarely fail to bring art and life into perilous juxtaposition. In 1601, an immediate consequence of this imaginative traffic in the dramatist's mind was the play that would finally make Shakespeare 'Shakespearean': *The Tragical History of Hamlet, Prince of Denmark.*

PART FOUR, 1600–1609:

Shakespearean

Shakespeare becomes 'Shakespearean', the 'soul of the age', and his greatest work makes its claim on posterity.

Fourteen

'DISTRACTED GLOBE'

The best actors in the world, either for tragedy, comedy,
history, pastoral, pastorical-comical, historical-
pastoral, tragical-historical, tragical-comical-historical-
pastoral, scene individable or poem unlimited.
Hamlet, 2.2.398

1.

In 2015, anticipating the imminent 400th anniversary of
Shakespeare's death, the Globe Theatre in Southwark began
touring a small-scale production of *Hamlet*, in what the
director Dominic Dromgoole described as a 'brain-defying,
logistics-confounding' transit of some 205 countries, from
Azerbaijan to Zambia.

In four hundred years, *Hamlet* has travelled through space
and time to every corner of the world's imagination, inspiring
all kinds of spin-off from *Rosencrantz and Guildenstern Are
Dead* to *The Lion King*. When it's staged at Elsinore, in
Kronborg Castle, on the edge of the sound separating
Denmark from Sweden, to the north of Copenhagen, the
play becomes something else again, an eccentric statement
of local pride, as well as a Shakespearean rite of passage.
Laurence Olivier has played Hamlet here, and so have
Richard Burton, John Gielgud and Kenneth Branagh.

A few years before Dromgoole's globe-trotting *Hamlet*,

and breaking away from the Shakespeare Club, which prefers to stay on English soil, I took the train to Helsingor to see Jude Law perform the role in an English-language production within the castle courtyard. The presence of Frederik, the perfectly sane crown prince of Denmark, in the audience on opening night added another layer to the aura of otherworldliness. For the Danish Shakespeare-lovers who queue up on summer evenings with picnic hampers and plaid rugs, *Hamlet* is their national play. What is Helsingor? A wind-swept crag brooding above a furious sea? Actually, it's a picture postcard: a seventeenth-century restoration overlooking a blameless suburban town, half an hour's train ride from Copenhagen, selling both booze and bard. This Helsingor festival exhibits the devotion of Gilbert and Sullivan fans at the Savoy Theatre. At every reference to Denmark, or the Danes, the audience politely applauds or, stranger still, titters knowingly; and the atmosphere becomes a mix of Glyndebourne and the Edinburgh Tattoo, an event both cultural and ceremonial.

For Jude Law, the experience was about his actor's relationship with a famous play. In one interview, having fretted about the familiarity of 'To be, or not to be', he exclaimed, 'Never underestimate the power of these lines. Our language is littered with words and phrases from this play, and we have not, in four hundred years, found a better way of putting things.'

'To be, or not to be' is a line that can thrill, chill or inspire. Like the tolling of a great bell, this massive inter-rogative will echo through the audience's imagination. History or romance; comedy or tragedy: Shakespeare's 'poem unlimited', the elusive and enigmatic summation of his genius, becomes his defining moment. To the unwitting London audiences who attended the Globe around 1600, the experience of seeing this play must have seemed like taking part in a collective nervous breakdown, made all the more acute by the slippery evasions of the playwright's art: every observation you might make about *Hamlet* is true – and so is its opposite.

From the moment the play opened at the Globe, probably during 1600–1, actors and audiences alike seem to have recognized they were in the presence of something utterly and uniquely new. Shakespeare, at once deeply read and instinctively original in dramatic strategy, would have known that, in the prince of Denmark, he had created a different kind of theatrical hero. He signals this during the scene where Hamlet asks Guildenstern to play a recorder. When his college friend insists he does not know how to do this, Hamlet makes this pointed retort: 'You would play upon me, you would seem to know my stops, you would pluck out the heart of my mystery . . . Call me what instrument you will, though you can fret me, you cannot play upon me [3.2.353–60].'

There are as many arguments about the date of *Hamlet*'s composition and first performance as about its dramatic intentions. At first, as if to anatomize the heart of the tragedy, Shakespeare opens with the challenge of the dramatic present: 'Who's there?' But few answers follow. Just as the opening scene contrasts brilliant clarity with baffling opacity, so the beginnings of *Hamlet*, the script, are boldly set forth in two quarto editions, 'bad' and 'good', each wrapped in doubt and controversy. Almost the only certainty is that the uncut text of Shakespeare's longest play runs to about 4,000 lines, has its origins in European folklore, and might also be a reworking of an *Ur-Hamlet* from the 1580s, which some scholars contend may have been one of Shakespeare's own early drafts.

Beyond these issues, however, *Hamlet* is an unprecedented theatrical achievement, a primal Shakespearean masterpiece, sometimes referred to as his *Mona Lisa*. With a life of its own, *Hamlet* stands next to the work of Aeschylus, Euripides, Virgil, Dante, and Tolstoy as the worldwide symbol of the playwright's genius. After 1600, Hamlet the universal hero will speak to successive generations as their contemporary with his own independent life and feelings. The world's literature has few genuine turning points, but this is certainly one of them.

Hamlet is swift, allusive, and thrilling. Shakespeare's new play demonstrated his most brilliant qualities from its opening line: for T. S. Eliot that first scene is 'as well constructed as that of any play ever written'. From the bone-chilling shadows of Elsinore's battlements to its bloody, chaotic, and cathartic climax, *Hamlet* is simultaneously of its time, and for all time: a ghost story, a revenge thriller, and an inquiry into the nature of being. It marries themes of public and private breakdown, domestic and state madness, reflecting the drama surrounding the fall of Essex as well as Shakespeare's mid-life sensibility after the tragic loss of his eleven-year-old son Hamnet, and immediately before the death of his own father, John Shakespeare. Aptly, the play falls at the midpoint of his career. With the Globe for a theatre workshop, he was writing as the acclaimed author of *Romeo and Juliet* and *Henry V*. Later, the lessons of *Hamlet* would propel him towards *Othello, Macbeth, King Lear, Antony and Cleopatra, Coriolanus, Othello, The Winter's Tale* and

The Tempest, the greatest sequence of original new plays in European theatre history.

Appropriately for such an innovative drama, *Hamlet* will showcase more than six hundred new words, from *gibber* to *remorseless*. Shakespeare also dazzled his audiences with those quotable lines that would pass into the mainstream of common English speech, from 'The play's the thing,' and 'Frailty, thy name is woman!' to 'More in sorrow than in anger,' 'Brevity is the soul of wit,' 'Conscience makes cowards of us all,' 'The lady doth protest too much,' and 'The rest is silence.'

Above all, *Hamlet* resounds to the clash of those dramatic antitheses with which Shakespeare animated his stagecraft. It is a play of noble simplicity and majestic complexity. Once he has introduced his tragic, coming-of-age protagonist, Shakespeare frames humanity's greatest existential challenge in the English of the street, words that every theatregoer, from the groundling to the gallery, can understand:

> To be, or not to be; that is the question:
> Whether 'tis nobler in the mind to suffer
> The slings and arrows of outrageous fortune,
> Or to take arms against a sea of troubles,
> And, by opposing, end them.
> [3.1.58–62]

Sometimes Shakespeare will provoke and console in the same breath, with his extraordinary capacity for the creative resolution of opposites. This is yet another reminder that, writing at the dangerous edge, he is always making uncanny connections with our deepest hopes and fears through poetry and story, and asking the simplest, most fundamental questions in plain English: Where do I come from? Why am I here? Who am I? and, Where am I going?

In its afterlife, this play renews itself by making a unique demand upon its audience. From the groundlings in the pit to the 'better sort' seated in the galleries, the playgoer is invited to enter into the heart and mind – the consciousness – of the play's protagonist. This had never happened before, to such a compelling extent, on the English stage. Thus, *Hamlet* becomes a demonstration of theatrical 'inwardness' in which the principal characters – notably Claudius and young Hamlet – express their secret thoughts and emotions in some great soliloquies, those dazzling arias of blank verse. This was the breakthrough moment towards which Shakespeare had been working since the death of Marlowe, a period described by the critic Frank Kermode as 'unparalleled in the history of anglophone poetry'.

2.

Years before his move to the Globe, Shakespeare had begun experimenting with the ways in which his characters might wrestle with thoughts and feelings onstage. In *Richard II*, he had presented a king examining both his private and public self:

What must the King do now? Must he submit?
The King shall do it. Must he be deposed?
The King shall be contented. Must he lose
The name of King?
[3.3.142–5]

By the end of that history, this new inwardness had become the anguished self-expression of a broken man 'studying' to compare 'this prison where I live unto the world [5.5.2]'. Meanwhile, the playwright who'd put 'self' into his sonnets began to explore the drama of eroticism in *Romeo and Juliet*. By 1599, in *Julius Caesar*, in his complex portrait of Brutus, Shakespeare had also imagined his bookish assassin wrestling with states of molten self-consciousness and dread, 'between the acting of a dreadful thing' and the deed itself. For Brutus, the self-aware protagonist becomes a 'little kingdom' suffering 'an insurrection [2.1.63–9]'.

In *Hamlet*, these strands are united. To weaponize the dramatic impact of this approach, Shakespeare braids the theatrical staple of 'revenge' – an old trope – with the more modern concept of 'memory', the faculty which, in Renaissance thought, liberates mankind's independence. Hamlet has already told his audience that the moods which can 'denote me truly' are unreliable, and that the inner man can never match his outward presence:

They are actions that a man might play;
But I have within that which passes show –
These but the trappings and the suits of woe.
[1.2.84–6]

Next, he personalizes his confession. 'Remember thee? Ay, thou poor ghost . . . [1.5.95–6]'. This urgent dramatization of memory becomes a short route into Hamlet's introspection. Shakespeare's concern as a playwright is to grapple with Hamlet's state of mind. His audience becomes trapped in the vortex of a new sensation, the tragedy in which Shakespeare explores both a new language, and a new sensibility. From the arresting moment of Hamlet's first soliloquy, the Globe was pitched into a radically unfamiliar universe of dramatic self-consciousness:

> O that this too too solid flesh would melt,
> Thaw, and resolve itself into a dew,
> Or that the Everlasting had not fixed
> His canon 'gainst self-slaughter! O God, O God,
> How weary, stale, flat, and unprofitable
> Seem to me all the uses of this world!
> [1.2.129–34]

In *Hamlet*, this turn-of-the-century audience witnessed Shakespeare discovering the intoxicating theatrical potency of mixing the 'self' with its articulate consciousness – through memory, conscience, and revenge – all within the first act. As if to hammer home that message, the Ghost says – several times – 'Remember me.' Shakespeare then pulls these themes together into a single speech that connects memory, the theatre and Hamlet's troubled mind in his anguished confession:

> Remember thee?
> Ay, thou poor ghost, while memory holds a seat
> In this distracted globe. Remember thee?
> Yea, from the table of my memory
> I'll wipe away all trivial fond records . . .
> [1.5.95–9]

The playwright's image for the prince's mind – 'this distracted globe' – a metaphor drawn from the theatre in which Hamlet is standing, short-circuits the playgoers' experience of the tragedy itself, but he still has some voltage in reserve. In *Hamlet*, Shakespeare withholds his most revolutionary moment of solitary self-examination with exemplary stagecraft. 'To be, or not to be' will be deployed to maximum effect, after the audience has been exposed to many iterations of Hamlet's inwardness. At the beginning of the third act, Hamlet's state of mind, overtly suicidal, focuses on his 'sea of troubles'. Now, having committed his audience to a new kind of experience, Shakespeare can begin to anatomize his 'madness'. Polonius' advice to Claudius opens a debate about the prince's sanity that will never be resolved. What, exactly, is the meaning of that 'antic disposition'? Polonius thinks he has the answer:

> Your noble son is mad –
> 'Mad' call I it, for to define true madness,
> What is't but to be nothing else but mad?
> [2.2.93–5]

Shakespeare is always a writer with a deep and instinctive humanity. If Hamlet is mad, he wants his audience to see that he's also alert to the human condition, and in thrall to depression, or (as we might see it) his existential angst:

> I have of late – but wherefore I know not – lost all
> my mirth, forgone all custom of exercise; and indeed
> it goes so heavily with my disposition that this goodly
> frame, the earth, seems to me a sterile promontory.
> This most excellent canopy the air, look you, this brave
> o'erhanging, this majestical roof fretted with golden

fire – why, it appeareth no other thing to me than a foul and pestilent congregation of vapours.
[2.2.296–304]

Before Shakespeare, no one had ever explored the intuition that we are just ourselves, but that other people also feel the same way – that they too are unique. Shakespeare's grasp of doubleness opens a door into the state of mind we now call 'empathy'. After his admission of insecurity, Hamlet moves to make a late-Renaissance statement of man's sovereign individualism:

What a piece of work is a man! How noble in reason, how infinite in faculty, in form and moving how express and admirable, in action how like an angel, in apprehension how like a god – the beauty of the world, the paragon of animals! And yet to me what is this quintessence of dust?
[2.2.304–9]

Hamlet's tormented humanity, articulated as never before, moves swiftly through a raw sequence of emotions: grief, conscience, despair, and the 'antic disposition' which hovers at the edge of reason. Each of these speeches is framed by its theatrical context. There is the prince's thespian glee: 'The play's the thing / Wherein I'll catch the conscience of the King [2.2.606–7].' Then, inspired by the example of the Player King, his subsequent admission of stage fright: 'Thus conscience does make cowards of us all . . . [3.1.85]'.

This supremely dramatic exposition is underpinned by a subtle and exquisite piece of theatre. In *Hamlet*, as in *A*

Midsummer Night's Dream, Shakespeare delights in the stagecraft of placing a group of actors-playing-actors – the Player King and his troupe – in the engine room of the plot, co-opting the conventions of popular theatre and its players.

Actors who perform Shakespeare are members of a theatrical elite who will enrich his lines with humanity, instinct, magic, and memory. His lines become part of their being as they, in turn, inhabit his roles, and become part of *Hamlet*'s afterlife. Jude Law, for instance, was aware of his recent predecessors – Kenneth Branagh, Jonathan Pryce, David Tennant, Simon Russell Beale, Benedict Cumberbatch – each of whom will have been conscious of following Garrick, Kean, Irving, Beerbohm Tree, Gielgud, Olivier and Schofield. Every one of these artists will have their own relationship to the Shakespeare who was possibly the first to express how strange is the transaction between player and playwright.

In *Hamlet*, the prince puzzles over the artistry of the Player King, contrasting his own inadequacy as 'a rogue and peasant slave' with the 'dream of passion' exhibited by the actor:

Tears in his eyes, distraction in 's aspect,
A broken voice, and his whole function suiting
With forms to his conceit? And all for nothing.
For Hecuba!
[2.2.557–60]

Hamlet can only marvel at this gift. 'What's Hecuba to him, or he to Hecuba?' In Hamlet's mind, there is even something questionable about an art form that can 'make mad the guilty and appal the free' as if, for a moment, Shakespeare is channelling the Puritan opposition to the theatre, while at the same time celebrating the democracy of the playhouse.

3.

In *The Empty Space*, Peter Brook explains the raw and modernizing power of what he calls 'popular' (or 'rough') theatre:

> It is dirt that gives the roughness its edge; filth and vulgarity are natural, obscenity is joyous: with these the spectacle takes on its socially liberating role, for by its nature the popular theatre is anti-authoritarian, anti-traditional, anti-pomp, anti-pretence. This is the theatre of noise, and the theatre of noise is the theatre of applause.

The players, like Hamlet himself, are in the middle of an acute contemporary career crisis. Their livelihood is threatened by competition from the popular 'boys' companies'. As actors, they are up against it. Moreover, the Player King has a second purpose (in many productions he will also play the part of the Ghost). First, he must represent, with poignant nobility, the profession to which Shakespeare has devoted his life. Actors, says Hamlet, in a heartfelt speech, should be 'well used': 'They are the abstracts and brief chronicles of the time. After your death you were better have a bad epitaph than their ill report while you live [2.2.527–9].'

Not only do they keep us honest, actors are in touch with their deepest feelings in a way that Hamlet ('a muddy-mettled rascal'), to his deep regret, is not. Further, the actors' skills are polyphonous. Here, Shakespeare allows Hamlet to give a masterclass in verse-speaking:

> Speak the speech, I pray you, as I pronounced it to you – trippingly on the tongue . . . Suit the action to the word, the word to the action, with this special observance: that you o'erstep not the modesty of nature. For anything so overdone is from the purpose of playing, whose end, both at the first and now, was and is to hold as 'twere the mirror up to nature.
> [3.2.1–22]

Secondly, exploiting the 'cunning of the scene', Hamlet will use the play he calls 'The Mousetrap' to nail Claudius' guilt once and for all.

As a revenge tragedy, *Hamlet* should be home and hosed by the end of Act Two. It's the measure of Shakespeare's radical renewal of the genre that, from one point of view, it has scarcely begun when, curtailing the play-within-the-play, Claudius calls for 'Lights, ho!' In the third, fourth and final acts, the illumination of the world Shakespeare has created now comes from the faltering light of some very disturbed sources. It will be the rejected Ophelia who makes the moving summary of her lover's tormented condition:

> O what a noble mind is here o'erthrown!
> The courtier's, soldier's, scholar's eye, tongue, sword,
> Th'expectancy and rose of the fair state . . .
> [3.1.153–5]

This troubled, elegiac sweetness brings the audience back to the present, and a reminder that some of this play strikes a note that's far from innovative. Shakespeare's observation that Hamlet's time is 'out of joint' signals a regret for the turning of the century.

How weary, stale, flat, and unprofitable
Seem to me all the uses of this world!
[1.2.133–4]

It's as if, in this expression of the prince's inexplicable loss of mirth, Shakespeare is already grieving for his queen.

4.

The death of Elizabeth I in March 1603 saw a new dynasty advancing centre stage, with James VI of Scotland's dramatic move south to Whitehall. Already, the instability of Jacobean England had been prefigured in the disruptions of 1599–1603. Not only had Essex plotted against the Crown, but the headstrong Earl's rebellion had scarcely been snuffed out before Elizabeth herself began to fail. Once the old queen was dead, there were new men with unfamiliar accents supplanting the hallowed nobility of late-medieval England. A way of life through which Shakespeare had come of age, and in which he had flourished as its dramatist, was becoming 'an unweeded garden / That grows to seed [1.2.135]'. It's no surprise that Hamlet hesitates over the Ghost's summons to retribution. In theory, he should sweep to his revenge by the close of Act One, but it is not obvious where, precisely, his enemy is to be found. Is it the new king? Or is it his duplicitous associates, sinister counsellors like Polonius, corrupted friends like Rosencrantz and Guildenstern, or that creepy 'waterfly', Osric?

Beyond the walls of the court, there is yet more uncertainty and confusion. The common people, formerly a bulwark of loyalty to the status quo, have become 'muddied, Thick and unwholesome in their thoughts [4.5.79]'. Shakespeare's apprehensions about 'the people' are turning towards the darker anxieties he will put into *Coriolanus*. There, the crisis is as acute as in Elsinore, but not confined to court circles. The people are starving, oppressed, and angry. Coriolanus, indifferent to their plight, matches their rage with his majestic 'I banish you [3.3.127]', words that Claudius possibly internalized, but never expressed.

Both these plays end as human, not political, tragedies. The 'people' will always be the toys of history, spectators to the catastrophes of an elite. On that more intimate scale, the carnage which brings *Hamlet* to a climax is the only redemption Shakespeare can suggest, a bloodbath followed by invasion and a military occupation. Typically, Shakespeare reconciles Hamlet to this nihilistic conclusion – a nihilism that will grow in his imagination throughout the 1600s – through the prince's Anglo-Saxon stoicism, uttered in limpid monosyllables: 'If it be now, 'tis not to come. If it be not to come, it will be now. If it be not now, yet it will come. The readiness is all [5.2.166–8].'

Soon after these lines, his audience would have stumbled out onto the streets of London, wondering what on earth they had just witnessed, a play about Denmark, or something closer to home? Shakespeare himself had already encrypted a message about his own state of mind in Hamlet's words to Gertrude during their frantic bedroom scene:

It is not madness
That I have uttered. Bring me to the test,
And I the matter will reword, which madness
Would gambol from.
[3.4.132–15]

Throughout the coming decade, Shakespeare would progressively 'reword' his 'matter'. At odds with his time, and ageing throughout the decade, he would take his art into another dimension, a radically new interpretation of reality. In the process, he would transform his dramatic gifts into something timeless, abstract, modern, and 'Shakespearean'.

Fifteen

'WHAT YOU WILL'

VIOLA: Then think you right: I am not what I am.
OLIVIA: I would you were as I would have you be.
Twelfth Night, 3.1.139

1.

Across four centuries, the afterlife of *Hamlet* has acquired many manifestations. At first, the play swiftly became a topic for discussion within literary London. Around 1600, for instance, one scholar noted that, while the younger generation 'takes much delight in Shakespeare's *Venus, & Adonis*', it was 'his tragedie of *Hamlet, Prince of Denmarke*' that pleased 'the wiser sort'. As befitted a theatrical hit, *Hamlet* became a fixture in the Globe's repertoire.

Shakespeare himself, meanwhile, had moved on to a new project. *Twelfth Night* is another play about the identity of the self in a world turned upside down by the irruptions of misrule. It has a similar mix of unrequited love, madness, melancholy and even court intrigue, suffused with a kind of joyous levity, a comedy that's as infectious, dark and original as *Hamlet*, whose antic mood it seems at times to share. There's the same collision of memory with emotion when Viola (in the guise of Cesario) flirts with Orsino in the spirit of *Hamlet*, describing the history of her love affairs, and her secret communing

207

with melancholy, the fashionable affliction of the late-Elizabethan gallant:

> She pined in thought,
> And with a green and yellow melancholy
> She sat like patience on a monument,
> Smiling at grief.
> [2.4.112–5]

With the negligent ambiguity Shakespeare now culti-vates after 'As You Like It', he gave this latest comedy a throwaway subtitle – 'What You Will' – conscripting the audience to his purposes while at the same time indicating that the playgoers at the Globe could anticipate a pleasing entertainment, not a tragedy, even if the one is a half-cousin to the other. In the humiliation of Malvolio, there's a sense in which *Twelfth Night* might be a cruel comic out-take from *Hamlet*: Olivia's 'steward' could have found a minor role at Elsinore. Hereafter, Shakespeare's expression of 'comedy' will become abstract romances, seasoned with bitter darkness.

From Viola's first question – 'What country, friends, is this?' – *Twelfth Night* propels the audience into a world of speculation: about identity, gender, place, position, and faith. Above all, it's about love, the subject of its opening line: 'If music be the food of love, play on.' The mood is conditional, with hints of the fairy-tale. Once Viola has been told that she's in Illyria, Shakespeare transports us to a sunshine province – half real, half unreal – rich in Arcadian connotations, which becomes another semi-abstract society smitten with reveries of desire and courtly romance. Viola finds herself in a dream world peopled with sixteenth-century English reprobates, such as Sir Toby Belch and Sir Andrew Aguecheek, who make specific reference to London landmarks like 'the Elephant' (3.3.39) and enjoy the kind of city slang ('Westward ho!') familiar to theatregoers being ferried across the Thames to Southwark.

Twelfth Night is the dark comedy that also inspired *Shakespeare in Love,* another brilliant confection of moods and themes. The new world in which Viola finds herself becomes the highly artificial setting for an intoxicating dialogue about the identity of the self as it's expressed by a young woman (played by a boy) who has disguised herself as a boy (Cesario) and gets wooed by another woman, Olivia (played by a boy). The duality (and its associated confusions) that runs through almost every scene inspired some of its loveliest poetry:

> Make me a willow cabin at your gate
> And call upon my soul within the house,
> Write loyal cantons of contemned love,
> And sing them loud even in the dead of night;
> Halloo your name to the reverberate hills,
> And make the babbling gossip of the air
> Cry out 'Olivia!'
> [1.5.257–63]

There's an intensity to Viola's vision of herself as a lover wooing a disdainful mistress, an introspective fervour that derives from the innovations Shakespeare had explored in *Hamlet.* The travails of the self as a microcosm of humanity would become a dominant theme throughout the 1600s, in which Shakespeare would embark on several dramas of identity: sexual (*Measure for Measure*), regal

(*King Lear*), political (*Coriolanus*), and magical (*The Tempest*), locating each in a half-imagined world. When the Romantic movement rediscovered Shakespeare, it would be the poet's snail-horn sensitivity to selfhood, and the ecstatic celebration of free expression through nature, that transformed the author of *Hamlet* into the god of the Romantics' idolatry.

2.

Initially, even the 'good' quarto editions of *Hamlet* did not outsell Shakespeare's fashionable poetry. The resonant importance of *Hamlet* became established over centuries. Indeed, the first record of *Hamlet* in performance abroad occurs in 1607 when the *Red Dragon*, an East India Company vessel, anchored off Sierra Leone, 'gave the tragedie of Hamlett' to a scratch audience of sailors, merchants and mystified local thrill-seekers. Thereafter, it was performed at court in 1619, and 'diverse times . . . in the cittie of London'.

In his study of 'Hamletomanie' Andrew Dickson describes how *Hamlet* first became 'Shakespearean' in France and Germany during the eighteenth century, a by-product of the fashionable Anglomania adopted by the self-styled philosopher and satirist known as 'Voltaire'. Jean-Marie Arouet had fled to England, escaping French absolutism. Soon, his discovery of the *Complete Works* inspired him to pay Shakespeare the compliment of devout imitation. Voltaire's 'Hamlet', which appeared in 1726, was followed by versions of *Julius Caesar* and *Othello*. (Eventually, he would turn against Shakespeare.)

After this strange marriage of Shakespeare and French Enlightenment sensibility, it was Germany and the Germans who embraced his work as their own. Later, it would be

Tolstoy's claim that Shakespeare's renown was 'got up' by German professors and 'thence was transferred to England'. More prosaic, and perhaps less polemical, it was through the fervour of the philosopher and critic Johann Gottfried Herder and his essay on Shakespeare that England's national poet was hailed by Herder's disciples as *unser Shakespeare* ('our Shakespeare'), and an English dramatist became canonized as an unacknowledged German writer. Above all, it was Goethe who translated the prince of Denmark into a romantic hero for his generation in *The Sorrows of Young Werther* (1774). Goethe had lit an eternal flame, but it would be his acolytes, Schiller and Schlegel, who fired up the cult of the Bard. The young Schiller was obsessed with Shakespeare. His masterpiece *Don Carlos*, a tragic tale of the doomed heir to the Spanish throne who falls in love with his stepmother and is drawn into a fatal struggle with his tyrannical father was, he admitted, a play with the 'soul of *Hamlet*'.

Schiller was fiery; but for A. W. Schlegel, Shakespeare was a sober Germanic figure, a dedicated craftsman inspired by his reverence for art, *die Kunst*. Schlegel's translations, the *Dramatische Werke*, transformed Shakespeare into a great German writer. In an impossible fantasy, Schlegel came to believe that his translations could hew so closely to the original that it would be as if Shakespeare himself had actually written in German. As a result of these ambitions, an exuberant, sometimes vulgar kind of popular entertainment, rooted in the English vernacular, driven by sex, politics, and violence, seasoned with money, jealousy, and lust, became the symbol of a high-minded bourgeois culture, a romantic sensibility expressed in one word: *Shakespearomanie*.

This German cult of Shakespeare culminated in 1844 with a poem by Ferdinand Feilgrath, which began, *Deutschland ist Hamlet* ('Germany is Hamlet'), and described an introspective people, incapable of action. This notion also had its English adherents. When the great Romantic Samuel Taylor Coleridge first visited Gottingen in 1798–9, he soon fell under the spell of an Aryan Shakespeare.

Coleridge's trip to Germany inspired the idea of a native 'Shakespearean' aesthetic. In 1808, imitating Schlegel, Coleridge embarked on two series of literary talks whose unintended consequence was to fix Shakespeare and his work in the amber-gold of a feverish Romantic thesis about the poetic 'Imagination'. Coleridge was fascinated with the idea of 'the one power in the world of the senses', and proposed to address this in twenty-five lectures on Chaucer, Milton, Pope and Wordsworth, a series that, returning to the 'poetic principle', identified Shakespeare as an artist with a godlike creative ability to transform himself into infinite variety, 'to become by power of Imagination another Thing'.

Three years later, Coleridge's second lecture series, advertised as 'the Principles of Poetry', and promoted in *The Times*, was launched before a crowded audience in the Corporation Hall, just off Fleet Street, in November 1811. Once again, it was all about Shakespeare, but in a more personal key, recognized as history in the making. Coleridge's appearance, reported the *Sun*, 'constitutes a prominent feature in the Literature of the times'.

Coleridge was less interested in the detail of a Shakespeare playscript than in its overall effect, especially the playwright's command of 'dramatic illusion'. Coleridge entered into the consciousness of the crowd. 'We choose,' he declared, 'to be deceived,' aided by the artistry of players and playwright in which Shakespeare's theatre sponsors a sustained condition of 'inward excitement' – a mirror to the actors' experience. According to one account, he declared that Shakespeare 'is not the creature of the day, to disappear with the day, but the representative and abstract of truth which must ever be true, and of humour which must ever be humorous'. Coleridge went on: there are those 'who read his works with Feeling and Understanding'; and then there are those who become the recipients of the poet's power, 'a Thrill which tells us that, by becoming better acquainted with the poet, we have become better acquainted with ourselves'. Finally, in January 1812, Coleridge plunged into *Hamlet*. Subsequently, he would declare that '*Hamlet* was the play, or rather Hamlet himself was the character, in which I first made my insight into the genius of Shakespeare.'

In the words of his biographer Richard Holmes, Coleridge's central argument was this: Shakespeare had consciously transformed the old, crude convention of the Elizabethan revenge play into a supremely poetic meditation on the inner workings of the imaginative mind, a study of moral paralysis. At the same time, Shakespeare had created 'an archetypal Romantic hero – Hamlet as Everyman – who also seemed extraordinarily like Coleridge himself'. *Hamlet* criticism was never quite the same again. To the end of his life, Coleridge would claim, 'I have a smack of Hamlet myself, if I may say so.'

Coleridge might be dogged by accusations of plagiarism, but the larger point is that the poet, identifying himself so completely with Hamlet, had transformed the play for his audience into a 'Shakespearean' experience. Among the other English Romantics, no one was more Shakespeare-obsessed than John Keats, who decided that the ambiguous Shakespeare was a 'chameleon poet' (not unlike himself), who took 'as much delight in conceiving an Iago as an Imogen'. Keats even composed a sonnet in 1818 ('On Sitting Down to Read *King Lear* Once Again') about his dialogue with the complete works:

> Adieu! For, once again, the fierce dispute
> Betwixt damnation and impassioned clay
> Must I burn through; once more humbly assay
> The bitter-sweet of this Shakespearean fruit.

Keats was drawn towards Shakespeare's tantalizing absence. As he wrote to his brother George in 1817:

> The fire is at its last click – I am sitting with my back to it with one foot rather askew upon the rug and the other with the heel a little elevated from the carpet . . . Could I see the same thing done of any great Man long since dead it would be a great delight: as to know in what position Shakespeare sat when he began 'To be or not to be'.

Heart on sleeve, Keats was also fascinated by Shakespeare's personality as a writer, especially the poet's trademark opacity. In December 1817, walking back to Hampstead with two friends after a Christmas pantomime, Keats experienced a sudden insight of suggestive brilliance. As he trudged up the hill, the conversation turned to Shakespeare, and he got into a 'disquisition':

Several things dovetailed in my mind, & at once it struck me, what quality went to form a Man of Achievement especially in Literature & which Shakespeare possessed so enormously – I mean Negative Capability, that is when man is capable of being in uncertainties, Mysteries, doubts, without any irritable reaching after fact & reason . . .

Keats's 'Negative Capability' is precisely the kind of subtle interpretative idea Shakespeare might have recognized, a concept that captures the way he worked, and also the way in which his work plays on the mind of his audience. In February 1818, Keats developed this notion in a second letter:

We hate poetry that has a palpable design upon us – and if we do not agree, seems to put its hand in its breeches' pocket. Poetry should be great & unobtrusive, a thing which enters into one's soul, and does not startle it or amaze it with itself but with its subject.

After the Romantics, there would be wilder expressions of 'Shakespearomanie'; more, and madder, jubilees. In the USA, this expressed itself in conspiracy theories, notably from Delia Bacon, vain attempts to argue that Shakespeare could not have written Shakespeare. Rarely, in any literature outside scripture, has so much microscopic attention been focused on the relics of a literary life and its work. This obsessive and progressively global scrutiny of the writer and his art eventually provoked the mid-Victorian poet Matthew Arnold to compose 'Shakespeare', an exasperated mixture of paean and protest which began:

Others abide our question. Thou art free.
We ask and ask. Thou smilest and art still,
Out-topping knowledge.

3.

In the decade before he wrote *Hamlet*, Shakespeare's career as a gifted young poet and playwright had been replete with negative capability. He was both 'great and unobtrusive', and yet quite at home with being 'in uncertainties, mysteries, doubts'. Shakespeare's apparently effortless command of his own mystery is both tempting and provocative. In our own time, the appeal of Keats' 'negative capability' has been repurposed in Stephen Greenblatt's formulation of Shakespeare's 'strategic opacity', his refusal to elucidate vital aspects of plot and character in his plays. Here, Iago's 'Demand me nothing,' seems to capture the playwright's attitude towards his creative privacy.

Shakespeare the risk artist had always gravitated towards the dramatic fulcrum of maximum jeopardy, but the Essex rebellion, illustrating how close to the edge of darkness Shakespeare and his players could stray, demonstrated the need for a survival instinct. With the arrival of James Stuart from Scotland in the spring of 1603, there was a new and higher premium on the Shakespearean exercise of artistic cunning. This took shape, in the coming decade, as a quality we might call 'negligent ambiguity'. His modus operandi in perilous times, this became the newest iteration of the playwright's determination somehow both to 'please' his audience and his patron while preserving his dramatist's appetite for the creative clash of opposites.

The tenor of the farewell Shakespeare strikes in Feste's

plangent adieu at the close of *Twelfth Night* is something strangely reflective, even nostalgic:

> When that I was and a little tiny boy,
> With hey, ho, the wind and the rain,
> A foolish thing was but a toy,
> For the rain it raineth every day.

In the spirit of 'what you will' and negligent ambiguity, Shakespeare signs off with a resilient mix of nonchalant 'hey-ho' and English pragmatism, never once forgetting that he has a local audience to satisfy:

> A great while ago the world began,
> With hey, ho, the wind and the rain,
> But that's all one, our play is done,
> And we'll strive to please you every day.
> [5.1.385–406]

During the coming decade (1600–9), at home in 'the wind and the rain', Shakespeare would search out theatrical risk in the remote and mythical past. As usual, his inspiration would come from the dangers inherent in the here and now. Under a new regime, his plays become turbocharged with dramatic daring, the antidote to the frustrations of middle age, and the vicissitudes of show business in a new generation. His next two plays – both tragedies – would subject their protagonists to the most hostile environment, testing them in storms that 'trifled former knowings'. In his last years as a playwright, Shakespeare was diving the depths, in his lifelong search for the truth about our identity.

Sixteen

'TELL ME WHO I AM'

I fear I am not in my perfect mind.
King Lear, 4.6.56

1.

After his breakthrough with *Hamlet* and the dramatization of the self, Shakespeare went deeper and deeper into the 'inward' mind, his own as much as his characters', reflecting some disrupted times. As this Jacobean decade unfolded, Shakespeare was immersing himself more and more in extreme states of personal and political consciousness.

In *Hamlet*, he had asked 'Who's there?'; now, in the subsequent tragedies of the 1600s, he was asking, 'Who are we?' Both questions seal his grip on the contemporary audience. These plays are the Himalayas of Shakespearean drama. Predictably enough, *King Lear*, with *Hamlet*, is a Shakespeare Club favourite, even if we are as often disappointed as transfixed. Actors and directors who attempt to scale these peaks need a head for heights. The *Lear* we particularly treasure is Derek Jacobi's performance at the Donmar in 2010, an intimate production that seemed to bring the drama to life as if the ink on the script was scarcely dry. Equally, Simon Russell Beale's interpretation of the role at the National Theatre in 2014, directed by Sam Mendes, also had some spine-tingling moments associated with the king's dementia, especially in the killing of his Fool. On this occasion, our Club, flirting with the mystery of performance, and tempted by the starry matrix of a great production, arranged to meet Simon Russell Beale after the show. This contemporary master of Shakespearean interpretation had already been a notable Hamlet, but to play Lear is to take another step up Parnassus. Like *Hamlet*, performing *King Lear* is a marathon. The mad old king will be on stage – with only one good break, during Act Four – for more than three hours. The role is massive, 22 per cent of the script, 188 separate speeches, and ten great scenes, some of them gruelling feats of endurance.

And now, here he was – Simon Russell Beale – in jacket and jeans, affably in our midst, backstage at the National, with a pint of bitter to quench his thirst, on the balcony of the actors' bar. Showing few signs of fatigue, the actor patiently answered our questions, and chatted amiably about the part with several ironical asides about the inexplicable madness of the king, and the opacity of Shakespeare's plotting.

This was a rare encounter for the Club. We are among Nature's fans, and prefer to remain anonymous, even detached; nor are we especially avant-garde in our tastes, and generally incline towards the mainstream. The other directors whom we have followed, from afar, have been the established West End names such as the late Peter Hall, Nicholas Hytner, Declan Donnellan, Marianne Elliott, Trevor Nunn, Michael Grandage, Sam Mendes, and Adrian Noble. Through sheer longevity, the Club has seen theatrical history being made on the London and Stratford stage: the launch of the Globe; Phyllida Lloyd's all-female productions of *Henry IV* and *Julius Caesar*; and even a complete reading of the Sonnets, with Harriet Walter and friends at the Royal Festival Hall. The tangible excitement of a great production scores a double hit: it not only modernizes Shakespeare, but also renews the art form itself. At its best, our Club has known some sublime stage moments derived from Shakespeare's taste for novelty.

As a poet, Shakespeare could never switch off his curiosity, or, as a playwright, his appetite for creative risk. Identity in crisis was always his subject, but – with fresh patrons to satisfy – he had to find new modes of dramatic expression. Increasingly, in a more reflective and autumnal, even wintry mood, he became drawn towards another aspect of introspection, the ageing mind *in extremis*. This was not just the last frontier of the unexamined self, it was *his* mind: he was bound to be engaged. With a change of dynasty, and the emergence of a British state, coinciding with his late-life maturity, Shakespeare's anatomy of the self became deeper, darker, and more abstract. At the same time, in his final years, the politics surrounding the Stuart succession delivered the particular kind of dramatic material to which it was impossible to be indifferent. His country was troubled, and so was he.

Some of the plays of the 1600s – *Measure for Measure*, *Timon of Athens*, *Pericles*, *Cymbeline*, *The Winter's Tale*, *The Tempest* – resist easy classification. Are they tragedies, comedies or 'romances'? (The First Folio is often a poor guide.) They do, however, share a common theme. Each is animated by the search for a meaningful self amid the confusions of the present. These are plays which portray men and women, especially men, at the limits of reason. It's here – most piquantly – that an intriguing neurological aspect of Shakespeare's genius brings art and life closer together.

The American novelist Marilynne Robinson, a lifelong Shakespeare scholar, has enjoyed speculating about 'the profound complexity of the brain'. In one of her more suggestive recent asides, she writes:

> The old humanists took the work of the human mind – literature, music, philosophy, art, and languages – as proof of what the mind is and might be. Out of this has come the great aura of brilliance and exceptionalism around our species that neuroscience would dispel.

But there are tangible limits to that 'aura of brilliance'. Robinson continues:

> If Shakespeare had undergone an MRI there is no reason to believe that there would be any more evidence of extraordinary brilliance in him than there would be of a self or a soul . . .

The same humiliation doubtless awaits Mozart and Einstein, but this is not just a failure to be laid at the door of either contemporary neuroscience or human evolution. More deeply, the image of our greatest writer, strapped in for an fMRI examination, brings us up against what Francis Crick called 'the Hard Problem', the baffling dichotomy between our physical brain on the one hand (approximately 1.4 kg of 'grey matter'), and our human consciousness (an infinity of imagination, thought and feeling) in all its fathomless complexity, on the other. This is also the subject of Shakespeare's greatest play, *King Lear*.

2.

At the Globe, after 1604, aside from the hazards of regime change, there was that familiar cycle of old worries about finding a new play for the next season. At some point around the coronation of James I, Shakespeare began to consider the infirmities of ageing in relation to temporal – and possibly, creative – power. Three particular stories attracted his attention. As usual, Shakespeare preferred to work from existing sources: a mix of old drama, contemporary fact and recent fiction.

The first was a script which Shakespeare may have known from his days at the Rose Theatre, an anonymous play about a mythological Celtic king, the early Briton known as Leir. In 1605, for reasons that are unclear, this had been published in a quarto edition as *The True Chronicle History of King Leir, and his three daughters, Gonorill, Ragan, and Cordella. As it hath bene divers and sundry times lately acted.*

Shakespeare's borrowing from *King Leir* is characteristically omnivorous but – yet again – he transformed the old material into something wholly Shakespearean, an existential portrait of a mind at the end of its tether. Besides, he had other material to add to the mix. A second, factual source supplied a more recent plot, the notorious 1603 lawsuit involving the two daughters of a doddery old knight (Sir Brian Annesley), a case which had made a powerful contemporary impression, and with which Shakespeare, in lodgings neighbouring the Inns of Court, would have been familiar.

Finally, Shakespeare reimagined the drama of *King Leir* in yet a third way, to make it his own by adding the Gloucester-Edgar-Edmund plot as a mirror to the family breakdown of Lear-Goneril-Regan. Sir Philip Sidney's

Arcadia (1590), the tale of a kingly father and his two sons, good and bad, lingered in Shakespeare's memory as a late-Elizabethan literary sensation. One scene, in particular, was outstanding in Sidney's prose romance: the moment when the blind, destitute and desperate old man is led to the edge of a cliff by his good son. The fusion of this theme (the blinding and saving of Gloucester) with the climax of Lear's redemption (the king's madness and reconciliation with Cordelia) sees Shakespeare at his finest, and it holds the key to the astonishing power of his new play's fifth act.

Not only was Shakespeare reworking *King Leir*, he was also returning to some favourite themes. In a very early play like *Titus Andronicus* he had already tackled the deranged self-destruction of a tyrannical patriarch. Around the same time that he was writing *King Lear*, he was also exploring the breakdown of a man of wealth and power, and his flight into exile, in *Timon of Athens*. In Lear, however, the drama is deepened and humanized through the complex relationship between the old king and his three daughters.

Lear is all too conscious of waning powers. It's this frailty which has inspired the misguided division of his kingdom. In the first act, as well as sketching the kingdom's tormented politics, Shakespeare introduces the king's fear of dementia, renewing the theme of madness. When the Fool tells the king that 'Thou shouldst not have been old till thou hadst been wise,' Lear's response is plaintive, raw, and terrified:

O let me not be mad, not mad, sweet heaven!
Keep me in temper. I would not be mad.
[1.5.45–6]

The poignancy of Lear's tortured self-awareness is essential to the greatness of *King Lear*. Shakespeare unfolds the king's unravelling identity in a sequence of speeches that range from the manic to the magisterial:

We are not ourselves
When nature, being oppressed, commands the mind
To suffer with the body. I'll forbear,
And am fallen out with my more headier will,
To take the indisposed and sickly fit
For the sound man.
[2.2.279–84]

This is regal, and coherent. The king, humane in his distress, also shows himself to be alert to the condition of his kingdom:

Poor naked wretches, wheresoe'er you are,
That bide the pelting of this pitiless storm,
How shall your houseless heads and unfed sides,
Your looped and windowed raggedness, defend you
From seasons such as these ?
[3.4.28–32]

Thereafter, the speed of Lear's disintegration is horrifying, but all too plausible. Madness and flashes of reason become strangely contiguous. When he flees from his 'pelican daughters' into the storm on the heath with that geriatric howl of anguish, 'O, reason not the need [2.2.438]', his audience will be on his side. Families caring for Alzheimer's sufferers will know the ferocity with which the affliction can strike, often after a long, slow gestation.

Shakespeare conveys his understanding in a single speech, which begins, almost philosophically, in the king's consideration of routine welfare:

> Our basest beggars
> Are in the poorest thing superfluous.
> Allow not nature more than nature needs,
> Man's life is cheap as beast's.

As his dementia strikes, the king becomes almost inarticulate with rage, denouncing his daughters:

> No, you unnatural hags,
> I will have such revenges on you both
> That all the world shall – I will do such things –
> What they are, yet I know not; but they shall be
> The terrors of the earth.

Finally, the king recovers himself, before dissolving into terrified self-pity:

> You think I'll weep.
> No, I'll not weep. I have full cause of weeping,
> But this heart shall break into a hundred thousand
>   flaws
> Or ere I'll weep. O Fool, I shall go mad!
> [2.2.452–9]

At this midpoint, Shakespeare signals the chaos of the king's mind with the sudden frenzy of nature, an apocalyptic storm. In Derek Jacobi's remarkable performance of 2010, directed by Michael Grandage, Lear modernized

'Blow, winds, and crack your cheeks' by coming downstage to *whisper* his lines, a master-stroke. Thereafter, as the action of the play unfolds, Lear is progressively gibbering, until he becomes purged of his anger and appears in a kind of second childhood, festooned with wild flowers, and challenging imaginary wildlife. Nevertheless, he's still conscious of his old self when he concedes [4.5.189], 'I am cut to the brains.'

In the next scene, when Cordelia resists his pathetic attempts to demonstrate his love for his daughter ('You must not kneel'), he does not rage, as he might have done before. Instead, he concedes his frailty:

Pray do not mock.
I am a very foolish, fond old man,
Fourscore and upward,
Not an hour more nor less, and to deal plainly,
I fear I am not in my perfect mind.
[4.6.52–6]

Here, at this point of enfeebled self-knowledge, Shake-speare can extract wisdom and pathos from Lear's condition, and proceeds to do so in speeches of great insight and beauty. Lear tells his former 'pelican daughter', Cordelia, with whom he is now reconciled, that in prison, 'We two alone will sing like birds i'th' cage.' No longer vexed by power, they'll gossip about it instead, 'Who loses and who wins, who's in, who's out'. Then comes Shakespeare's concluding summary, when Lear declares that he and his daughter will 'take upon us the mystery of things' – linking the complexity of the brain, even *in extremis*, to something greater than its human dimensions – 'as if we were God's spies [5.3.17].'

There is not much more to be said. With deft and faultless economy, Shakespeare has nailed the tragedy of old age, its fears and fretfulness, and pinned it to a larger drama that gives it both meaning and consequence. In a highly modern twist, Lear is neither redeemed nor absolved by his sufferings, his death is brought on by the torments of grief for the loss of his child, Cordelia, and the breaking of an old man's heart. Shakespeare does not say this – he does not need to – but the sovereign individual without the comforts of reason or the love of family has no future. The contemporary neurologist knows this, but Shakespeare got there first.

King Lear seems to have been recognized as a remarkable new tragedy from its first production. In 1608, a quarto edition came into circulation, entitled the *True Chronicle Historie of King Leir and his three Daughters*. The King's Men, whose play this was, made no attempt to distinguish their *King Lear* from the older *King Leir*. There is, however, a significant new detail. At the head of the title page, with top billing, and in the largest font, the eye is drawn to the not-so-humble author, 'M. William Shak-speare'.

The king whose candour about being 'cut to the brains' is so direct and modern, and the play which takes its characters so vertiginously to the limit, have inspired many comparisons with the work of such avant-garde playwrights as Ionesco and Samuel Beckett. Lear's 'Let me not be mad,' could be a line from *Endgame* or *Waiting For Godot*. In the 1960s, the Polish writer-director Jan Kott became quite explicit about this. 'It is odd,' he writes, 'how often the word "Shakespearean" is uttered when one speaks about Beckett . . . [whose work] has more similarities to

Shakespeare than to nineteenth century drama.' For Kott, the striking feature of Beckett's 'new theatre' is the 'grotesque quality [which] deals with problems, conflicts and themes of tragedy such as: human fate, the meaning of existence, freedom and inevitability, the discrepancy between the absolute and the fragile human order. For Kott, 'grotesque means tragedy rewritten in different terms.'

Beckett and Shakespeare have this in common: their fearless trade in risk and originality. It was in response to this quality that the young Harold Pinter was moved to express his admiration for the constancy of Beckett's artistic vision in a letter to a friend:

The farther he goes, the more good it does me. I don't want philosophies, tracts, dogmas, creeds, ways out, truths, answers, nothing from the bargain basement. He is the most courageous, remorseless writer going and the more he grinds my nose in the shit the more I am grateful to him . . . His work is beautiful.

As *King Lear* demonstrates, Shakespeare's creative instincts, similarly, would always take him towards contemporary danger zones, but in ever more tantalizing ways. In politics, Shakespeare presents the conundrum of a writer who, while powerfully identified with England and English history, together with the English landscape and its language, remains hard to pin down without equivocation. During these later years, Shakespeare's grasp of historical geography became metaphorical. Henceforward, he would use each location – Illyria, Sicily, Bohemia, even ancient Rome – for his own dramatic purposes, the state of the nation and the popular mind, for example in *Coriolanus*, a tragedy whose protagonist is every bit as wilful and irrational as King Lear.

Amid the nihilism of the 1600s, he would always reduce his dramatic crises to a great reckoning in a little room. In *Macbeth*, his protagonist will be 'cabined, cribbed, confined [3.4.23]'. The mature artist, now installed at the court of King James, was a writer for whom – as *Macbeth* suggests – history and geography come into play from dramatic considerations, and for imaginative purposes. Simultaneously, he began to locate another 'ancient British' drama in the semi-mythical landscape of 'Albion', the setting for *Cymbeline*, a landscape even more abstract than his 'Scotland'.

3.

As Britain's national playwright, Shakespeare has become a touchstone, albeit a fickle one. In April 2019, Michael Roth, Germany's Europe minister, followed an exasperated tweet with a speech in which he described Brexit as 'a big shit-show. I don't know if William Shakespeare could have come up with such a tragedy.' This intervention inspired the Shakespeare scholar Emma Smith to imagine 'a Shakespearean cast' of 'wounded, self-deluded, malign' characters hurtling the nation towards destruction. Occasionally, during the interminable Brexit debates of 2016–19, both sides turned to the *Complete Works* for affirmation, but usually came away with a mixed message. None of this prevented the former prime minister Gordon Brown from pronouncing Shakespeare 'a Remainer' or Labour's one-time deputy leader, Tom Watson, from tweeting 'Shakespeare, the Greatest Englishman 400 years ago, was wholly deeply [*sic*] European.' And when the first phase of the Brexit agony concluded with the Conservative election victory of December 2019, *The Times*'s political sketch-writer saluted the new prime minister's performance in the House of Commons with some familiar imagery: 'Mr Johnson was reaching for the paternalistic, balmy tone found at the end of Shakespearean plays after three hours of limb-hacking vengefulness.' As the new year turned, some commentators began to grapple with the possibility of a Shakespearean side to the new administration. The *Guardian*'s columnist, for instance, turned to the histories:

> At the close of *Henry IV*, as Prince Hal is about to be crowned king, he stuns his former drinking companion Sir John Falstaff by telling him: 'Presume not that I am the thing I was, / For God doth know, so shall the world perceive, / That I have turned away my former self.' In Johnson's case it is hard to be sure whether he has turned his former self away. And these are very early days in what may be a very long premiership . . .

It is easy enough to pilfer support for either side of any political argument from the history plays, or to find Shakespeare masquerading as John Bull, the red-blooded patriot. The final scene of *King John*, a neglected play, is often quoted to stress the playwright's presumed nationalist credentials, for example, in the words of half-French Philip the Bastard:

> This England never did, nor never shall,
> Lie at the proud foot of a conqueror.
> [5.7.112–13]

In context, crucially, he is holding forth after the death of the king, intoning the kind of platitudes politicians turn to at moments of pomp and circumstance. In the same tone, Philip the Bastard closes *King John* with: 'Nought shall make us rue, If England to itself do rest but true [5.7.117–18].'

More unequivocally patriotic, John of Gaunt's soliloquy in *Richard II* appears to find the playwright wrapped in the cross of St George:

This royal throne of kings, this sceptred isle,
This earth of majesty, this seat of Mars,
This other Eden, demi-paradise . . .
This happy breed of men, this little world.
[2.1.40–45]

On the Brexit side of the argument, do not look to the Club for any special insight. During the twenty-something years we have met to watch Shakespeare's plays – years of war, banking crisis and, finally, national nervous breakdown – I do not recall a single contemporary political discussion. For us, the play's the thing, and it's the code of the Club to focus on the work in hand, preferably with reference to a well-thumbed script. I would guess that, as metropolitans, we are broadly in sympathy on the pressing issues of British national importance, but who knows? We are doubtless pro-European, but we also cheerfully accept that Shakespeare's earthier characters never mince their words when describing their European neighbours.

From Falstaff down, the red-blooded English have no time for 'hasty Germans and blunt Hollanders', nor 'the bragging Spaniard'. Greece is 'insolent', Denmark 'rotten', and France 'a dog-hole'. For the French, indeed, there is only contempt. In *The Merry Wives*, Dr Caius is presented as prickly, lecherous and snooty, with a high-class list of patients, 'de earl, de knight, de lords, de gentlemen'. Dr Caius also massacres the King's English: 'Vetch me in my closet *un boîtier vert* . . . [1.4.42]'. In the histories, which are stiff with anti-Gallic propaganda, the 'confident and over-lusty French' are arrogant, touchy, pompous, comically unable to speak English, and treacherous: ''Tis better using France than trusting France [4.1.41],' declares Hastings in *3 Henry VI*.

Against such cartoon insularity, there's the abundant evidence of Shakespeare's deep and lasting debt to European literature and thought. He was steeped in translations of Ovid, Plutarch, and Montaigne, and well versed in Europe, especially Italy, the setting for one-third of his plays. Indeed, Shakespeare probably spoke passable Italian, had read the works of Giovanni Boccaccio and Matteo Bandello, and may have fallen in love with Italy in the form of the 'dark lady' addressed in the sonnets – some say the wife of John Florio, who taught the Elizabethan court to speak Italian.

At the same time, Shakespeare's negligent ambiguity meant that while, as an Elizabethan, he could write characters to beat the drum for English national pride – intensifying his appeal as the national poet – in these years, he also expressed himself in a more abstract, existential key. In his prime, Shakespeare would morph the secret history of everyday life into the public dramas of English history by way of humanity's preoccupations with birth, procreation and death. This now took him, in search of a resolution to contemporary predicaments, to the whirling wilds of a Scottish heath. In the expression of a warning against the 'shameful conquest' of a troubled country, Shakespeare had discovered a thrilling new metaphor – apocalyptic, even supernatural, jeopardy – to illuminate the condition of England.

Seventeen

'SHAMEFUL CONQUEST'

Alas, poor country!
Almost afraid to know itself.
Macbeth, 4.3.164

1.

As the dramatist of English politics, Shakespeare seems always to have understood the nation's capacity for snatching defeat from the jaws of victory. In *Richard II*, John of Gaunt's celebrated paean to 'this royal throne of kings [2.1.40]' is also an admonition to the current generation that 'this dear dear land' has become 'leased out . . . like to a tenement or pelting farm [2.1.57–60]' and, in conclusion – words that, during 2016–19, came to have an eerie resonance – a warning from history:

England that was wont to conquer others
Hath made a shameful conquest of itself.
[2.1.65–6]

For many observers, Brexit and its associated vicissitudes, from the fall of one prime minister to the rise of another to the top of the greasy pole, became a pantomime of national humiliation conducted on the very edge of an abyss in which any hope for a coherent future seemed to be threatened by the imminent prospect of domestic chaos. And yet, who was to say that this emergency was any more perilous than the famous disruptions of 1688 or even 1603? Soon after the Jacobean succession, possibly while he was working on *King Lear*, Shakespeare became caught up in a tide of English history in which, by indirection, he examined the condition of a 'poor country' that had become 'almost afraid to know itself [*Macbeth*, 4.3.164–5]', an island state threatened by enemies within.

In the ancient Scottish history Shakespeare could read about in Raphael Holinshed's *Chronicles* (1587), he had discovered an apocalyptic metaphor to illuminate the condition of England, but he hardly dared stray south of the border. Where once, in the histories, he had revelled in the specifics of the political context, now he appropriated whatever he required from an abstract setting in which Dunsinane Wood would be almost the only recognizable feature. The virtue of this approach for Shakespeare, in a play like *Macbeth*, was that he could experiment with risk, and retain control of a vision that enabled him to be on both sides of any argument.

Despite many anxieties about the new regime, at first the dynastic transition from the Tudors to the Stuarts, from the sinister, arteriosclerotic dread of Elizabeth I to the witch-hunting paranoia of James I, passed off with unanticipated smoothness. Within hours of the queen's death on 24 March, James was proclaimed king in London, where the news was received without disturbance. Early in April 1603, James left Edinburgh for London, promising to return home every three years, and progressed slowly south, from town to town, hunting with hounds whenever he could. Along his route, James I's new subjects flocked to see him, grateful that the succession had triggered neither unrest nor invasion. 'In an hour, two nations were made one,' exulted Thomas Dekker, and even 'wild Ireland became tame on the sudden'. The king's coronation in his new capital was delayed by an outbreak of the plague, but English resilience took this in its stride.

When, finally, a year late, the king entered London, the crowds of people, one observer reported, were 'so greedy to behold the King that they injured and hurt one another'. James's coronation took place in July 1604, replete with elaborate poetic allegories provided by fashionable metropolitans such as Dekker and Jonson. London was temporarily *en fête*. 'The streets seemed paved with men,' wrote Dekker. 'Stalls instead of rich wares were set out with children, open casements filled up with women.'

This move from the archetypical Englishness of the Tudors to the incipient Britishness of the Stuarts occurred at a crucial moment in Shakespeare's development as a poet and playwright. He was turning forty, and was widely recognized for his recent masterpiece. *Hamlet* had demonstrated a soothsaying gift for marrying his personal story with his country's to strike a chord that chimed with contemporary experience. But it always remained a deniable vision. Throughout this decade, he perfected the art of writing plays about himself and his country that, transcending self and nation, became Shakespearean.

With a privileged vantage point close to the heart of the state, Shakespeare the player was far from threadbare, while Shakespeare the poet was no longer an upstart. At the accession of James to the English throne, the Lord Chamberlain's Men had become the King's Men. Shakespeare, Burbage, and their associates at the Globe were now authorized in letters patent, dated 17 May 1603, 'freely to use and exercise the art and faculty of playing comedies, tragedies, histories, interludes, morals, pastorals, stage plays, and such others like as they have already studied . . . for the recreation of our loving subjects as for our solace and pleasure.' Kitted out in the scarlet livery of a groom of the bedchamber, Shakespeare became a member of the royal household, a significant promotion.

At the court of Elizabeth I, Shakespeare had remained a detached observer, mastering an airy textual ambivalence that gave his plays an intangible but potent universality. When James I, the author of *Daemonologie*, a dialogue about witchcraft, arrived in London with his Scottish retinue, bringing with him fresh infusions of royal paranoia about assassination and witches, Shakespeare responded by developing a new repertoire of negligent ambiguity, possibly inspired by his changed circumstances.

In 1606, following his transition from outsider to insider with *Antony and Cleopatra*, and building on the duplicity examined in *Hamlet*, Shakespeare self-satirized his new professional environment in a comic interlude buried in the heart of the play. Pompey has thrown an impromptu banquet, at which Antony and his rival triumvir Lepidus (who is drunk) fall into party chat about the exotic wonders of Africa:

LEPIDUS: What manner o' thing is your crocodile?
ANTONY: It is shaped, sir, like itself, and it is as broad
    as it hath breadth. It is just so high as it is, and
    moves with its own organs. It lives by that which
    nourisheth it, and the elements once out of it, it
    transmigrates.

LEPIDUS: What colour is it of?
ANTONY: Of its own colour too.
LEPIDUS: 'Tis a strange serpent.
ANTONY: 'Tis so; and the tears of it are wet.
[2.7.40–49]

Octavius Caesar, overhearing, asks, 'Will this description satisfy him?', a teasing inquiry that evokes Touchstone's anatomy of 'the Lie Direct' in *As You Like It* [5.4.68–80]. But being, as it were, within close range of the crocodile's jaws, it also hints at the jeopardy of court life. For a writer whose creative DNA had long been nourished by the untrammelled freedom of the natural world, and the exuberance of the English vernacular, Shakespeare's courtier role posed an artistic threat. To continue to be Shakespearean, running with the hare and hunting with the hounds, he would have to be vigilant vis-à-vis the demands of his new patron.

But he would never renege on his creative addiction to risk. Quite the reverse: in one of the first plays he wrote for James, who was an enthusiastic playgoer, Shakespeare doubled down on his lifelong instincts as a playwright. He continued to engage his curiosity to the full, to locate his drama at the crossroads of maximum danger, taking his devoted audience on another perilous journey. To do this before the king his master would require all the most slippery arts of theatrical duplicity at his command. Almost at the same time as *Antony and Cleopatra*, apparently writing at top speed, Shakespeare began to work on the play that would place such 'equivocation', literally and metaphorically, centre stage. Rarely, in his see-saw career, had art and life come together with such propitious synergy; rarely, if ever, had the proto-British state been exposed to such peril from within; and never in his career was Shakespeare placed so close to such an outstanding moment of national jeopardy.

By chance, scarcely two years after the coronation, the wheel of history had delivered an outrageous event of such astonishing peril to the new king that James I would be transfixed by a dread unknown at court since the Spanish Armada. Once again, Shakespeare was writing both to answer his own artistic needs, and to provide a reassuring narrative line for his new patron, while at the same time giving his regular London audience the consoling explanation of acute historical disruption for which he was renowned.

The event – or rather, the outstanding non-event – that would inspire Shakespeare to mobilize all his gifts as a dramatist and poet was the spectacular and audacious conspiracy known to history as the Gunpowder Plot of 5 November 1605.

2.

As an ex-officio groom of the royal bedchamber, Shakespeare would have noted how, in the unravelling of a great treason, there were moments when time and fear seemed to stand still, while 'the hour' – the relentless tick-tock of history – ran on 'through the roughest day [*Macbeth*, 1.3.160]'. Shakespeare was familiar with routine court life in Whitehall. But on this occasion he would have witnessed a new kind of state emergency.

On 31 October, James I had returned to London for the State Opening of Parliament amid rumours of a mysterious letter recently brought, hotfoot, before the Privy Council. For two or three days, there was a dreadful 'interim'.

Meanwhile, the king, hypersensitive about attempts against his life, had read the anonymous correspondent's warning of 'a terrible blow' during the course of this parliament, and its advice to the recipient to 'devise some excuse to shift your attendance'. James, obsessed with assassination, immediately grasped the sinister meaning of this strange communication. More delay ensued. The authorities wanted to investigate a potential crime scene at a moment when the state's enemies, the secret forces of Roman Catholic opposition, were most committed to their 'horrid deed'.

On 4 November, when the great vault beneath parliament was searched, it was found to be heaped with 'piles of billets and faggots', and – even more suspicious – watched over by a 'very tall and desperate fellow'. Further investigations that same night uncovered some thirty-six barrels of gunpowder. The 'desperate fellow', who identified himself as 'John Johnson', was also found to be concealing 'three matches and all other instruments fit for blowing up the powder'. No question: without this search, about a ton of gunpowder would have been detonated; and the opening of parliament on 5 November would have witnessed a sulphurous explosion whose 'thought-executing fires' would have annihilated the king, his family and his court, together with the leaders of church and state assembled in parliament.

Under interrogation, 'John Johnson' betrayed his master Thomas Percy, a member of the royal household with powerful Catholic connections. Percy had been a trusted go-between in the negotiations between London and Edinburgh in the run-up to James's accession. A manhunt was launched and a royal proclamation identifying Thomas Percy hurried into print. The Crown appealed to all good citizens 'to apprehend [him] by all possible means, especially' – this latest 'interim moment' of delay was a dramatic master stroke – 'to keep him alive, to the end the rest of the conspirators may be discovered.'

Once the cat was out of the bag, England fell into conspiracy fever, a mood Shakespeare would shortly mobilize for use in his next two plays:

> But cruel are the times when we are traitors
> And do not know ourselves; when we hold rumour
> From what we fear, yet know not what we fear.
> [*Macbeth*, 4.2.18–20]

As news of the terrible – as yet unexplained – plot filtered into the capital from the court, London went onto high alert: bell-ringing, bonfires lit at street corners, and widespread panic. One foreign witness described a city 'in great uncertainty: Catholics fear heretics and vice versa, both are armed. Foreigners live in terror of the mob that is convinced that some foreign princes are at the bottom of the plot.' Shakespeare, exposed to the king's paranoia in Whitehall, would find even greater dread at home among the French Huguenots with whom he was lodging on Silver Street in the City.

This atmosphere of suspicion was propagated by King James, who was convinced that any explosion would have killed some 30,000, and described 'a spectacle so terrible and terrifying that its like has never been heard of'. Scarcely four days after the discovery of the Gunpowder Plot, the king's speech to parliament sustained a brilliant strategy: to ramp up an atmosphere of such nameless dread as to justify the state's counterterrorist reprisals against suspect English

Catholics. It was now, in the first weeks after 5 November, that the threats of this conspiracy became clear to the government in general, and to Shakespeare more particularly.

Never, in the course of a life lived in the shadow of violent death, had the playwright found himself, inadvertently, at such acute personal risk. 'The frame of things' was disjoint; more nerve-wracking, the epicentre of this upheaval was in Shakespeare's home town. Elsewhere in Warwickshire, a short ride from Stratford, the theft of ten horses had alerted the authorities to 'some great rebellion'; many local Catholic recusants were now under suspicion, with Shakespeare's county and its anxious citizens on terror alert. In his new play, the character Ross would provide a running commentary on this dread, from his description of 'strange images of death [1.3.95]' to his grim comparison of everyday life to a kind of plague scene:

> Where sighs and groans and shrieks that rend the air
> Are made, not marked; where violent sorrow seems
> A modern ecstasy. The dead man's knell
> Is there scarce asked for who, and good men's lives
> Expire before the flowers in their caps,
> Dying or ere they sicken.
> [*Macbeth*, 4.3.169–74]

The king, meanwhile, sent an army to crush the Catholic uprising. Once 'John Johnson' had confessed under torture to being 'Guido Fawkes', the Midlands part of the conspiracy was quickly broken, despite some last-ditch resistance around Stratford. Soon there was a grim procession of manacled prisoners being transported across the Avon towards a more savage interrogation in London. Some of these suspects were

Shakespeare's friends and relations; the mastermind, Robert Catesby, and his co-conspirator Francis Tresham, were both related to his mother Mary's Arden family.

On 27 January 1606, eight surviving plotters were taken from the Tower to face the Crown's justice in Westminster, another show trial. By the end of the month, Fawkes and the principal conspirators had been hanged, drawn and quartered, and their severed heads placed on spikes in view of London Bridge. But the aftershocks of the 'Powder Treason', as it was known, continued to send shudders through the Jacobean state.

While Fawkes and his fellows suffered horrifying retribution in the Tower, government agents had been in relentless pursuit of Francis Tresham's Catholic circle, in particular the Jesuit Henry Garnet. This brave priest had been sent from Rome in 1586 on a dangerous mission to support the cause of English Roman Catholicism. Garnet had not only survived the paranoid final years of Elizabeth's reign, he had prepared himself for the wily defence of his faith, in the event of interrogation. In 1598, he had composed a handbook, entitled *A Treatise of Lying and Fraudulent Equivocation*, that instructed English Catholics how to lie under oath without peril to their souls. During December 1605, in the frenzy of investigation that followed the discovery of the plot, the Crown's searchers unearthed Garnet's 'treatise'. At once, the state's officers placed this document at the centre of the case against the Jesuit, who had been run to ground in rebellious Warwickshire in the new year of 1606.

In an ominous climax to 'that heavy and woeful tragedy which is commonly called the Powder Treason', Garnet was brought to judgement on 28 March, a trial witnessed by King James from behind a screen. The case turned on the issue of 'equivocation', which the prosecution established as code for high treason. Garnet was condemned, and sentenced to execution. On the scaffold in St Paul's Churchyard he declared, in words that gave 'equivocation' the afterlife of a warning from beyond the grave: 'It is no time now to equivocate; how it is lawful and when, I have shown my mind elsewhere; but I do not now equivocate, and more than I have confessed I do not know.' These were the fateful words to which the Porter in *Macbeth* would allude in his boozy, free-associating pre-dawn ramblings:

Knock, knock! Who's there, in th'other devil's name? Faith, here's an equivocator that could swear in both the scales against either scale, who committed treason enough for God's sake, yet could not equivocate to heaven. O, come in equivocator.
[2.3.7–11]

When Shakespeare slips his most edgy topical references into this comic monologue, in an elaborate joke about equivocation and the trial of the equivocating Jesuit, the contemporary dialogue of literature and events becomes unmistakable. Later, in the summer of 1606, the state prosecutor Edward Coke not only addressed Garnet's 'hellish sophistry', and linked equivocating to 'the traitorous, detestable, tyrannical, bloody, murderous villainy' of the Gunpowder Plot, but also made deeply Shakespearean allusions to John of Gaunt's speech in *Richard II* [2.1.40–60]. Shakespeare's vision was once again conjured to provide a moment of coherence in the midst of a great disruption: 'I do not know what to speak,' declared Coke, 'because I want words . . . Only this, had their [the plotters'] horrible attempt taken place . . . This so well planted, pleasant, fruitful, world's-accounted Eden's Paradise, should have been by this time, made a place disconsolate, a vast and desert wilderness.'

Coke was not alone in recognizing his country being rescued from a dreadful fate as 'a vast and desert wilderness'. The plays – notably *Macbeth* – that Shakespeare would write after the Gunpowder Plot express an acute dread of a rebellion in which 'present fears are less than horrible imaginings [1.3.147–8]'.

In early middle age, Shakespeare was wrestling with matters of good and evil in humanity: what is the nature of existence? How is it that dreams become bloody nightmares? What is the role of violence within ambition? And what the place of conscience in human affairs? These existential issues were joined by some urgent political questions: how should a good king conduct himself? And what is treachery? Despite professional risk to himself, Shakespeare went unerringly to the core of the horror unleashed by the plot of 5 November. He would be at his most Shakespearean in choosing to write – for a Scottish king who lived in dread of assassination, and was obsessed with witchcraft – a new play about dynastic succession in which the protagonist, a psychopathic Scottish regicide, makes rendezvous with witches and himself invokes the supernatural in a satanic rhapsody:

Stars, hide your fires,
Let not light see my black and deep desires;
The eye wink at the hand; yet let that be
Which the eye fears, when it is done, to see.
[1.4.50–53]

Shakespeare would illuminate this new dramatic subject by exploiting to the limit his penchant for dramatic antitheses while at the same time probing close to the heart of his royal patron's paranoia in the 'Scottish play', a tragedy steeped in English politics.

3.

From its first line, a play obsessed by the state of England assails audience and actors alike with questions: 'When shall we three meet again?'; 'What bloody man is that?'; 'Is execution done on Cawdor?'; 'Where hast thou been?', and so on. These challenges bring no consolation. From the opening scene of *Macbeth*, there are few good options for the participants in the unfolding tragedy. Any future rendezvous must take place 'in thunder, lightning, or in rain'. This bleak prospect will be compounded from the moment the weird (or 'weyard') sisters, a.k.a. the three witches, step through the 'filthy air' to announce that 'fair is foul, and foul is fair'. With these words, *Macbeth* becomes the play in which Shakespeare will dazzle, provoke and disturb his new royal patron with his most daring and transgressive exploration of kingship and ambition.

Cunningly, in the first instance, Shakespeare disguises his intentions within the abstract confusion of the witches' world. *Macbeth* opens with 'the instruments of darkness [1.3.122]' in a fever of antithesis:

'When the battle's lost and won [1.1.4].'

'Not so happy, yet much happier [1.3.64].'

'Lesser than Macbeth, and greater [1.3.63].'

'Cannot be ill; cannot be good [1.3.130].'

Finally, these multiplying contradictions and inter-rogatives collide in Banquo's question to Macbeth:

Good sir, why do you start and seem to fear
Things that do sound so fair?
[1.3.49–50]

In the unearthly meeting of the witches, English drama's arch-equivocator creates a memorably weird, ambiguous and supernatural *coup de théâtre* that sets the tone for everything that follows, and accompanies the plot of the play to its merciless, nihilistic conclusion. Next to the oppressive menace of the witches and the supernatural, the dominant mood of *Macbeth*, from the first appearance of the king and his retinue, is one of routine slaughter evocative of the recent eviscerations on Tyburn hill. 'What bloody man is that? [1.2.1.]' asks Duncan, almost casually. The captain's answer speaks of 'bloody execution [1.2.20]', and seems more to suggest the ritual 'quartering' of the scaffold than the frenzy of the battlefield:

Till he unseamed him from the nave to th' chops
And fixed his head upon our battlements.
[1.2.22–3]

His protagonist's conduct, which reprises King James's response to the 'powder treason', is apocalyptic, with 'noble Macbeth' choosing 'to bathe in reeking wounds' as if he would 'memorize another Golgotha [1.2.40]'. Moreover, Shakespeare offers no respite. The action of *Macbeth* moves at speed. By the middle of Act Three, its murderous protagonist, regretting his 'hangman's hands' and floundering in a political abattoir, confesses to being 'in blood', through a poignant and famous metaphor:

Stepped in so far that, should I wade no more,
Returning were as tedious as go o'er.
[3.4.136–7]

He has been driven mad by the blood shed in Duncan's chamber: 'It will have blood, they say. Blood will have blood [3.4.121].'

In a few deft strokes, Shakespeare has reminded the audience in the Globe where they are. It's less twelfth-century Scotland, more a country – a Scots king's contemporary England – wracked with questions about its future. Other snatches of local colour are derived from the unsettling turbulence of the Essex rebellion. Shakespeare's audience would instinctively recall Essex's reported death in Malcolm's account of Cawdor's execution:

I have spoke
With one that saw him die . . . Nothing in his life
Became him like the leaving it. He died
As one that had been studied in his death
To throw away the dearest thing he owed
As 'twere a careless trifle.
[1.4.4–11]

No sooner has the bloody context of the play been established than the next scene adds a precisely opposite dimension of insubstantiality to the visceral clarity of the opening. Macbeth now meets the 'weyard sisters' in all their compelling ambiguity as 'imperfect speakers'. After a sequence of mysterious utterances, they vanish 'into the air' so comprehensively that Banquo, who's with Macbeth as a military companion, wonders aloud if he and his fellow haven't both gone mad.

'Have we eaten on the insane root that takes the reason prisoner? [1.3.86–7]' he asks. In the aftermath of 5 November 1605, this is a world that Shakespeare's audience will understand with the shock of recognition, a world in which 'nothing is, but what is not [1.3.152]', and in which a remorseless clock delivers the merciless consequences of history, without interruption: 'Time, and the hour, runs through the roughest day [1.3.160].'

4.

Put 'blood' and 'witchcraft' together, and the upshot will be 'murder'. When Macbeth and his wife contemplate the assassination of the king, who can say if this impulse comes from within their demonic souls, or from the inevitable consequence of mixing with witches? Shakespeare, opaque as ever, never addresses this. He is chiefly concerned to narrate Macbeth's descent into Hell, and to do this through a scene of such comical banality – the Porter opening up the castle gate – that it's only on the thunderous knocking – 'knock, knock, knock' – from without that we, the audience, realize what a world it is that we are spying on.

Add 'time' to 'murder' and it's a short step to the psychology of violence. This was the wonderful insight of the Romantic essayist Thomas De Quincey's 'On the Knocking at the Hell Gate in *Macbeth*' of 1823, which identifies for modern audiences the all-important and psychologically significant role of Act Two.

De Quincey was first inspired to write by a gruesome East End murder. For the essayist, the finer points of the police investigation on the Ratcliffe Highway were unimportant. Struck by the audacity and mystery of these East End crimes, he found imaginative collateral in *Macbeth*, a play in which he could explore the mind of the killer and consider the working of a violent 'imagination'. It was the conjunction of risk and creativity – the quotidian enigmas of the present, *in extremis* – that inspired De Quincey's invocation of Shakespeare in the quest for meaning.

The porter scene takes place in the dead of night, interrupting the Macbeths' tormented post-mortem into their assassination of Duncan. Macbeth is anguished as he never will be again. While the regicide expresses his remorse for the murder of Duncan, Shakespeare is at pains to make his message unequivocal:

Will all great Neptune's ocean wash this blood
Clean from my hand? No, this my hand will rather
The multitudinous seas incarnadine,
Making the green one red.
[2.2.58–61]

The vernacular of that last line elucidates its orotund predecessor, country language trumping court, for the benefit of the groundlings. *Multitudinous* is also a reminder that the vigilant snapper-up within the playwright's mind will never miss an opportunity to flash his linguistic booty in front of an appreciative royal audience. By contrast, Lady Macbeth, who becomes deranged and sleepless, is pitiless and cold-blooded:

> A little water clears us of this deed.
> How easy is it then! Your constancy
> Hath left you unattended. Hark, more knocking.
> [2.2.65–7]

From this moment forward, almost all the action of the play will take place in, or approaching, the hours of darkness, another 'interim' moment that Macbeth welcomes:

> Come, seeling night,
> Scarf up the tender eye of pitiful day,
> And with thy bloody and invisible hand
> Cancel and tear to pieces that great bond
> Which keeps me pale.
> [3.2.47–51]

Hereafter, this wild darkness becomes, for Shakespeare, an existential condition, a sleep-deprived psychic prison that affects all the principals, including Macbeth's rival, the wakeful, doomed Banquo, who will be murdered at nightfall:

> A heavy summons lies like lead upon me,
> And yet I would not sleep. Merciful powers,
> Restrain in me the cursèd thoughts that nature
> Gives way to in repose.
> [2.1.6–9]

Banquo is all-important to Shakespeare, who was using *Macbeth* for a very specific purpose: to reaffirm the legitimacy of the Stuart dynasty after the shock of the 'powder treason'. Macbeth consults the 'weyard sisters' on this very question:

Tell me, if your art
Can tell so much, shall Banquo's issue ever
Reign in this kingdom?
[4.1.117–19]

Such 'equivocation' is vital: Shakespeare's Banquo is King James's upright, brave, and wronged ancestor, the scion of a noble bloodline, a figure more vivid in the playwright's imagination than in the historical record. Here, this second meaning of 'blood' to legitimize a new, and seemingly upstart, dynasty becomes the subtext of the play, Shakespeare's reconciliation of Scottish and English political rivalries, and the long-term transition to 'Britishness'. By chance, this would coincide with the beginnings of a new audience in the New World.

Eighteen

'BRAVE NEW WORLD'

Where America, the Indies?
The Comedy of Errors, 3.2.136

1.

As the 1600s unfolded, the terrible shock of the 'powder treason' slowly faded from public consciousness until a playground refrain, 'Remember, remember, the fifth of November,' would be the only surviving trace of this crisis in the national psyche. More than Essex, the 'marvellous Earl', the emblematic figure of the age was now that adventurer and man of letters, Sir Walter Raleigh. Overseas exploration raised English eyes from the obsessive contemplation of a domestic crisis to foreign adventure and the hopes of booty from abroad. Throughout this decade, there was a 'brave new world' to be discovered. Ironically, for a writer who apparently had no difficulty in making global journeys of the mind, the playwright never visited, and hardly even alludes to, America, a new country that would become as Shakespearean as England.

This is surprising. Superabundant in curiosity, Shakespeare had plenty of opportunity to nurture an interest in the New World. As a courtier and man of business, he knew the restless figure of Raleigh well enough to satirize him in *Love's Labour's Lost*. His patron,

Southampton, took an active interest in global exploration. Anyone crossing the Thames to attend the Globe Theatre on the south bank, as Shakespeare habitually did, could have watched seasoned English and European merchant vessels preparing to set sail abroad in search of treasure. Despite such provocations, however, he eschewed colonial adventures, preferring to set his plays in foreign parts that were either mysterious, such as Illyria, or Bohemia; unfamiliar, as in Vienna; or downright legendary, for instance Albion. In 1613, there's just one other late reference to transatlantic life. In *Henry VIII*, also known as *All Is True*, one of his comic porters makes a jocular allusion to a 'strange Indian', demanding: 'Is this Moorfields to muster in? Or have we some strange Indian with the great tool come to court, the women so besiege us? [5.3.31–3]'

As a young man, Shakespeare had been responsive to the social impact of global capitalism, and intrigued by the consequences of overseas adventure. In *Titus Andronicus*, his first African character, Aaron, is described as a villainous 'blackamoor' with a 'fleece of woolly hair', who embodies both African and Moorish heritage. To the Elizabethans, it was the Mediterranean and perhaps West Africa – populated by exotic characters, and rich in strange beasts, fabulous fruits, unearthly landscapes and wild weather – that seemed the most fantastic parts of the known world.

Shakespeare's silence on colonial affairs is all the more striking in contrast to some of his greatest contemporary competitors, who were exploiting these new opportunities for all they were worth. Under James I, there had been a sea change. Looking across the Atlantic, London had begun to buzz with stories about the fabulous opportunities of the New World. In 1605, Ben Jonson collaborated on a play, *Eastward Ho!*, in which Seagull, a sea captain, tantalizes a would-be emigrant, Spendall, with the latest news from Virginia:

> A whole country of English is there, man. I tell thee, gold is more plentiful than copper is with us . . . Why man, all their dripping pans and their chamber-pots are pure gold, and for rubies and diamonds, they go forth on holidays and gather 'em by the sea shore . . . [3.3.14–24]

Finally, says Seagull, echoing Jack Cade, 'You shall live freely there, without serjeants, or courtiers, or lawyers.' That same year, inspired by similarly tempting promotions, three ships crossed the Atlantic, cruised in the West Indies and then headed up the East Coast. In April 1607, these pioneers sailed into Chesapeake Bay. After about a month they reached the James River, where they moored in six fathoms off a wooded island which they promptly named Jamestown.

Such adventures found echoes in the poetry of the day. Shakespeare's near-contemporary, John Donne, known as 'a great frequenter of plays', coined the perfect erotic metaphor, the comparison of a lover's devotion to his mistress's body with a transatlantic crossing:

> And sailing towards her India, in that way
> Shall at her fair Atlantick Navell stay . . .

'O my America!' exclaims the poet, 'my new-found-land.' Shakespeare would have recognized a homage to his own youthful American reference in *The Comedy of Errors* when one of the Dromio twins, in bawdy conversation with his master Antipholus about a 'spherical' maidservant, finds himself comparing parts of her body to the globe:

ANTIPHOLUS: Where Spain?
DROMIO: Faith, I saw it not, but I felt it hot in her breath.
ANTIPHOLUS: Where America, the Indies?
DROMIO: O, sir, upon her nose, all o'er embellished with rubies, carbuncles, sapphires, declining their rich aspect to the hot breath of Spain, who sent whole armadas of carracks to be ballast at her nose.

[3.2.134–41]

That had been written as long ago as 1594. Otherwise, on the subject of 'America', the inveterate snapper-up of unconsidered trifles kept his pickers and stealers to himself. Then, in June 1609, while Shakespeare was at work on *Cymbeline*, the Earl of Southampton commissioned a small fleet of ships under the Virginia Company to set sail to the new American colonies with the promise of fabulous rewards. On board the flagship, the *Sea Venture*, was the admiral Sir George Summers, together with a future governor of Virginia. In July, however, when a sudden storm off Bermuda scattered the fleet, Summers and all on board were assumed to have been lost at sea.

But there was a miracle. Nine months later, in May 1610, two small vessels carrying the crew of the *Sea Venture* landed at Jamestown with an extraordinary tale to tell. Their ship had actually run aground on Bermuda ('the isle of devils') but they had escaped ashore. Despite rumours of cannibalism by the natives, the shipwrecked sailors had found an island paradise: a lovely climate, plenty of food and shelter, and enough timber to construct the vessels in which they had completed their crossing to the Virginia settlement. There was, after all, a 'brave new world'.

What use Shakespeare would make of this event says a lot about his imaginative focus during this decade. In the first scene of *The Tempest*, he confined himself to the perfect expression of natural jeopardy: a storm at sea and a shipwreck. This famous opening bears the hallmark of research, but the island on which Ferdinand, Antonio, Gonzalo and the rest will scramble ashore is a fantasy, patterned after Mediterranean models. Shakespeare would never get closer to Virginia than Ariel's topical allusion to 'the still-vexed Bermoothes [1.2.230]', which became Bermuda, the second English colony in the New World. Within a century, the first Americans would discover that Shakespeare spoke to their new society with an unanticipated candour and urgency.

The Tempest, staged in 1611, and marking the climax of Shakespeare's work in the theatre, has a colonial subtext, but no deeper penetration of the New World. Five years later, he was dead. Within seven years of his death, not only had the Founding Fathers set sail in the *Mayflower* from Plymouth (1620), but Heminges and Condell had published the First Folio (1623). Eventually, by a nice irony, the volume that preserved forever the finest literature of Tudor and Stuart England came to exercise a special hold over the American mind. The evolution of this transatlantic Shakespearean inheritance was more than a century in the making; the First Folio would become a canonical text in the making of the United States, though not at first.

Nineteen

'A WORLD ELSEWHERE'

Not a soul
But felt a fever of the mad, and played
Some tricks of desperation.
The Tempest, 1.2.209

1.

The men and women who first embarked for the New World on board the *Mayflower* in 1620 were a mixed bunch, driven by a tangle of idealistic, colonizing, self-interested and religious aspirations. A minority went to America to find an austere wilderness in which to establish the kingdom of God. Other Puritans, like John Winthrop, were prompted by the ambitions that had once galvanized Walter Raleigh and the first Virginians. To them, as to Coriolanus, this was 'a world elsewhere'.

Both Northerners and Southerners were inspired by the dream of a fresh start. As an emigrant community, however, they missed their mother country. Next to the Holy Bible, Shakespeare's complete works became the colonial settlers' domestic reading, a wistful mix of consolation and souvenir. At first, his American popularity was curbed by Puritan hatred of 'licentiousness'; by the eighteenth century, however, there was a new mood afoot.

The first American performance of Shakespeare took

place in New York City with a production of *Romeo and Juliet* in 1730. Before the American Revolution, Shakespeare was mainly staged by itinerant British players, who had to contend with colonial opposition to the 'extravagance and dissipation' of the theatre. In Philadelphia the ban against play-acting was not lifted until 1789; God-fearing Americans remained prejudiced against actors as 'idle persons'.

1776 was the watershed. Ever since Thomas Jefferson drafted the Declaration of Independence, US society has been built on fine words, constantly reshaped by popular rhetoric. The new Americans turned to Shakespeare as a guide, philosopher and friend. The quest for a new language and sensibility with which to define American culture and society inspired the appropriation of Shakespeare's greatest plays. The Old World dramatist became a kind of honorary Yankee, rich in language, and alert to the political potency of the banal rhetoric that flourishes in times of easy money and conspicuous consumption.

In *Timon of Athens*, for instance, Shakespeare mirrors a quasi-American ambivalence towards capitalism: half celebrating and throwing parties; half hating the world and withdrawing into isolation. In the end, anticipating his imminent death, and with a kind of existential fury, Timon advertises a belated self-knowledge, while urging the project forward: 'Nothing brings me all things. Go, live still [5.2.73].' This experimental study of man's place in a better-organized society – the American dilemma – has been described as, 'as schematic as Beckett and unashamedly analytic as Bertolt Brecht,' a play for today.

A generation after the Revolution, Shakespeare was a settled feature of post-colonial life. In *Democracy in America* (1835), de Tocqueville observed: 'There is hardly a pioneer hut in which the odd volume of Shakespeare cannot be found. I remember reading the feudal drama *Henry V* for the first time in a log cabin.' Meanwhile, in literary circles, there was a lively debate about Shakespeare's role as an American as much as an English national poet. The forgotten Charles Sprague composed a prize poem on Shakespeare which culminates in the declaration that Shakespeare must inspire America's poets. 'Thy name, thy verse, thy language shall they bear,' wrote Sprague:

> Once more, in Thee, shall Albion's sceptre wave,
> And what her mighty Lion lost, her mightier Swan
> shall save!

Such bombastic lines speak to a sore cultural anxiety: the mid-century challenge for a rising generation of American writers was to equal, if not surpass, the playwright's achievement.

This task was already being addressed in many American schools. Ubiquitous texts like *McGuffey's Reader* (1839) assigned Shakespearean extracts to children studying public speaking, seeding his words in the minds of successive generations. James Shapiro, whose anthology *Shakespeare in America* reproduces many key passages, offers this explanation: 'In a nation wrestling with great issues, Shakespeare's works allowed Americans to express views that may otherwise have been hard to articulate – or admit to.' Shapiro describes the history of Shakespeare in the New World as 'a history of America itself . . . expressed through two-and-a-half centuries of essays, parodies, burlesques, poems, speeches, short stories, letters, musicals, novels, reviews, films and staged performances.'

Shakespeare's legacy, once Puritan scruples had been consigned to history, became a topical issue. American fascination with 'the bard of Stratford-upon-Avon' inspired a quixotic attempt by P. T. Barnum, the showman credited with 'there's a sucker born every minute', to acquire Shakespeare's (nearly derelict) 'birthplace' anonymously and ship it across the Atlantic to New York as part of his Museum of Curiosities. This plot was foiled with the help of Charles Dickens, no fan of American cultural piracy. Meanwhile, the show carried on. Across the States – in metropolitan theatres, saloons, church halls and even mining camps – there were frequent performances of Shakespeare plays. To a bard-struck society, brushing up your Shakespeare – the *Kiss Me Kate* show-stopper – was essential to civilized life:

> Brush up your Shakespeare,
> Start quoting him now.
> Brush up your Shakespeare,
> And the women you will wow.

2.

Cole Porter knew what he was talking about. Throughout the nineteenth century Shakespeare had been written into the canon of American literature by ambitious new writers anxious to shake off or outdo English influence. Cultural nationalism came in various guises.

In August 1850, for instance, a group of literati set out to climb Monument Mountain in Massachusetts. The party included Nathaniel Hawthorne, the author of *The Scarlet Letter*, and a young Herman Melville, who was struggling to complete an unwieldy coming-of-age tale about a South

Seas whaler. Melville and Hawthorne had never met. But after a day in the open air, a quantity of champagne, an exchange of Shakespeare quotations, and a sudden downpour, the younger man was enraptured with his new friend who had 'dropped germinous seeds into my soul'. Rarely in Anglo-American literature has there been such a meeting, the attraction of opposites.

Hawthorne, from an old New England family, was careful, cultivated and inward, a 'dark angel', according to one. Melville was a ragged, voluble, romantic New Yorker from mercantile stock. Both writers had hovered on the edge of insolvency, and each was a kind of outsider. One outcome of this strange encounter was a quasi-ecstatic exploration of Shakespeare and his works, especially from Melville, about the literary question that was troubling patriotic writers in the United States: to what extent should an American writer strive to emulate Shakespeare?

Melville's answer was twofold: he would study the *Complete Works* (his seven-volume edition of Shakespeare has almost five hundred passages marked for special consideration). Equally, he would celebrate, as he put it, 'the things that make Shakespeare, Shakespeare', the qualities he believed that he and Hawthorne shared, those dark qualities he would emulate in *Moby-Dick*: 'Through the mouths of the dark characters of Hamlet, Timon, Lear, and Iago, he [Shakespeare] craftily says, or sometimes insinuates the things which we feel to be so terrifically true . . .' Having boldly declared that 'Shakespeares are this day being born on the banks of the Ohio,' Melville did not merely want to identify with Shakespeare, he wanted to compete with him, as an American: 'If Shakespeare has not been equalled, he is sure to be surpassed, and surpassed by an American born now or yet to be born.' For Melville, the writing of *Moby-Dick*, one of the most Shakespearean novels in the American literary canon, became a conscious effort of literary one-upmanship.

From its clarion first line, 'Call me Ishmael,' *Moby-Dick* is consciously elemental and exhilarating, building towards an apocalyptic climax by pitting the outsider Ishmael against the infinity of the ocean while stirring up all the big questions of existence. But there's another, equally Shakespearean *Moby-Dick*, full of rough humour and witty asides. When forced to share a bed with the tattooed harpooner Queequeg, Ishmael alludes to Trinculo's encounter with Caliban in *The Tempest*: 'Better sleep with a sober cannibal,' he says, 'than a drunken Christian.' Not unlike Shakespeare, Melville (having died in obscurity), had to wait almost a hundred years before his novel's importance was fully acknowledged by readers and critics. *Moby-Dick* is now regarded as one of the greatest works of American literature. Its dialogue with the *Collected Works* becomes just another way in which Shakespeare gets remodernized by generations of new readers.

3.

In the United States, Shakespeare's lines were often consoling but also provocative. Occasionally, they accompanied outbreaks of nineteenth-century American violence, first in New York at Astor Place (1849); and secondly, in the assassination of Abraham Lincoln (1865). In New York, the feud between theatrical enemies William Charles Macready and Edwin Forrest was linked to rival productions of *Macbeth*, leading to street violence in which a score of New Yorkers died and hundreds were injured. In

Washington, Lincoln's assassin John Wilkes Booth, who identified strongly with Shakespeare's Brutus, justified the killing by quoting from *Julius Caesar*.

Before Lincoln fell, Shakespeare (already quoted by the president in his First Inaugural) had also been cited on Civil War battlefields. The Confederate commander Jefferson Davis, quoting *Richard III*, urged his troops to look forward to a time when 'grim-visaged war would smooth her wrinkled front . . .' Shakespeare's remarkable propensity to be adopted by all kinds of American, from Malcolm X and Stephen Sondheim to Bart and Homer Simpson, is exemplified by his popularity out west. *Hamlet*, *Richard III*, and *Macbeth*, regularly performed in California, were well known to gold rush audiences. In the words of one San Francisco journalist in 1857, there was 'hardly a newspaper boy in the city who does not understand the playable plays of Shakespeare, so often have they been ranted on the boards'.

By the 1870s, garbled versions of Shakespeare were sufficiently commonplace for Mark Twain to include the 'rightful duke of Bridgewater's' performance (with a fellow impostor, the 'King of France'), in *The Adventures of Huckleberry Finn*. At first, in this famous parody, 'the duke' initiates a discussion of *Hamlet*:

'Oh, I've got it – you can do Hamlet's soliloquy.'
'Hamlet's which?'
'Hamlet's soliloquy, you know; the most celebrated thing in Shakespeare.'

Eventually, having struck 'a most noble attitude' and 'frowning horrible every now and then', the duke performs, as described by Huck Finn:

All through his speech he howled, and spread around, and swelled up his chest, and just knocked the spots out of any acting ever I see before. This is the speech – I learned it, easy enough, while he was learning it to the king:

To be, or not to be; that is the bare bodkin
That makes calamity of so long life;
For who would fardels bear, till Birnam Wood do
    come to Dunsinane . . .

All this becomes 'a consummation devoutly to be wished . . .' until the duke declaims his farcical climax:

But soft you, the fair Ophelia:
Ope not thy ponderous and marble jaws,
But get thee to a nunnery – go!

According to Huck, 'the duke . . . mighty soon got it so he could do it first-rate . . . It was perfectly lovely the way he would tip and tear and rair up behind when he was getting it off.'

Meanwhile, just at the moment when the young Samuel Clemens was beginning to explore his comic imagination as 'Mark Twain' in gold-rush California, a precisely opposite reading of Shakespeare was emerging on the East Coast.

By 1850, the essayist and prominent Transcendentalist Ralph Waldo Emerson was ready to publish his seminal essay 'Shakespeare; or, the Poet'. Towards the end of his life, Emerson would declare the playwright to be a man who 'dwarfs all writers without a solitary exception', but in 'Shakespeare; or, the Poet' Emerson mixed praise and criticism. He also nailed the 'authorship' debate in a couple of sentences: 'Shakespeare is the only biographer of Shakespeare . . . So far from Shakespeare's being the least known, he is the only person in all modern history fully known to us.'

Towards the climax of his argument, he threw aside all his doubts and saluted Shakespeare's universality in words that still resound with meaning and good sense:

> He . . . drew the man of England and Europe; the father of man in America: he drew the man, and described the day, and what is done in it: he read the hearts of men and women, their probity, and their second thought, and wiles; the wiles of innocence, and the transitions by which vices and virtues slide into their contraries: he could divide the mother's part from the father's part in the face of the child, or draw the fine demarcations of freedom and of fate: he knew the laws of repression which make the police of nature: and all the sweets and all the terrors of the human lot lay in his mind . . .

But how to explain such mastery, or decode this mystery? As authors of 'the book of life', Emerson concluded, Shakespeare and his contemporaries, from Marlowe and Jonson to Beaumont and Fletcher, had been lucky to grow up 'in a time when the English people were importunate for dramatic entertainments . . . The people had tasted this new joy . . . It had become a national interest.'

Emerson's invitation to American readers to make similar discoveries soon elicited an enthusiastic response in the precursor to the modern 'book club'. From the 1880s to the 1940s, there was a States-wide network of some five hundred Shakespeare Clubs, mainly for self-improving women, in which his plays were read and discussed. This was just another way in which Shakespeare became the means by which Americans could engage with the difficult issues of gender, race and power. In every subsequent decade, some of the most creative minds in America would continue to explore the cultural fault lines beneath the surface of the national conversation, through Shakespearean allusions.

PART FIVE, 1610–1616:

'Exit Ghost'

Shakespeare, facing the endgame, becomes freed from constraints of time and place, to take his work to new heights.

Twenty

'CHAOS IS COME AGAIN'

Farewell the tranquil mind; farewell content.
Othello, 3.3.353

1.

When, during the summer of 2016, I attended an open-air production of *Henry V* in Nashville's Centennial Park, the setting was the American Civil War. An onstage gospel choir sang spirituals between the acts, and no one in the audience seemed to find it surprising that the forces of France were kitted out in Confederate uniforms, or that the production promoted itself as a contemporary re-examination of the war between the states. Here in the USA, I was witnessing yet another iteration of 'negligent ambiguity'.

Shakespeare's appeal to twenty-first-century America is rooted in his polyvalent qualities. Neither one thing nor another, he both is – and is not – American. As the outstanding poet of the English language and its literature, he has a natural hold over the American imagination. Equally, as an Elizabethan from across the Atlantic, he is exotic, remote, and sometimes barely intelligible. Yet, as a near-contemporary of the Pilgrim Fathers, he has an automatic entrée to the opening scenes of the American experiment – perhaps because he never wrote an explicitly

American play – while his words and characters have been stitched into the American dream as something precious that's at once foreign and familiar.

Ever since the first draft of the Declaration of Independence, a society tormented by issues of race has wrestled with a coherent narrative line through the chaos and inhumanity inflicted on American life by the slave trade and its bitter aftermath. *Othello, the Moor of Venice* speaks to an unresolved national trauma, and the performance history of Shakespeare's play demonstrates the afterlife of a theme that's proved susceptible to almost infinite reinterpretation with some bizarre manifestations.

In January 1846, for instance, when the US Army was stationed at Corpus Christi, Texas, 'the most murderous . . . God-forsaken hole' in the south, according to one correspondent, its commander turned to Shakespeare for entertainment. US troops had been dispatched south by Congress after the annexation of Texas, to provoke a war with Mexico. As they waited for action, and out of concern for his men's welfare, General Magruder (known as 'Prince John' for his thespian manner) commissioned the construction of an 800-seat theatre, and was soon immersed in rehearsals for *Othello*. This extraordinary production starred (as Desdemona) a young officer named James Longstreet, eventually 'Old War Horse', a renowned Confederate general.

Down in Corpus Christi, there was, however, a problem. Longstreet, a strapping six-footer, was hopelessly miscast. So Magruder decided to give the role to the slender, slighter figure (5ft 8in) of Lieutenant Ulysses S. Grant (subsequently the eighteenth president of the USA), who was, Longstreet observed, 'very like a girl dressed up'. To the troops in

Corpus Christi, *Othello* was understood as a play about soldiers going off to war. In the deep South, the tragedy of a black general eloping with a white woman might seem taboo. Actually, the record shows that *Othello* was often staged there before the Civil War; in the slave states of the Confederacy, many young black men were named Othello. (In Corpus Christi, eventually, Grant was replaced by a professional actress when the soldier cast as Othello objected to a cross-dressing Desdemona. Thereafter this show fades from view.)

There's another aspect of *Othello* – equally addictive to American audiences – that transcends colour. This is the disturbing portrait Shakespeare paints of a world disrupted by inexplicable un-reason. On this reading, Iago becomes the malign enigma whose 'Demand me nothing' only promises further disorder. To this defiance, Graziano replies that 'Torments will ope your lips [5.2.312]', a line which acquired a special resonance during the Bush administration's use of torture in the war on terror.

Othello's message is bleak: there will be no restoration of the status quo. Shakespeare does not flinch from this; he is at pains to emphasize the protagonists' predicament. Brabantio, correctly predicting 'naught but bitterness [1.1.164]', attributes this to 'practices of cunning hell'. How else can he explain to himself the conundrum of his daughter, who is 'in love with what she fear'd to look on [1.3.98]'?

Such scenes become harbingers of the play's desolation. Othello's mind spirals out of control as he gets caught up in a world without meaning, the prisoner of his identity, struggling to keep Desdemona:

Excellent wretch! Perdition catch my soul
But I do love thee, and when I love thee not,
Chaos is come again.
[3.3.91–3]

Once Othello's world turns against him, he is doomed.
After the murder of Desdemona, in anguished conversation
with Iago's wife Emilia, he blames supernatural and celestial chaos for his tragedy:

It is the very error of the moon,
She comes more nearer earth than she was wont,
And makes men mad.
[5.2.118–20]

On so many levels, to such a variety of Americans,
Othello remains a fundamental text; *Coriolanus* is another.
In contrast with the histories, where the people had been
understood as a dangerous, unruly mob, the plebeians'
opposition to Coriolanus appeals to the American mind:
it is articulate and reasoned. Especially in this late work,
Shakespeare's New World audience gets hooked on existential public themes. What happens when a governing
clique fights the restrictions imposed by democratic government? Who makes our public story, he asks, and how?
More Shakespearean questions: Is history – that mundane
record of events – just the outcome of chance, or do we
play a part in its cycles, and does it answer to human
agency? Is there not, after all, some free will in play here?

In 2016, when African-American riots broke out in
Ferguson, Missouri, there was a new madness in the
air. During the closing year of the Obama presidency,

overburdened by unresolved issues of colour, *Othello* was again a touchstone. During that divisive summer, amid the confusion of America's cultural and political elites coming to terms with an inexplicable insurgency, there was one notable source of wisdom – the commentary of those Shakespearean scholars who could articulate a language through which to analyse the crisis. With disruption on all sides, I arranged to visit Michael Witmore, the director of the Folger Shakespeare Library, in Washington DC.

2.

The Folger, the world's greatest archive of First Folio editions, located in the shadow of the Capitol, is as much the Vatican of Shakespeare studies in the USA as is the Shakespeare Birthplace Trust in Britain. I was heading there to see its treasures, but also, in conversation with its director, to reflect on Shakespeare's place in American culture.

As we descended through the library's bank-vault security to the strongroom holding the Folger's treasures, it was the Shakespearean themes of the moment, as much as the sober majesty of Heminges' and Condell's work, that dominated our discussion. We turned the pages of one First Folio, marvelling at the whiteness of its paper, its grandeur and elegance, while Witmore spoke about the way in which, to voters who felt powerless, it would be a character such as 'Poor Tom' (Edgar) in *King Lear* who could best express the frustrated rage of those 'left behind' in contemporary America. 'These great issues that continue to trouble us,' Witmore observed, with some passion, 'are Shakespearean.'

Witmore lives and breathes Shakespeare. For this youthful and energetic head of a venerable Washington institution, it is as though 'the preamble to American life' was written by Shakespeare himself. From this Folger perspective, it's those qualities so vital to the founding and creation of the United States – individualism, curiosity, and intellectual passion – that Shakespeare never fails to address. This, Witmore suggests, is how Shakespeare persists as a contemporary voice within American consciousness. Further, in conversation, he argues that Shakespeare enabled the first Americans to explore 'quite dangerous subject matter'.

Among the many historical examples of Shakespeare's mediating role in contemporary American life remembered at the Folger, none is more poignant than the story of the Shakespeare statue in Central Park, New York City. This pensive bronze stands on rising ground not far from East 66th Street. In 1864, this monument to the 300th anniversary of Shakespeare's birth had been inaugurated by a well-known theatrical family, the Booth brothers. But then, there was an unforeseen crisis.

A few months after the successful launch of their plans, the youngest Booth brother, the actor John Wilkes, descended into infamy at Ford's Theatre in Washington DC, on the night of 14 April 1865. Lincoln's assassin fled the scene, and was hunted down, dying several days later in a shoot-out. Seven years passed before his brothers could revive their project. Eventually, on 23 May 1872, a large crowd turned out in Central Park to inaugurate a statue which stands still as a symbol of American reconciliation. In the words of James Shapiro, an out-and-out New Yorker, 'Shakespeare remains at the centre of the things we fight over and disagree about.'

As 2019 ended, more than two years after the brouhaha

(in the park) over *Julius Caesar*, Shapiro would complete his contemporary examination of this theme, *Shakespeare in a Divided America*. For Shapiro, Shakespeare's appeal to modern America is 'all about belonging and national identity'. On this reading, the inclusive Latin motto found on American coins – *E pluribus unum* ('One out of many') – finds a correlation in the Shakespeare canon. For Witmore, as well, Shakespeare becomes a moderating player in America's culture wars, arbitrating 'issues of race, class, privilege, entitlement and opportunity'. His plays gather up those threads of theme, character and plot that satisfy diverse American audiences. In performance, the theatre will become unified into a coherent whole – 'one out of many'. In Washington, according to Witmore, Shakespeare's popularity is attributable to his role as a lightning rod for political debate. Especially in troubled times, members of Congress increase their visits to the Folger. 'They feel,' says Witmore, 'that Shakespeare is somehow part of their story.'

In June 2019, during the contentious aftermath of the Mueller report, Shakespeare was invoked yet again when the special counsel's investigation into the president's alleged collusion with Russia came under sustained public attack from the White House. Mueller's supporters, regretting his failure to publicize the truth, turned instinctively towards an immediate comparison. 'This is a Shakespearean-level tragedy,' observed Patrick Cotter, a former federal prosecutor. 'It is the tragedy of the principled person, constrained by principle, being opposed by the completely unprincipled – the president and his lackeys.' Cotter's summary: 'The principled are chained, and the unprincipled romp free.'

According to Witmore, when leadership is found wanting in the White House, among members of Congress there will always be a renewed appetite for *Henry V*, *Troilus and Cressida*, and *Coriolanus*. We can see that, from Nixon to Trump, amid the excesses and vanities and the stench of cronyism surrounding the presidency, plays such as *Richard III* and *Julius Caesar* have become a useful and necessary conduit through which a larger, more fractious debate can be ventilated with safety. To some Americans, these channels of reconciliation can be found throughout Shakespeare. In December 2019, blogging on the influential Lit Hub, Liesl Schillinger used *Love's Labour's Lost* to explore the *Shakespearean Drama at the Heart of Impeachment* under the headline 'High Comedy and Misdemeanours'.

The story of Shakespeare in America that Folger tells is richly encrusted with many varieties of heterodox reinterpretation. After *Huckleberry Finn*, Mark Twain's imagination, for instance, continued to mash up Shakespeare and his works throughout his career. He became one of several prominent Americans (subsequently to include Charlie Chaplin and Orson Welles) who believed in a 'Shakespeare' written by a more obviously educated writer, such as Sir Francis Bacon. In 1909, Twain and his circle decided that it was possible to detect the coded signature FRANCISCO BACONO in a sequence of letters from the First Folio.

In fact, some years before Twain, the idea that the true and secret hand behind the plays belonged to Francis Bacon had already become lodged in the obsessive imagination of a charismatic American bluestocking, coincidentally named Delia Bacon, who mobilized the assistance of Nathaniel Hawthorne (as United States Consul in Liverpool).

Hawthorne helped Bacon publish *The Philosophy of the Plays of Shakspere Unfolded* (1857), a gallimaufry of 'demented allegorizing' submerged in almost unreadable prose that, at first, gained little traction. By most rational criteria, Sir Francis Bacon was an unlikely candidate as 'Shakespeare'. He had long been recognized as a Renaissance great: scientist, courtier, philosopher, jurist – and writer. On a conventional analysis, just about the only things at which he did not try his hand were plays or poems.

None of this presented a problem for Delia Bacon. Her close reading of Shakespeare, she declared, revealed the collective effort of a 'little clique of disappointed and defeated politicians' fighting a desperate covert battle against the 'despotism' of Elizabeth and James I. Delia Bacon was a formidable advocate for her namesake: of course no one individual could possibly have written the plays attributed to Shakespeare. He was little better than a 'pet horse-boy at Blackfriars', 'an old showman and hawker of plays', an out-and-out 'stupid, illiterate, third-rate play actor'. Other American pioneers of the 'authorship question' threw chronology to the winds and advanced the claims of Christopher Marlowe and Edward de Vere (seventeenth Earl of Oxford), to name two leading contenders in a field that also includes Sir Walter Raleigh, John Donne and even the Virgin Queen herself.

The case for Marlowe is a farrago of wishful thinking. The most improbable of all the anti-Stratfordian theories (Marlowe died in 1593), it was wittily spoofed in Tom Stoppard's screenplay (co-written with Marc Norman), *Shakespeare in Love*. Only slightly less loopy is the suggestion, from the 'Oxford' caucus, that Edward de Vere is the true author of the canon. Despite his inconveniently early death in 1604 – before *Macbeth*, *King Lear*, *Coriolanus*, *The Winter's Tale* and *The Tempest* were written and/or staged – de Vere continues to fascinate the anti-Stratfordians (notably Roland Emmerich whose 2011 film, *Anonymous*, bundles this nonsense into an absurd cinematic fantasy), for whom the plays are the surrogate autobiography of a secretive literary earl. This sub-sect also derives a good deal of its confidence from the advocacy of Sigmund Freud. Possibly more embarrassing to the father of psychoanalysis, Freud's views are based on one volume, *Shakespeare Identified* by Thomas Looney, another Victorian obsessed by 'Who Wrote Shakespeare?'.

The obvious answer, supported by a surprising quantity of Elizabethan and early Jacobean documents, is that Shakespeare wrote Shakespeare. By the mid-nineteenth century, however, the authorship debate had the unintended consequence of placing Shakespeare's life and work at the centre of the finest American literary criticism.

3.

The Folger also trades in truth as much as in reconciliation. Deep in its vaults, Witmore's colleague, the curator Heather Wolfe, is a Shakespeare detective who has brought her forensic skills to bear on many disputed aspects of Shakespeare's biography. A bright-eyed manuscript scholar, she's a palaeographer specializing in Elizabethan England who in certain moods of candour might put you in mind of Portia. Penetrating the mysteries that surround his genius, Dr Wolfe has clarified our appreciation of the poet and playwright as a man. For years, despite a tantalizing mass of documents that survive from the late sixteenth century, the historical Shakespeare had continued to slip through scholars' fingers. In 2016, however, Wolfe made a discovery that transformed our understanding of Shakespeare's biography.

Before Dr Wolfe, all that scholars could be certain about was that a man named Shaxpere, or Shakespear, was born in Stratford in 1564, that he was an actor whose name is printed in the collected edition of his work published in 1623, and also that he married a certain Anne Hathaway, and died in 1616 – according to legend, on his birthday, St George's Day. The so-called 'Stratfordian' case for Shakespeare rested on a few other facts, but basically, that was it. In the absence of reliable data, a mountain of speculation had morphed into those weird fantasies about authorship.

In simple terms, Wolfe delivered the *coup de grâce* to the conspiracy theorists. She has no time for their speculations. 'Without hard evidence for other contenders,' she says, 'it's hard for me to engage with that line of inquiry.' Dr Wolfe's appetite for manuscript corroboration has led her into many dusty corners of the Elizabethan archives, an instinct that first led her to reopen the file on the coat of arms granted to Shakespeare's father, the small-town glover, in 1596.

John Shakespeare, from Stratford-upon-Avon, was ambitious to rise in the world. Among his contemporaries in Stratford, he was a figure of fun for his social climbing. His son, who would continue the quest for official recognition, also attracted metropolitan disdain as the 'upstart crow'. In 1601, after his father's death, the upwardly mobile 'W. Shake-speare' renewed his family's application for a coat of arms. He had made a good living in the theatre, and was buying property in and around Stratford to consolidate his claim as a 'Gentleman'. Under the rules that governed the court of Elizabeth I, only the queen's heralds could grant this wish.

A much-reproduced sketch for a coat of arms crystallized Shakespeare's hopes for legitimacy in the antique jargon of heraldry: 'On a Bend Sables, a Speare of the first steeled argent. And for his Crest, a falcon, his winges displayed Argent, supporting a Speare Gould . . .' The needy applicant also attached a motto: *Non Sanz Droit* ('Not without right'). All this, and much more, is buried in the London archive of the College of Heralds, the court officials who administered the rituals governing the lives of the knights and earls surrounding Queen Elizabeth I.

In 1602, within the College of Heralds, a bitter rivalry broke out between Sir William Dethick, the Garter King of Arms, and another herald, Ralph Brooke, when Brooke released a list of some twenty-three 'mean persons' whose applications for crests (he claimed) had been wrongfully preferred by Dethick. When 'Shakespeare the Player' found himself on this list, his campaign for social advancement was plunged into doubt. It's at this point that Heather Wolfe discovered what she describes as 'the smoking gun'. In the Brooke–Dethick feud, it becomes clear that 'Shakespeare, Gent. from Stratford' and 'Shakespeare ye player' are the same individual. In other words, that 'the man from Stratford' is indeed the playwright. Crucially, in the long-running 'authorship' debate, this had been a fiercely contested point. Wolfe's research nailed any lingering doubts in which the Shakespeare deniers could take refuge. For Wolfe, it's Shakespeare the man who breaks cover here. 'He's defending his legacy not only as a playwright, but most importantly to him, as a gentleman,' she says. The derogatory references to the arms belonging to 'Shakespeare ye player' show that he was playing 'the same game as everyone else in that period, purchasing land in Stratford to support his case to "ancient" gentility, rather than through his astonishing professional success.'

Professor Shapiro describes Wolfe as 'a Sherlock Holmes of the archives' who 'has had the intellectual independence to see what others have overlooked. Make no mistake: her recent finds are consequential, and sharpen our sense of Shakespeare's dogged pursuit of upward mobility,' he says. 'It is one more nail in the coffin of those who can't bring themselves to acknowledge that the glover's son from Stratford was also the successful man of the theatre who left us so many extraordinary plays.' For Dr Wolfe, her work is all about an accurate biographical portrait. 'Additional finds will help us understand his life,' she says, renewing his appeal to contemporary America as an historical figure as much as a poet and playwright of genius. The marriage of these qualities would inspire his Shakespearean afterlife.

Twenty-One

'OUR REVELS NOW ARE ENDED'

I love a ballad in print, a life, for then we are sure they are true.
The Winter's Tale, 4.4.258

1.

After 1609, the outline of a 'Shakespearean' myth begins to emerge from the story of the playwright's final years, intensifying the debates surrounding his last exit. In this mysterious process, the publication of the sonnets comes at a crucial point, the moment when he was being challenged by the rising generation, writers such as Jonson, Middleton, Beaumont, and Fletcher.

For twenty-odd years, he had worked incessantly at the dangerous edge, smuggling an occluded self into his work, and perhaps never more so than in the sonnets. On 20 May 1609, this investment returned an unexpected and imperfect dividend, more by accident than design, when the printer Thomas Thorpe, known for his unscrupulous methods, registered 'a booke called Shakespeares sonnettes' with the Stationers' Company.

These 'sugared Sonnets' had been a word-of-mouth phenomenon since the turn of the century, and this quarto edition – unauthorized by Shakespeare – was a publishing coup: an astonishing sequence of 154 sonnets plus a long poem entitled 'A Lover's Complaint'. Priced at sixpence, this slim volume was prefaced by an enigmatic dedication – the most famous in English literature – whose eccentric use of full stops was possibly intended to suggest a certain marmoreal permanence:

TO.THE.ONLIE.BEGETTER.OF.
THESE.INSVING.SONNETS.
M^r. W.H.   ALL.HAPPINESSE.
AND.THAT.ETERNITIE.
PROMISED.
BY.
OUR.EVER-LIVING.POET.
WISHETH.
THE.WELL-WISHING.
ADVENTURER.IN.
SETTING.
FORTH.
T.T.

Only a maverick like Thomas Thorpe ('T. T.') could have devised such a grandiose and garbled page. Worse, the typesetting from page to page was of a piece with this preliminary matter. Unlike *Venus and Adonis* and *The Rape of Lucrece*, whose publication Shakespeare had overseen, Thorpe's edition was peppered with misprints. But it becomes a founding document in the emergence of the Shakespearean story. From this moment forward, his life and work will become framed by the many mysteries of an inscrutable record. In 1609, perhaps strangest of all, the publication of Thorpe's opportunistic text attracted virtually no attention, and quickly faded from view. Only thirteen copies of the first edition survive.

Mysterious 'Mr W. H.', however, has enjoyed a long afterlife. From a career replete with puzzles, the sonnets have excited centuries of speculation to equal the riddle of the Sphinx. In the words of the poet Auden, 'More nonsense has been talked and written on the sonnets than on any other literary work in the world.' Much of this debate has swirled around the identity of the dedicatee. If 'Mr W. H.' is another of Thorpe's misprints, goes one argument, might it not be the poet 'W. S.' himself? Or was it perhaps William Herbert, Earl of Pembroke (dedicatee of the First Folio)? Or Shakespeare's former patron, Henry Wriothesley, Earl of Southampton? Or – after Oscar Wilde – 'William Hughes'?

The enigmas surrounding the sonnets indicate the way in which, as a writer, Shakespeare moved from metropolitan renown to the grandeur of myth with few of the intervening irritations of celebrity. A year after the sonnets comes the apocryphal tale of Shakespeare's contribution to the King James Bible, a translation 'authorized' by the king, which had been delegated to teams of scholars from London, Oxford and Cambridge. There's no evidence that Shakespeare had any connection with these clerics, but a riddle buried in Psalm 46 ('God is our refuge and strength: a very potent help in trouble') is said to put the playwright in their midst.

The case goes as follows: the 46th word of Psalm 46 is 'shake' (*the mountains shake with the swelling thereof*) and the 46th word from the end is 'spear' (*cutteth the spear in sunder*). As a clincher, the committee on which Shakespeare is alleged to have sat may have numbered forty-six participants. In 1610, the year when the translation was completed, the poet himself was forty-six years old: QED. (This is probably among the least fanciful of the many bizarre theories surrounding the playwright's life and work.) At this stage in Shakespeare's career, with much of his future behind him, the temptation to extract biographical collateral from the last nuggets of his *Complete Works* can become overwhelming. However, setting aside some wishful thinking, what do we know for certain?

At the age of forty-six, Shakespeare was still active as a senior member of the King's Men; his greatest tragedies, from *Hamlet* to *Macbeth* and *Coriolanus*, had been written, performed, and, in several cases, published. Time, no longer on his side, had become something of an obsession. In fact – we have this advantage – he has barely seven years to live.

Will Shakespeare, groom of the bedchamber, was both a servant of the Crown and a theatrical impresario, poet, playwright and actor – a significant contemporary artist – replete with as much acclaim as the age could bestow on a mere 'player'. Among some aficionados of creative danger such as Graham Greene, whose fervent loyalty was to the romance of betrayal, such honours were suspect. In 1969, accepting Germany's Shakespeare Prize with a lecture about 'disloyalty', the novelist used the occasion to criticize Shakespeare for being too complicit with the state in the persecution of the poet Southwell, accusing him of being an accomplice in repression. It was, declared Greene, the writer's duty to make 'a virtue of disloyalty':

> The writer is driven by his vocation to be a protestant in a Catholic society, a catholic in a Protestant one . . . He stands for the victims, and the victims change . . . Loyalty confines you . . . but disloyalty encourages you to roam through any human mind; it gives the novelist an extra dimension of understanding.

In failing a fellow poet, argued Greene, Shakespeare had flunked a fundamental test: 'We revolt against this bourgeois poet on his way to the house at Stratford and his coat of arms . . .' For Greene, there was the temptation to use Shakespeare against Shakespeare – 'You have too much respect upon the world,' the accusation flung at Antonio in *The Merchant of Venice*: 'They lose it that do buy it with much care [1.1.74–5].'

'If only he had lived a few more years,' exclaims Greene, 'we could have seen the great poet of the Establishment defect to the side of the disloyal.' These comments say more about the novelist than the playwright, but this lecture does raise a fundamental concern about the latter's deepest political sympathies. One answer to the question, 'How conservative was Shakespeare?' is that the mature writer was now embedded in the court of James I. This was not such a cosy move. Even Whitehall had become a place where everyone – high or low, king or scullion – lived in fear of the plague (more than 3,000 deaths a week during the worst of the latest outbreak), which dominated the first seven years, 1603–10, of the new reign.

Allusions to the plague are scattered throughout Shakespeare's Jacobean works, notably *King Lear* and *Coriolanus*, indicating a heightened awareness of the risks inherent in city life. During *Antony and Cleopatra*, when a soldier in battle is asked who's winning, he reports that all is lost, 'like the tokened pestilence, Where death is sure [3.10.9–10]'. Such ill winds had unintended consequences: the virulence of the plague had also decimated the 'boys' companies' whose popularity had so bedevilled London's theatre world since 1599.

The plague also sponsored a new kind of venue less

vulnerable to the perils of the climate or the crowd. In August 1608, the King's Men made a leasehold agreement with the landlord of the Blackfriars, a site the Burbage family had coveted since 1596. The Blackfriars monastery, abandoned during the Reformation, was on the north bank of the Thames, across the river from the Globe: a cluster of buildings with obvious potential as an indoor theatre. Above all, Blackfriars had a roof: here, Shakespeare and his fellow players could perform year-round.

2.

After the Globe (which was retained for summer business), Blackfriars, lit by candles and seating an audience of about seven hundred, offered a sheltered space, liberated from the groundlings in the pit. By 1610, the King's Men, performing at Blackfriars, were attracting a sophisticated audience with a taste for the intimacy that comes with candlelight. Shakespeare became inspired by the challenge of a better class of audience. Moreover, his investment brought him a one-sixth share of the business, a profitable deal.

The creative impact of Blackfriars is instantly discernible. In the public playhouses there were no breaks in the action, and the drama was freewheeling. In private theatres, plays became divided into five acts, not least because the candles had to be trimmed or replaced. During these breaks, musicians would perform 'sweet airs'; a superior kind of music became characteristic of Blackfriars.

The move across the Thames and the publication of Shakespeare's sonnets coincided with a new mood, an appetite for abstract, and timeless, romance. Not long after the opening of Blackfriars, Shakespeare made his own telling shift: new lodgings close to the theatre where he could work on his late plays – *Cymbeline*, *The Winter's Tale*, and *The Tempest* – exploring the potential of this new performance space, and experimenting with new ways to stage his work. When, in *Cymbeline*, Iachimo creeps into Imogen's bedroom to spy on her asleep, he can express sentiments that would have played more awkwardly at the Globe:

> How bravely thou becom'st thy bed! Fresh lily,
> And whiter than the sheets! That I might touch,
> But kiss, one kiss!

These lines also incubate an evolution in literary technique. The playwright exploits the Blackfriars' staging ('the flame o' the taper') so that his audience shares a transgressive moment like voyeurs:

> 'Tis her breathing that
> Perfumes the chamber thus. The flame o' the taper
> Bows toward her, and would underpeep her lids,
> To see th'enclosèd lights, now canopied
> Under these windows, white and azure-laced
> With blue of heaven's own tinct.
> [2.2.15–23]

Cymbeline has several such unforgettable moments, and some notorious absurdities. Meanwhile, the magic of *The Winter's Tale* and *The Tempest*, both works of fierce originality, reflects the darker vision of Shakespeare's mature years. There's also his brilliant way – through the character of Imogen – with 'inwardness', and some heart-stopping poetry, including Posthumus' tribute: 'Hang there like fruit, my soul, Till the tree die [5.6.263–4].' The audience for *Cymbeline* might conclude that they were witnessing a dramatized poem as much as a play. This suggestion brings Shakespeare back to *Venus and Adonis* and his beginnings.

Cymbeline also contains one of my favourites, the loveliest, and most moving of all Shakespeare's songs, a consolation for death:

> Fear no more the heat o' th' sun,
> Nor the furious winter's rages.
> Now thy worldly task hast done,
> Home art gone, and ta'en thy wages.
> Golden lads and girls all must,
> As chimney-sweepers, come to dust.
>
> Fear no more the frown o' th' great,
> Thou art past the tyrant's stroke.
> Care no more to clothe and eat,
> To thee the reed is as the oak.
> The sceptre, learning, physic, must
> All follow this and come to dust.
> [4.2.259–70]

This was never the kind of verse suited to the Globe's raucous apron stage. In the same setting, we also find Shakespeare yet again breaking new ground with theatrical convention. *The Winter's Tale* ('a sad tale's best for winter') shows Shakespeare at the top of his game – borrowing, cutting, revising and inventing. The play's source is almost an in-joke, a proud assertion of creative dominance by an ageing master. *Pandosto: The Triumph of Time* had been a popular novella by Shakespeare's former nemesis Robert

Greene, from whom he now borrowed freely. On this occasion, however, Shakespeare reimagines it with intense creative daring. Once more, he revisits sexual jealousy, a favourite theme. Leontes' suspicions of his wife Hermione, and his fury towards her in the opening scenes of the play, become a headlong dramatic exposition, mixed with passages of highly wrought poetry. Hermione's bitter teasing of her jealous husband is tense and abbreviated by repressed feeling:

What, have I twice said well? When was't before?
I prithee tell me. Cram's with praise, and make's
As fat as tame things. One good deed dying tongueless
Slaughters a thousand waiting upon that.
[1.2.92–5]

The Winter's Tale expresses Shakespeare's 'late' style – a complex, tightly wired, and psychologically rich portrait of family relationships and deep old friendships. Actors often dislike the contortions of these late plays, not least because Shakespeare seems to have lost interest, as Lytton Strachey puts it, in 'who says what to whom'.

The Winter's Tale is also outstanding for three exceptional moments of theatrical risk, ranging from the notorious to the heartbreaking. First, in Act Three, there's the scene where Antigonus, arriving on 'the coast of Bohemia' with the baby Perdita ('counted lost forever'), is surprised by the wild, and makes his fatal exit 'pursued by a bear', a crisis that leads to the discovery of Leontes' baby daughter by the Old Shepherd.

Soon after this, there's another Shakespearean innovation, the introduction of 'Time', as a chorus, in order to move the action of the play from Sicily to Bohemia sixteen years later. Shakespeare executes this manoeuvre with an audacious appeal to his audience:

> Imagine me,
> Gentle spectators, that I now may be
> In fair Bohemia, and remember well
> I mentioned a son o'th' King's, which Florizel
> I now name to you; and with speed so pace
> To speak of Perdita, now grown in grace
> Equal with wond'ring.
> [4.1.19–25]

Finally, most avant-garde of all, there's Shakespeare's famous *coup de théâtre*, the return to life of Hermione's statue. Having withheld all information about her fate after an explosive first act, this becomes a moment of sublime innovation that inspires some of his most moving dramatic poetry. Standing before the lifelike statue of his wife, Leontes decides it must be cold stone, and concedes his fault:

> I am ashamed. Does not the stone rebuke me
> For being more stone than it?
> [5.3.37–8]

In one of the riskiest reconciliation scenes Shakespeare ever wrote, Leontes confronts his shame, coming to terms with an ocean of regret. Finally, he reaches out to the statue with a line that actors love:

> O, she's warm!
> If this be magic, let it be an art

Lawful as eating.
[5.3.109–11]

There's little more to be said. This is the mature playwright fully in command of his stage, his audience and his art.

3.

Despite the appeal of the Blackfriars' potential intimacies, with the Globe still in business, there was no resisting the dramatic thrill of a shipwreck. Once gifted the news of a true-life seafaring miracle, Shakespeare exploited an unexpected theatrical bonanza with his usual relish.

When, during May 1610, the crew of the *Sea Venture* finally turned up in Jamestown with their tale of an extraordinary escape, London became seized by a tabloid sensation. First, one of the crew rushed out a pamphlet (*A Discovery of the Bermudas, Otherwise called the Isle of Devils*), cashing in on the story. To retain commercial advantage, the Virginia Company countered with *The True Declaration of the Estate of the Colony in Virginia*, subtitled *A confutation of such scandalous reports*. This was followed by William Strachey, from the *Sea Venture*, who circulated his version of events in the form of a letter. Shakespeare is known to have read Strachey in manuscript, and he probably also studied both the other pamphlets. Wholly suited to his current mood, here was the perfect scenario: remote, abstract, magical, and thrilling. Better still, the drama of *The Tempest* matched a plot to which he had always been drawn – the recovery of old identities and the repossession of a lost inheritance.

This became one of the rare occasions when Shakespeare obeys the rules: not since *The Comedy of Errors* in 1594 had he paid such attention to the classical unities. *The*

Tempest adheres to the dictates of time and place to an almost obsessive degree. The playwright signals the moment, just after noon, when Alonso's ship is wrecked, and will sign off, at evening, around six o'clock, when the characters go off to dine together, with every complication resolved by the storm and its aftermath. Having turned their world upside down, Prospero will bewitch his ship-wrecked brother and his associates, marry off his daughter, suppress a slave rebellion, and prepare for a return to Milan, all in the space of three hours.

As a demonstration of his art, the marriage of risk and innovation, *The Tempest* becomes a masterclass. From the storm itself ('We split, we split!') to the sudden serenity of Prospero and his daughter in their island seclusion ('Lie there, my Art'), Shakespeare's juxtaposition of idyll with jeopardy runs through every line of the play like a refrain. It colours Prospero's love-hate relationship with Ariel, and places the threats of Alonso and Antonio next to the romantic harmony of Ferdinand and Miranda. On this reading, *The Tempest* is a play the audience can experience in two ways, almost simultaneously, as a work of terrifying nihilism, beset with thunderbolts, as well as an enchanting poem, full of 'sweet airs'. Thus, it's at once lyrical and brutal ('There's wood enough within') and yet Arcadian and fantastical ('How many goodly creatures are there here!'). Who can say what Shakespeare intended, or which theme was closest to his heart? 'Of all the plays,' writes Peter Brook, 'none is so baffling and elusive as *The Tempest* . . .' Once more, Shakespeare's 'negligent ambiguity' remains fully deployed.

The Tempest is so rich in valedictory poetry and the imagery of retirement, so fabled in composition as the last play written by Shakespeare alone, and so favoured by the First Folio, where it is placed at the head of the contents page, that it has been hard for many audiences and commentators not to see it as part of the playwright's exit strategy. The autobiographical association of Prospero and playwright seems both easy and natural: surely this is Shakespeare's farewell testament? Is Prospero not, as Coleridge puts it, 'the very Shakespeare himself, of the tempest'? A famous speech in Act Five seems to vindicate this interpretation:

> Graves at my command
> Have waked their sleepers, oped, and let 'em forth
> By my so potent art. But this rough magic
> I here abjure. And when I have required
> Some heavenly music – which even now I do –
> To work mine end upon their senses that
> This airy charm is for, I'll break my staff,
> Bury it certain fathoms in the earth,
> And deeper than did ever plummet sound
> I'll drown my book.
> [5.1.48–57]

Prospero's valediction presents a problem. Is this – or is this not – the poet speaking? Is his message changing? Shakespeare scholars recoil at the association of life and art, but creative correlations are tempting. Besides, there are other ways of looking at this strange, hypnotic play. For some, in post-imperial times, it has been all about Caliban – that monstrous protagonist – as an icon of colonial oppression. The dominant motifs of master and slave, and a 'brave new world', a primitive island inhabited by a 'savage', visited by Europeans, and veiled by storms, can seem to hint at empire. For Coleridge, nevertheless, it is purely 'romantic . . . a species of drama which owes no allegiance to time or space' by a writer who had already 'surveyed all the impulses of human nature'. It was, in Coleridge's words, a summation:

> The language in which these truths are expressed was not drawn from any set fashion, but from the profoundest depths of [Shakespeare's] moral being, and is therefore for all ages.

For others, there is also, in Prospero the magus, one last, covert nod to Christopher Marlowe, the 'dead shepherd' whose murdered spirit haunts so much of Shakespeare's career. Prospero, like Doctor Faustus, is a man of books. Where Faustus, in his struggle with Mephostophilis, promises to burn his books, Prospero – in that great renunciation of his 'art' – plans to drown his. Moreover, Shakespeare has not lost his old instincts. In an explicit borrowing of Medea's invocation, he even paraphrases Ovid (from the *Metamorphoses*) in one of Prospero's closing speeches:

> Ye elves of hills, brooks, standing lakes and groves,
> And ye that on the sands with printless foot
> Do chase the ebbing Neptune, and do fly him
> When he comes back . . .
> [5.1.33–6]

This is hardly a benign conclusion. On a dispassionate reading, Prospero is a ruthless, unsentimental operator, imposing his will, bullying Ariel and Caliban ('a thing of

darkness') to the bitter end, and finally expressing a mood
of angry resignation when he declares 'Our revels now are
ended [4.1.148]'. To this star player, his fellow actors ('all
spirits'):

> Are melted into air, into thin air;
> And like the baseless fabric of this vision,
> The cloud-capped towers, the gorgeous palaces,
> The solemn temples, the great globe itself,
> Yea, all which it inherit, shall dissolve;
> And, like this insubstantial pageant faded,
> Leave not a rack behind.
> [4.1.150–56]

If Prospero is Shakespeare, then his vision is nihilistic,
not uplifting: 'We are such stuff as dreams are made on.'
His closing words, ambiguous as ever, offer only the most
provisional respite:

> And my ending is despair
> Unless I be relieved by prayer,
> Which pierces so, that it assaults
> Mercy itself, and frees all faults.
> [5.1.Epilogue.15–18]

'My ending is despair' is a line that will not have escaped
the notice of James I, a keen playgoer. Adding to the play's
mysteries, there are very few records of contemporary
performances: it became, within a very few years, a central
part of the Shakespearean myth, with playwright and
Prospero united in sympathy and sensibility, and with the
'despair' of his 'ending' lost in time and oblivion.

Twenty-Two

'SANS EVERYTHING'

No longer mourn for me when I am dead
Than you shall hear the surly sullen bell
Give warnings to the world that I am fled
From this vile world with vilest worms to dwell.

Sonnet 71, 1

1.

Throughout his life as a poet, Shakespeare toyed with one classical obsession more than any other: the verdict of posterity. Sonnet 71 had playfully inverted this conceit with 'Do not so much as my poor name rehearse'. Now, in a new decade, sequestered in the antechamber to extinction, few ironies remained.

In his prime, Shakespeare often played the ghost, and had used the stage direction 'Exit Ghost' three times (in *Julius Caesar*, *Hamlet* and *Macbeth*). By 1611, life was catching up with art; his own exit loomed. As long ago as 1599, in *As You Like It*, he had anticipated this 'last scene' of humanity's 'strange, eventful history' as 'second childishness and mere oblivion', coining a famous summary of old age: 'Sans teeth, sans eyes, sans taste, sans everything [2.7.166].' Now the mind and imagination, the creative fire, that had driven Shakespeare for so many years of incessant literary and theatrical labour, began to betray the faintest hint of weary old age. Approaching fifty, however, there was life still to be lived, and Shakespeare's endgame was yet to come. His own simple summary, in *Hamlet*, is pre-emptive: 'If it be not now, yet it will come [5.2.166].'

In English literary life, houses are sometimes a better guide to creative intentions than books. If, after *The Tempest*, Shakespeare seriously entertained the idea of playing Prospero, and retiring to his library at home in the country, the record of his property dealings tells a different story. On 10 March 1613, Shakespeare, the wealthy gentleman owner of New Place in Stratford, made a highly significant commitment to a metropolitan future. For the substantial sum of £140, he acquired his first London property, a gate-house in Blackfriars, the neighbourhood that was now integral to his daily life as a playwright, where like Prospero in Milan he could live among his books.

This 'dwelling house or tenement' had been built above a 'great gate' at the top of the street that ran down to the Thames by Puddle Wharf, where the city's boatmen waited to ferry customers to Bankside. Close to the King's Men's new theatre, the Blackfriars gatehouse was a perfect location for Shakespeare. His new address has been described as both 'a pied à terre and an investment', and was part of the old priory complex riddled with 'sundry back-dores and bye-wayes'. This new home mirrored Shakespeare's elusive habits, but also signalled that, on the verge of his sixth decade, he was as fully engaged as ever with his work in the theatre.

Actually, at this juncture, Shakespeare, the author of those late 'romances', had just returned to a new collaboration, co-writing another history play, *The Life of King*

Henry the Eighth (or *All Is True*), with the young John Fletcher. After five years' torment, the plague had abated, and city life was returning to normal. Now was not the moment to retire; he would revert to the collegiate ways of Elizabethan theatre, and work with Middleton, Wilkins and Fletcher, while still devoting more time to his estates, and perhaps his wife and their two daughters.

The decisive turning point in these final years was less to do with property or family – matters of great interest to an elderly man worn out by many seasons of non-stop theatre work as a playwright and a 'sharer' – than the vicissitudes of show business. On 29 June 1613, there was a disaster when, in an eerie echo of Prospero's speeches, the Globe was burned to the ground during an afternoon production of *All Is True*, an event that inspired a flurry of ephemeral squibs.

The blaze was an obvious hazard of live performance. When, with trumpets and drums, a cannon had been fired to signal Henry's glorious arrival at the home of Cardinal Wolsey – the prelude to the king's first meeting with Anne Boleyn – the linstock for igniting the charge had started a fire in the Globe's thatched roof, initially disregarded by the stage-struck audience as 'an idle smoke':

> their eyes more attentive to the show, it kindled inwardly, and ran round like a train, consuming within less than an hour the whole house to the very grounds.

Happily, the audience was unscathed. 'Nothing did perish but wood and straw, and a few forsaken cloaks.' One fellow, who got too close to the blaze, found his breeches catching fire 'that would perhaps have broiled him, if he had not by the benefit of a provident wit put it out with a bottled ale'. These dramatic events soon became a city joke; in the words of one contemporary ballad:

No shower his rain did there down force
In all that sunshine weather,
To save that great renowned house;
Nor thou, O ale-house, neither,
Had it begun below, sans doubt,
Their wives for fear had pissed it out.

For the King's Men, the spectacle of 'the great globe itself' dissolved by fire to ash and smoking debris was a short-term commercial crisis which – thanks to their royal patron and the nearby Blackfriars Theatre – was less acute than it might otherwise have been. Another Globe, with a tiled roof, possibly paid for by King James, was up and running within a year. But tellingly, on this occasion, the Globe's fifty-year-old playwright did not invest as a 'sharer'.

By 1614, moreover, Shakespeare had quit the scene: finally, he was back in Stratford. The record is patchy, but he appears to have continued his association with John Fletcher. Their latest collaboration became *The Two Noble Kinsmen*, a very late work – probably his last – that Heminges and Condell did not include in the First Folio for reasons that are unclear, but possibly relating to rights issues.

2.

The ambiguities surrounding Shakespeare's life and work never fade. Approximately from summer 1613 to spring

1616, his last exit, can be interpreted many ways. Anthony Burgess, who devoted so much creative energy, in fact and fiction, to the study of Shakespeare as man and artist, came closer than most to a plausible intuition about his return to Stratford, a move that Burgess associates with *Timon of Athens*:

> The mood of the tragedy is that of a man who has had enough of the great world, with its fawning, clawing and biting. Timon turns his back on Athens for ever. It was time for his creator to turn his back on London – not perhaps for ever. But for longer and longer periods of rural peace which should imperceptibly merge into a sort of retirement. Sort of: no writer ever really retires.

Contemporary Shakespeare scholars will reject such braiding of life and work, but Burgess's instincts derived from a lifelong dedication to the arts of literature. Linked to this reading, there's the myth of the poet's sunset years propagated in the eighteenth century by his first biographer, Nicholas Rowe: 'The latter part of his life was spent, as all men of good sense will wish theirs may be, in ease, retirement and the conversation of his friends.' Rowe admitted limits to his research. 'I could never meet with any further account of him,' he wrote, 'than that the top of his performance was the Ghost in his own *Hamlet*.'

Stripped of posterity's embellishments, what did Shakespeare's return home look like? There was, first of all, the strange renewal of old family ties and the renegotiation of his place in the community. A library of speculation about his relationship with Anne, his wife of more than thirty years, has never yet unlocked the mystery of that marriage, which only becomes more opaque with the publication and scrutiny of his last will and testament.

Home life provided few of his accustomed metropolitan pleasures, nor – in retirement – much productive work. There is no reliable record of how he passed his time in Stratford. The journey to London (never less than three days' ride) meant that he was confined to the town limits, and restricted to encounters with passing friends.

These were hardly good times for a reluctant family man and retired playwright; there are some apocryphal tales of Shakespeare's drunken old age. Offstage, there was the drumbeat of mortality: the deaths in the family included his aunt Margaret, and the passing of two brothers, both in their forties (Gilbert in 1612, and Richard in 1613). Within the family, he was becoming a sole survivor.

The belief that Shakespeare was content to withdraw in peace to New Place also has to contend with the record of his business transactions. Almost all his investments, made in and around Stratford, are long-term assets that suggest he expected to live to a ripe old age. In November 1614, he became caught up in a contentious legal battle over the forced enclosure for sheep farming of some tithe-bearing lands first acquired by his father. The enclosers were grasping and unpopular; and Stratford's council was prepared to support Shakespeare in resisting their proposal, but he seems to have decided not to fight the case. The playwright Edward Bond, whose play *Bingo* explores Shakespeare's final years, pointedly observes: 'He could either side with the landowners or with the poor who would lose their land and their livelihood. He sided with the landowners.'

At home, family life was equally vexatious. His first child Susanna was well married to a local doctor, John Hall, but thirty-one-year-old Judith, Hamnet's surviving twin, was still a spinster of the parish who now proposed to marry a younger man. Thomas Quiney, aged twenty-seven, was a sleazy publican who would eventually desert her. Judith's sudden wedding took place in February 1616, during Lent. The reasons for this became clear when, in March, an unmarried Stratford woman named Margaret Wheeler died in childbirth. On her deathbed, she named Quiney as the father of her child. Shakespeare had always enjoyed the comedy of the sexes, but the idea that his new son-in-law had seduced another woman while courting Judith would have brought no joy to his household. Worse, there was another possibility. Had Quiney proposed to Judith to avoid being compelled to marry Margaret? No father likes to see his daughter abused in such a way.

It was during these first distressing months of 1616 that Shakespeare began to write his last will and testament, a document that has attracted almost as much scholarly attention as any sonnet or play he wrote for his London audience. What, most contentiously, was the meaning of that bequest to his wife of his 'second-best bed'?

Shakespeare had summoned his lawyer, Francis Collins, to draft this document in January 1616, apparently in some haste. His signatures on the will indicate he's in failing health: there will always be debates about the nature of his afflictions. Was it Parkinson's? Was it syphilis, or simply *Anno Domini*? Whatever it was, he was on the way out.

If, during these final months, there'd been any professional, creative satisfaction to be had, following *All Is*

True, it came from his latest collaboration with John Fletcher on *The Two Noble Kinsmen*. In his prime, Shakespeare had drawn on Chaucer's 'Knight's Tale' for the characters of Theseus and Hippolyta in *A Midsummer Night's Dream*. Now, in old age, he returned to Chaucer for a tale of unrequited love, the story of Palamon and Arcite, a tragi-comedy. To the Romantic critic and great Shakespearean Charles Lamb, this shows the playwright outshining his junior partner:

> Shakespeare mingles everything, he runs line into line, embarrasses sentences and metaphors; before one idea has burst its shell, another is hatched and clamorous for disclosure.

This is another way of saying that his depiction of Theseus (so different from the Duke in *A Midsummer Night's Dream*) is a bitter, nihilistic figure whose laughter is forced, even defeated. And in *The Two Noble Kinsmen* are those lines – often quoted – that seem to suggest the playwright's ultimate valediction, Theseus' closing speech to the gods:

> O you heavenly charmers,
> What things you make of us! For what we lack
> We laugh, for what we have, are sorry; still
> Are children in some kind. Let us be thankful
> For that which is, and with you leave dispute
> That are above our question. Let's go off
> And bear us like the time.
> [5.6.131–7]

Bearing himself 'like the time', Shakespeare's own end is in character. There was, for instance, nothing to match Falstaff's passing, no last words, no contemporary account of a deathbed scene, just a scrap of gossip, recorded by the vicar of Stratford in the 1660s: 'Shakespeare, Drayton and Ben Jonson had a merry meeting, and it seems drank too hard, for Shakespeare died of a fever there contracted.'

So he leaves the scene, as he had always done, like a man who will find good company when he needs to, as an outsider. Shakespeare is a man who wants to please and entertain, and who'll never outstay his welcome, while preserving his privacy as a risk-artist. And, of course, he would ever pose that habitual and all-important question, understood by every writer: 'I would now ask ye how ye like the play . . .?'

After such an inquiry, Shakespeare always made peace with his audience, as in the Epilogue to *The Two Noble Kinsmen*, after a graceful bow, with courtesy, respect, and silence:

We have our end; and ye shall have ere long,
I dare say, many a better to prolong
Your old loves to us. We, and all our might
Rest at your service. Gentlemen, good night.

Twenty-Three

'THE UNDISCOVER'D COUNTRY'

What seest thou else
In the dark backward and abysm of time?
The Tempest, 1.2.49

1.

Were there, in those final Stratford years, any conversations with 'sweet Will' Shakespeare about posterity? Or perhaps, with ironic allusions to self-important Ben Jonson, awkward discussions about a 'Complete Works'? It is tempting to imagine a visit to New Place by John Heminges and Henry Condell with bundles of playscript.

Tempting but futile. Shakespeare sustains his lifelong enigma from beyond the grave, but there is one final documentary certainty. Towards the end of November 1623, the bookseller Edward Blount, who traded at the sign of the Black Bear near St Paul's, finally held in his hands the text of the massive volume (some 885,000 words) for which he had long been waiting: *Mr William Shakespeares Comedies, Histories & Tragedies Published according to the True Originall Copies.*

For me, as for most Shakespeareans, readers, scholars and critics alike, it is hard to overstate the importance of this literary, cultural and commercial moment. 'Shakespearean', the noun and adjective, derives from the book known as the

First Folio. In dedicating this magnificent volume to the patrons William and Philip Herbert, 'an incomparable pair of brethren', the editors make it clear to posterity that, on behalf of the author, they are in the legacy business:

> We have but collected them [the plays] and done an office to the dead to procure his orphans guardians, without ambition either of self-profit or fame, only to keep the memory of so worthy a friend and fellow alive as was our SHAKESPEARE, by humble offer of his plays to your most noble patronage.

Next, addressing 'the Great Variety of Readers', these editors confessed, it was 'a thing to have been wished':

> that the author had lived to have set forth, and overseen, his own writings. But since it hath been ordained otherwise, and he, by his death, departed from that right, we pray you do not envy his friends the office of their care and pain to have collected and published them.

Shakespeare's former partners may be hinting that he had planned to 'set forth' his collected works, but we have no proof of his intention to 'oversee' such a project. In the suggestive words of Stephen Greenblatt, the playwright always wrote 'as if he thought that there were more interesting (or at least more dramatic) things in life to do than write plays'. Nevertheless, the marmoreal 900-page outcome of whatever was – or was not – discussed between the playwright and his editors, retains the unequivocal power of black on white.

A labour of love, this first authoritative edition of his work established 'Shakespeare' for all time, in two principal ways. Notably, it collected some thirty-six plays, including eighteen scripts (especially *Macbeth*, *Julius Caesar*, *As You Like It* and *The Tempest*) which would otherwise have remained unknown. Almost as importantly, the First Folio definitively connects Ben Jonson (who now declared his rival to be 'the soul of the age') and many of the actors who had first performed these plays with the historical person, the playwright himself, a figure helpfully illustrated by a famous frontispiece, the engraving of the author (compared by some to 'a self-satisfied pork butcher') that's become the logo for Shakespeare studies.

George Orwell says that, at fifty, 'everyone has the face he deserves', but here, at the junction of Tudor and Stuart England, with several competing versions of the author on display, there's yet more ambiguity. Where Christopher Marlowe has one 'putative' portrait, Shakespeare has at least six in contention as his definitive likeness – six images in search of an author. Each has its sometimes vehement advocates; none has been identified conclusively as the authentic likeness; and only two really matter.

The first portrait, widely reproduced, whose fortunes have risen and fallen with the vicissitudes of fashion, is the so-called Chandos portrait. To modern eyes, this swarthy Jacobean fellow with the earring who makes fearless eye contact with his audience is perhaps the most appealing. Furthermore, the provenance of the Chandos canvas places it in the early seventeenth century, probably between 1600 and 1610. Better yet, it comes with some contemporary references to Shakespeare himself.

Sadly, this does not clinch the argument. As the National

Portrait Gallery's commentary puts it, the identification of Shakespeare as the subject of the Chandos picture 'says as much about the growing interest in images of Shakespeare in the late seventeenth century as it does about the actual identity of the sitter'. Even in posterity, he remains provocatively elusive. When Freud first stood in front of this portrait, he decided that 'Shakespeare looks completely exceptional, completely un-English,' and worried that he must be of French ancestry, his name a corruption of 'Jacques Pierre'. These Latin features, said Freud, only raised new doubts about Shakespeare's Stratford origins. For years to come, Freud would be tormented by the authorship question. On the other hand, the Chandos portrait has more credibility than its four rival contenders: the Grafton (1588); the Sanders (1603); the Janssen (c.1610), and finally the Flower, a nineteenth-century portrait based on the frontispiece to the First Folio, which had been executed by the Dutch engraver Martin Droeshout in the 1620s.

More than the Chandos, and more than all the other contenders, this Droeshout image – another icon of the Shakespearean afterlife – has three indisputable characteristics that deserve to be taken seriously amid a fog of speculation and misattribution. First, it comes down to posterity in three distinctly separate versions, indicating the care and attention lavished on the likeness by the editors of the First Folio. Second, published in 1623, the Droeshout engraving is contemporary with many of those who either knew, or had worked with, William Shakespeare at the Globe. Third, most decisively, this portrait, which has inspired many busts and effigies, faces a lavish encomium to the playwright by his great rival, Ben Jonson, expressed with all the swagger for which he is renowned, and dominating the opening page of the First Folio.

Garrulous, vain, argumentative, jealous, proud, and deeply committed to exposing hypocrisy and corruption, Jonson was never a man to kowtow to nobility or privilege. How does he describe Shakespeare? It is Jonson who generously declares that his rival is 'the applause, the delight, the wonder of our stage', and then – a few lines later – that he is 'not of an age, but for all time' and claims him, with affectionate certainty, as his 'gentle Shakespeare . . .' Here, beyond question, is one great literary figure paying posthumous tribute to another. In a rational universe, Jonson's lines would confound any conspiracy which says that 'Shakespeare' is just an alias. Once again, it is Anthony Burgess who makes the best observation about these competing Shakespearean images:

> We need not repine at the lack of a satisfactory Shakespeare portrait. To see his face we need only look in the mirror. He is ourselves, ordinary suffering humanity, fired by moderate ambitions, concerned with money, the victim of desire, all too mortal . . . We are all Will. Shakespeare is the name of one of our redeemers.

2.

After 1616, and especially after 1623, Shakespeare and his Works advance on a slow, sometimes confused, march across the English-speaking world. The First Folio created an artefact of incalculable potency, and the unexampled grandeur of this achievement, combined with its enigmatic character, has dazzled and perplexed a roster of great writers, from Melville to Borges.

For those in every generation who suffer (in Ariel's words) 'the fever of the mad' in their obsession with Shakespeare's authorship, there is this consolation: they are in good company. Their literary critical judgements often illuminate parts of the Shakespearean inheritance that might otherwise be neglected; and their starting point must always be the First Folio. As a challenging blueprint for the ambitious writer, this volume has provoked, among others, George Bernard Shaw, Mark Twain and even Sigmund Freud, who had to concede that, in many important senses, Shakespeare was there before him.

Here, in *Shakespearean*, the third part of a 'disruption trilogy', I concede in this record of a quest, an obsessive streak: my journey from acute ill health to this prolonged rendezvous with Shakespeare. As much as any consolation, there are dangers in the feverish private reading of the *Complete Works*. Two examples stand out: the curious case of England's poet laureate, and his 'hypothesis bug', a radical and idiosyncratic re-evaluation; and the fascinating example of the novelist Arthur Phillips and *The Tragedy of Arthur,* his provocative fabrication of 2010.

In the neglected case of the poet Ted Hughes, 'the fever of the mad' brought a great poet to the brink of oblivion. The backstory to Hughes's longest and most sustained work of prose is yet another modern parable of Shakespeare's eternal spell over the contemporary mind.

Hughes had devoted much of his career to reading Shakespeare. In 1990, towards the end of his life, he signed a contract for a magnum opus entitled *Shakespeare and the Goddess of Complete Being*, a radical and enthusiastic interpretation that offered the reader 'a sort of musical adaptation', a majestic song in which the plays become 'a single titanic work, like an Indian epic'. For Hughes, Shakespeare's characters are always battling their way through various incarnations in 'a vast cyclic Tragedy of Divine Love'. On this reading, the First Folio functions on the scale, and with the complexity, of the *Mahabharata*. When *Shakespeare and the Goddess of Complete Being*, Hughes's most sustained prose work, was published in 1992, the reviews were cruel. The poet himself said that his book had nearly killed him, telling one friend he was 'not sure I've ever got over it'.

Arthur Phillips would probably recognize the experience of being haunted by Shakespeare. However, in his dialogue with Shakespeare's afterlife, he cuts a more elfin figure. His audacious Shakespearean romp is offered as a novel in which a certain 'Arthur Phillips' saves approximately the last one hundred pages of his novel, *The Tragedy of Arthur*, for a five-act play, mostly in blank verse, entitled *The Tragedy of Arthur by William Shakespeare*.

It's here, so to speak, that the fun begins. Before publication, Phillips actually invited the Shakespeare Club to participate in, and host, an informal reading of this work. Strangely, within our fraternity, we have never encouraged play-reading; this was a request to which, shamefully, the Club failed to respond. Soon after, many enthusiastic American reviews for Phillips's work became their own silent reproach. As the *New York Times* critic observed, saluting a 'very gifted forger', this entertaining confection, based on Holinshed, one of Shakespeare's favourite sources, blends military adventure, political intrigue and romantic love, as if it had been 'written by the author of *The True Tragedy of Richard, Duke of York*, no trivial achievement'.

Phillips's text becomes an offbeat memoir of a disturbing

childhood, reminiscent of John le Carré's *A Perfect Spy*, a young man's coming of age in the shadow of a parent with criminal instincts, a charming but hopeless crook. Having established a brilliant rococo-cum-postmodern premise, Phillips now unpeels an 'argument' between 'Phillips' the author and his publisher. The fictional novelist has been commissioned to write an introduction to this newly discovered Shakespeare play, *The Tragedy of Arthur*. But 'Phillips' is convinced that this 'tragedy' is just another fraud. His publisher, who has acquired the book rights at great expense, is in no mood to listen to Phillips's case; he expects to make a fortune from a 'new play' by William Shakespeare, and insists on Phillips's contractual obligations . . . Many more reflecting mirrors further dazzle the reader. Arthur Phillips, the real-life author of this exceptional pastiche, has many clever points to make about the Shakespeare cult. To me, this feat of imagination triumphs as an apotheosis of 'Shakespearean' self-consciousness.

Like Phillips, the actor Phoebe Waller-Bridge turns out to be fixated on Shakespeare. At the end of 2019, promoting the newly published scripts of *Fleabag*, Waller-Bridge was quizzed by the *New York Times* on various matters, including the inevitable 'dinner-party' question: 'You're organizing a literary dinner party. Which three writers, dead or alive, do you invite?'

Waller-Bridge's answer becomes a timely coda:

Definitely Shakespeare. I want to look that guy in the eye. I'd tell him there were other people invited, so he would definitely come. But in the end there'd just be an intense little table in a tiny room, lit by a single candle and me saying: 'OK. Come on. How the f—'

Epilogue

'REMEMBER ME'

1.

In Shakespeare, the Epilogue is sometimes the moment when – with a clear exit – the playwright breaks cover, speaking to us as himself. Nonetheless, the writer who animated the self never gives much away; I suspect he was just as opaque to his fellows in the King's Men.

Shakespeare and the actors of the Globe, including Heminges and Condell, were a band of brothers who had survived many vicissitudes by the time their theatre burned down in 1613. Once their 'friend and fellow' the dramatist was dead, that lifelong enigma filled the echoing biographical void beside almost a million words of poetry and prose in the First Folio. This juxtaposition of the artist and his legacy becomes another twist of the 'Shakespearean' conundrum: the universal fame of the invisible writer.

William Shakespeare's anonymity is in keeping with his innate creative privacy. The contrast between the ceaseless drama of his stage, and the stark white silence of those spacious pages, speaks of the gap between inspiration and performance. In the Shakespeare Club we, who honour his life and work in our regular outings, are versed in the mysteries of the literary life. Sometimes, one or other of us will quietly intone Beckett's 'Ever tried. Ever failed. No matter. Try Again. Fail again. Fail better.' As a group, we've certainly tasted occasional disappointment.

316

When, for instance, the Club launched its blog in 2009, we anticipated an appreciative response from the Shakespeare-loving community. One or two of us even speculated with facetious optimism about house seats from grateful managements. We were, of course, dead wrong. No freebies materialized, from any quarter; possibly more killing, our blogging ambitions were comprehensively dashed.

To date, after more than a decade, our Shakespearean co-ordinate (https://shakespearoes.wordpress.com) defies the gravity of the World Wide Web with its own peculiar expression of airy nothingness. In brief, this luckless site has yet to elicit a single online response. Not one. Our devoted Archivist's postings on this lone blog – potentially so vulnerable to the fevers of social media – might as well be written in double Dutch, or a code known only to the Club. To the rest – the Novelist, the Journalist, the Academic, the Publisher, the Scriptwriter, and the Actor – this failure remains a mystery of our times, a source of ironic speculation among club members. As a collective, we are at home in self-deprecation, badinage and *sotto voce* repartee. Shyness masks arrogance: some part of the Club's pride in its Shakespearean record will be gratified to have a place in these pages. Not – heaven forbid – that any of us would ever concede this.

Sometimes, in contemplation of the thunderous, indifferent silence we've inspired, I like to think that William Shakespeare himself would concede a discreet nod of approval. Among the paradoxes of his tantalizing absence, none is more piquant than the playwright's immanence as a universal genius. Speaking personally, the more I've written about Shakespeare, the more he's become a man with a distinct and special character, a writer with a deep understanding of his own self, an artist untroubled by the kind of fame most renowned writers must endure today. Shakespeare was never tormented by literary prizes, book festivals, or the Twittersphere. However, he was a well-known figure at court. As such an artist, I believe he was comfortable with the creative limits. He knew where he began, and where he ended; where he could take a chance; and where on no account he should stray. My Shakespeare is a very clever man and a writer of genius (not necessarily the same thing).

It's said of Mozart that the conundrum of his music is explained if we think of his compositions as part of a conversation with himself and his circle. Similarly, for Shakespeare, some of his dialogue flows as naturally as common speech. Other passages he chiselled, and chiselled again, like a craftsman at his bench. But he could always step back from this theatrical life, unscathed. His plays were work in progress, shared with his fellow players, precious literary artefacts over which, at the end of the day, he could – so to speak – throw a dust sheet and retire.

In other ways, too, he was lucky. Despite some perilous politics, he was never racked, or seriously challenged. Even during the Essex affair, I imagine him turning the world's more intrusive inquiries aside with insouciance, or banter: the quips of an artist for whom a close personal scrutiny was no laughing matter. Besides, no one could ever ask him to withdraw from, or betray, his own self because no one knew where to find it – and he wasn't saying. Iago's 'Demand me nothing' hints at the fiery solitude of the poet's mind.

If this makes Shakespeare seem well defended towards

everyday life, there is – opposed to the immense care he took with his imagination – the example of a man and a writer, a true artist, who hungrily ingested the enthralling variety of the world around him. Shakespeare's curiosity about everything under the sun makes him uniquely seductive: omnivorous, witty, sophisticated, wise and – from page to page – the most wonderful company. His immense gifts were part of his self and that self was never mortgaged, banged up, or bankrupted. It's as if – at some early stage in life – Will Shakespeare took an oath of loyalty to his calling, and its craft. He would never perjure that vow.

He did not have to: his commitment to that precious gift, his 'imagination' and its free traffic, made him a free man, in a very English way. Shakespeare achieves his sense of self through himself and his art, without resort to witchcraft, philosophy, or religion. The 'Remember me' of *Hamlet* resounds through his afterlife as the cry of a proud man who has made good, a poet of the unequalled 'self' whose 'invisibility' and studied lack of self-consciousness becomes central to his greatness.

In a risky business, Shakespeare's well-adjusted career feeds back into his work; art and life formed a virtuous circle. He was rich and well connected, favoured by two monarchs, treasured by their dynasties, and at home in Whitehall, among the most brilliant and powerful men of the age. Once he'd left his family in Stratford, he found a substitute at the Globe in London. He had all the books he needed, no serious money worries, and only the burden of incessant work at the thing he loved – his poetry and plays – to complain about. His closest collaborators, his theatrical and business partners, became the community that nourished his art.

So what, you might ask, remains? One answer, derived from the catalyst of risk and originality I introduced at first, is the playwright's 'negligent ambiguity'. The key to Shakespeare's creative strategy is that he understands his genre, and its categories ('pastoral', 'comical', 'historical' etc.). He also knows his limits, and the limits of language. He seems to recognize that words alone can never fully nail madness, slavery or torture – or indeed any of the great dramatic themes he puts before us on stage. He has, in other words, none of the arrogance that would want even to make such an attempt. In this, too, he is effortlessly modern, and provisional. The felicity of language for Shakespeare lies in its intangible quest for something just beyond human utterance and understanding, possibly in the creative territory of silence. With Lear, he wants to take upon him 'the mystery of things'. This is all of a piece with what we can deduce about the poet and playwright from his complete works.

2.

The fellow known to the records as 'W. Shake-speare' cherished his originality by treating it with a kind of infectious glee. In this, he seems to have fathomed the conundrum defined by Albert O. Hirschman, who writes, in a gloss on Keats's 'negative capability', that:

> Creativity always comes as a surprise to us; therefore we can never count on it and we dare not believe in it until it has happened. In other words, we would not consciously engage upon tasks whose success clearly requires that creativity be forthcoming. The only way in which we can bring our creative resources fully into

play is by misjudging the nature of the task, by presenting it to ourselves as more routine, simple, undemanding of genuine creativity than it will turn out to be.

The alchemy of the creative life has many potent ingredients. In 'The Lady with the Dog', a favourite story of mine, Chekhov invests his character Gurov with reflections about infidelity, i.e. the tension between our inner and outer selves; in Gurov's case, as the lover of Anna, the lady: 'He had two lives,' writes Chekhov, 'one, open, seen and known by all who cared to know, full of relative truth and of relative falsehood; and another life running its course in secret.' Chekhov explains the importance of this secrecy:

Everything that was essential, of interest and of value to him, everything that made the kernel of his life, was hidden; and all that was false in him, the sheath in which he hid himself to conceal the truth – his work, his discussions at the club etc. . . . – all that was open . . . Personal life rested on secrecy, and possibly it was on this account that civilized man was so nervously anxious his personal privacy should be respected.

Shakespeare's intuition about the need for secrecy in art inspired his negative capability, that gift from which he acquired his command of opacity – his innate ambiguity.

The Shakespeare of 'negligent ambiguity' is a writer who treated playwriting as a regular job for someone who loved to read and write, and for whom authorship was merely part of everyday life. This was the quality that appealed to W. H. Auden, who admired the poet's 'attitude towards his work'. Auden continues: 'There's something a little irritating in the determination of the very greatest artists, like Dante, Joyce, or Milton, to create masterpieces and to think themselves important. To be able to devote one's life to art without forgetting that art is frivolous is a tremendous achievement of personal character. Shakespeare never takes himself too seriously.' This infectious English quality becomes another facet of his appeal to the contemporary theatre, actors and audiences alike. The ambiguous Shakespeare never fails to invite reinterpretation.

This embodies a pragmatic quality which recurs throughout English literature. Consider, for instance, Harold Pinter's acceptance speech for the Shakespeare Prize in 1970, in which he described a Shakespearean attitude to his own work. 'I'm a writer,' he declared, 'not a critic. When I used the word work I mean work. I regard myself as nothing more than a working man. If I am to talk at all,' he went on, 'I prefer to talk practically about practical matters . . .'

Which brings us back home. Speaking from the front of the stage, an appropriate move for an epilogue, I see that my journey has arrived at a natural conclusion. The 'disruption' that began with my 'right hemisphere haemorrhagic infarct' on 28 July 1995 (the subject of *My Year Off*), and was recapitulated in another emergency on 27 June 2014 (the subject of *Every Third Thought*), has run its course, culminating in the global pandemic of coronavirus. Here, in *Shakespearean*, the disparate threads of thought and feeling sponsored by those irruptions have come together in another new narrative, intrinsic to the human instinct to renew the 'self' shot to pieces twenty-five years ago.

In this moment of valediction, my ending is not despair,

but an inner yelp of recognition, which speaks to the closing of a book. In brief, everything seems in harmony: there's no collision of memoir, lit. crit., or *belles-lettres*. No more do I see, as some have seen, a conflict between Shakespeare the poet and Shakespeare the playwright. A play is more like a poem than a history, or a novel. Both poem and play achieve their power over their audience through metaphor and imagery as much as narrative. A great poem is not an 'airy nothing', but sharp, durable and precise. In resilient English, that's what Shakespeare gives us – again and again – his 'poem unlimited'.

Finally, these are just provisional statements, none of which add up to a conclusion: Shakespeare will remain . . . our Shakespeare, *Unser Shakespeare*, that timeless and elusive moving target. Few other conclusions are advisable, or even possible. The temptation to make grandiose claims for such a giant of the world's literature will always be rebuffed by Shakespeare himself, apparently the most modest of men, who is always so grounded in the common-place materials of everyday life. He, who invented a humane version of the self, will always remind us of our humanity.

Shakespeare, in telling us who we are, gives us a narrative line – a story – with which to address the experience we now call existence, i.e. Hamlet's 'outrageous fortune'. But that's not the whole story. As a great artist, Shakespeare knows that vanity kills creativity. He would never, it seems, allow himself to surrender to self-importance, except insofar as he will always be true to himself, as the most private of men, and the most practical of writers.

If any conclusion is possible, beneath such infinite vastness and variety, that is for you, the gentle reader, to

323

discover. Only one thing is certain: the deeper you go, the greater the risk, but the more you will find, in the work, and in yourself.

Harold Pinter, a great playwright with whom I was lucky enough to work as his editor and friend, always had one fierce inquiry about every new theatrical production. Whipping off his glasses, an alarming gesture he'd made inimitably his own, he would focus his glittering gaze on this overwhelming question: 'Does it remain?'

Shakespeare, and his book of life, remains.

(London, October 2017–November 2019)

POSTSCRIPT

While I was working on *Shakespearean* during 2018/19, the four horsemen of the Apocalypse often intruded on my thoughts and reading, as the outriders to so many of Shakespeare's themes. There were, of course, many correlations between the deaths, wars and famines of then and now. Only when my text was with the copyeditor in the first weeks of 2020 did the pale horseman of plague and pestilence irrupt into my narrative in the shape of Covid-19, the greatest global disruption of our time.

At once another new Shakespearean meme began to race through the internet, '*King Lear* was written in quarantine'. Scholarship, however, reports this verdict: not proven. Closer examination of some imperfect data suggests that *Lear* was more probably written during a hiatus in the plague conditions of the early 1600s. More telling, perhaps, is the realization first, that plague overshadowed Shakespeare's entire creative career, very many months in the years 1593–1610, and second, that several other Jacobean plays – notably *Macbeth*, *Coriolanus* and *Timon of Athens* – have many more prominent plague references.

And then there is this, a heart-stopping scrap of anecdotal evidence from a provincial Elizabethan town. In the summer of 1564, Oliver Gunner, a weaver's apprentice, died in Stratford-on-Avon. In the town's records, next to the fate of this unfortunate young man was an ominous marginal note: *Hic incipit pestis* (Here begins the plague).

This particular outbreak of a familiar, and terrifying, disease ripped through Stratford with the indifference to age, gender and status typical of viral pandemics. The outcome of plague was often cruel and inexplicable. One family might be annihilated, their neighbours spared. In one house on Henley Street, there was a young married couple who'd already lost two children to previous plague outbreaks. Their baby son was three months old when they locked their doors and sealed their windows, and hung out bunches of thyme and rosemary, the traditional precaution against pestilence. From bitter experience, they knew that children were especially vulnerable: but perhaps there'd be a miracle, and he'd survive.

As it turned out, John and Mary Shakespeare were lucky. When the plague was over, this couple could celebrate their good fortune. One fifth of the town's population was dead, but their young son was still alive. He would grow up to survive many kinds of extraordinary late-medieval emergency, some of which now seem closer to us than we can ever have imagined. The last word must be Shakespeare's, the closing lines of *King Lear*:

> The weight of this sad time we must obey,
> Speak what we feel, not what we ought to say.
> The oldest hath borne most; we that are young
> Shall never see so much, nor live so long.

[5.3.322–325]

NOTES

This is a personal inquiry into Shakespeare's life and work, a literary and biographical essay for the general reader, not a work of cutting-edge academic prowess for Shakespeare scholars, though I hope they will profit in passing, here and there. Accordingly, in identifying Shakespeare's Dramatis Personae, I have followed conventional spellings. In addition, to achieve a standard text of works cited, my quotations from Shakespeare's poetry and plays are taken from the Oxford Shakespeare edition of the *Complete Works* edited by John Jowett, William Montgomery, Gary Taylor, and Stanley Wells (second edition, 2005).

PART ONE, 1564–2016: 'WHO'S THERE?'

Prologue: Was This the Face?

p.3.   **sombre, transgressive motto** By chance, Shakespeare's sonnet 73 echoes this motto with 'consumed by that which it was nourished by'.

p.4.   **more than four centuries** Park Honan, the author of the most reliable biography, *Christopher Marlowe* (Oxford, 2005), explores the background to this 'putative portrait' (pp. 111–12), and also the relationship between Marlowe and Shakespeare, confessing (p. 2) that he had not been able 'to catch the two playwrights in conversation'. See also Charles Nicholl, *The Reckoning* (London, 1992), an enthralling portrait of Marlowe's final years in the Elizabethan secret state.

p.4.   **We took the picture** This restoration was carried out by the London firm of W. Holder & Sons, on the advice of Professor Bruce Dickins.

p.5.   **so distant, strange and potent** Susan Brigden, *New Worlds, Lost Worlds* (London, 2001), p. 309.

p.5.   **Shakespeare's hasty wedding** Germaine Greer, *Shakespeare's Wife* (London, 2007) is an entertaining, scholarly, and unpredictable account of what it might have meant to be married to William Shakespeare.

p.7.   **a world now otherwise lost** For Marlowe and the Elizabethans, see Lytton Strachey, *Elizabeth and Essex* (London, 1928), pp. 8–9.

p.7.   **The words with which we seek** George Steiner's 1964 essay, *Language & Silence* (London, 1967), pp. 224–38.

One: 'The Book of Life'

p.11.   **some weird shit** George W. Bush, *New Statesman*, 25–31 January 2019. This aside was widely reported by the 'fake news' media.

p.12.   **American critic Ralph Waldo Emerson** See 'Shakespeare; or the Poet', in James Shapiro (ed.), *Shakespeare in America* (New York, 2014), p. 105.

p.13.   **In May 2020, the actor** Robert De Niro on *Newsnight*, BBC TV in conversation with Emily Maitlis. 12.05.2020.

p.13.   **questions we have to address** In the world's libraries, there are tens of thousands of books, in every language under the sun, about Shakespeare and his works, a four-hundred-year-old literature to which many scholars have devoted their lives. The *Shakespeare Quarterly* keeps a record of every publication devoted to his life and work. Since the millennium, there have been several good new books about many aspects of Shakespeare: *Will in the World* by Stephen Greenblatt (London, 2004); a fine discursive essay *Shakespeare:*

The Theatre of Our World by Peter Conrad (London, 2018); a brilliant study of his style, *Shakespeare's Language* by Frank Kermode (London, 2009); a detailed analysis of one singular aspect of his career, *Shakespeare's Money* by Robert Bearman (Oxford, 2016); and yet again, fresh and original studies of his life and work – *1599: A Year in the Life of William Shakespeare* by James Shapiro (London, 2008), and *Soul of the Age* by Jonathan Bate (London, 2008).

Two: 'To Be, or Not To Be'

p.14.   **No fewer than three of his plays** *A Midsummer Night's Dream*, *King John* and *Richard III*.

p.15.   **remains an enigma** See Charles Nicholl, *The Lodger* (London, 2007), pp. 25–6. See also 'The Enigma of Shakespeare' (1964) by Jorge Luis Borges in *The Total Library* (London, 1999), pp. 463–74, and 'Todo y nada' in *El Hacedor* (Buenos Aires, 1960).

p.15.   **among contemporary witnesses** Later, in the first biographical writings of the eighteenth century, Shakespeare was remembered as more transgressive – poaching deer, insolent to his queen, cruel to an old friend, with a typically provincial 'rudeness' of manner.

p.15.   **In *Brief Lives*** See Oliver Lawson Dick (ed.), *Brief Lives* (London, 2016).

p.17.   **rediscovering life after a stroke** Robert McCrum, *My Year Off* (London and New York, 1998).

p.17.   **the title for a sequel** 'Every third thought shall be my grave' [*The Tempest*, 5.1.314] became *Every Third Thought: On Life, Death and the Endgame* (London, 2017).

p.17.   **I read Shakespeare *directly*** Virginia Woolf, 13 April 1930, *Diaries* (London, 1979).

pp.18   **One definition of 'plasticity'** This definition comes
–19.   from Merriam-Webster.

p.19.   **The artist is so steeped** Henry James, Introduction to *The Tempest* (New York, 1907).

Notes

p.19.　**I now have three editions** In *Shakespearean*, I will quote from the Oxford, but occasionally refer to Arden, Norton and the RSC.

p.19.　**a dedicated play-going circle** With profound, and heartfelt, thanks to my friends and associates, the members of the Shakespeare Club: Cressida Connolly, Ben Macintyre, Neil Mendoza, Roland Phillips, Simon Shaw, Rupert Walters, and Wynn Weldon.

p.21.　**The big thing was to try** Andrew Scott, quoted in the *Observer*, 17.06.2018.

p.21.　**The reason to do** Nicholas Hytner, *Balancing Acts* (London, 2017), pp. 155–9. I gratefully acknowledge a long interview with Hytner at the Bridge Theatre on 9 October 2019.

p.21.　**They will find themselves in good company** Peter Conrad, *Shakespeare: The Theatre of Our World* (London, 2018), p. 24.

p.21–2.　**Prominent bardo-phobes** Tolstoy's bitter assault on Shakespeare's 'wild ravings' is the subject of an entertaining 1947 essay, 'Lear, Tolstoy and the Fool' by George Orwell. See Orwell, *Essays* (London, 1984), pp. 401–16.

p.23.　**conjectural chronology** Until the eighteenth century, there was no attempt to date the sequence of Shakespeare's plays. Most subsequent chronologies must contain areas of speculation and expert guesswork.

Three: 'The Whirligig of Time'

p.24.　**In his 1998 novel** Philip Roth, *I Married A Communist* (London, 1998), p. 302.

p.25.　**Amid the repression of popular culture** See 'When Milton met Shakespeare', *Guardian*, 16.09.2019.

p.25.　**needed not the spectacles of books** John Dryden, 'Essay of Dramatic Poesy', 1667.

p.26.　**the composition of Shakespeare** See S. Schoenbaum, *Shakespeare's Lives* (Oxford, 1993), pp. 99–100. I owe an important debt to this magisterial volume.

p.27.   **Here Nature nurs'd her darling boy** One of several
Jubilee tributes, this was performed at Stratford's
Holy Trinity Church, home to the immortal remains
interred beneath a famous warning:
    Good friend, for Jesus' sake forbeare,
    To dig the dust enclosed here.
    Blessed be the man that spares these stones,
    And cursed be he that moves my bones.

p.27.   **The main Jubilee stage** Schoenbaum, op. cit. pp.
104–10.

p.28.   **The show ended with Garrick's Ode** John Brewer,
*The Pleasures of the Imagination: English Culture in
the Eighteenth Century* (London, 1997), pp. 327–9.

p.28–9.   **We all talk Shakespeare** Jane Austen, *Mansfield Park*
(1814), volume 3, chapter 34. See Kathryn
Sutherland (ed.), Penguin Classics edition (London,
1996), pp. 118, 312–13.

p.29.   **transformed traditional ways of reading Shakespeare**
Jonathan Bate (ed.), *The Romantics on Shakespeare*
(London, 1992), p. 195.

p.29.   **unofficial sponsor of the civilizing mission** cf.
Frank Kermode's ironical commentary on this
'cunning imperialist conspiracy' – an increasingly
large empire needed a suitably large poet and
Shakespeare was chosen for the job. From 'Writing
about Shakespeare' in *LRB Selections 1: Frank
Kermode* (London, 2019), p. 138.

p.30.   **Shakespeare is not a whit** This account of the 1864
tercentenary partly draws on the work of Andrew
Dickson in his Shakespearean tour de force *Worlds
Elsewhere* (London, 2016), pp. 3–4.

p.31.   **Wilde's scintillating short story** Schoenbaum, op. cit.,
pp. 320–24.

p.32.   **Shakespeare said everything** Orson Welles, 'On
Staging Shakespeare, and on Shakespeare's Stage', in
Everybody's Shakespeare (New York, 1934).

p.32.   **In the second half of the twentieth century** Peter
Brook, *The Empty Space* (London, 1968), p. 107.

p.33.   **pondered the inconceivable mystery** Schoenbaum, op. cit. p. vii.

p.33.   **Will the Shakespeare anniversary** G. Steiner, *Language and Silence* (London, 1967), pp. 224–36.

p.34.   **In this virtual-reality version** *New York Times*, 27.01.2019.

p.34.   **The protean audience** Adrian Noble, *How To Do Shakespeare* (London, 2010), pp. 2–3.

p.35.   **I just hate the idea** Andrew Scott, *Observer*, 17.06.2018.

p.35.   **In 2012, the British Library** See Dickson, op. cit., p. 261, for a thorough analysis.

p.35.   **Mandela himself is reported** Andrew Dickson, op. cit., pp. 260–310, also presents a persuasive alternative version to the Mandela story reported in the press.

p.36.   **and even Prince Charles** *Guardian*, 8.11.2018.

p.36–7. **Charles told the BBC** The Shakespeare biographer Anthony Holden reports that the prince's favourite Shakespeare lines come from *Henry V*:
    What infinite heartsease
    Must kings neglect that private men enjoy?
    [4.1.233–4]

p.37.   **created us all** See Conrad, op. cit. p. 12.

p.37.   **A five-ring opening circus** *New York Times*, 27.07.2012.

p.37.   **managed to feature a flock of sheep** Ibid.

p.38.   **uplifting celebration of Englishness** See Dickson, op. cit., p. xvi. See also the *New York Times*, 27.07.2012 and 28.07.2012.

Four: 'Something Is Rotten in the State'

p.40.   **To sign, or not to sign** Quoted in Shapiro (ed.), *Shakespeare in America*, p. 3.

p.41.   **Shakespeare's words** *New York Times*, 08.10.2016.

p.42.   **The other thing I took** *New Yorker*, 07.06.2017.

pp.42–3. **This was a show** *New York Times*, 11.06.2017.

p.44.   **No taxpayer dollars** *New York Times*, 13.06.2017.

p.44.   **Six months after these sensations** Michael Wolff, *Fire and Fury: Inside the Trump White House* (New York, 2018), p. 280. Bannon has some form as a 'Shakespearean' outrider. Having flirted with a film of Julie Taymor's *Titus Andronicus*, he adapted *Coriolanus* as a rap musical set in South Central Los Angeles during the Rodney King riots. *New Statesman*, 01–07.06., 2018.

p.45.   **How does a truly disastrous** Stephen Greenblatt, *Tyrant* (London, 2018), passim.

p.46.   **'Shakespeare's spell'** See Shapiro, op. cit., p. xviii.

p.46.   **fresh from Stratford** Shakespeare left school, presumably, in the late 1570s or early 1580s. The myth of his life says that he was apprenticed to his father, a glover. In 1582, he married Anne Hathaway who bore him a daughter, Susanna, in May 1583, and twins, Hamnet and Judith, baptized on 2 February 1585. Thereafter, he drops from the record into the biographical abyss known as 'the lost years'. From 1585 until 1592, when 'Shakespeare' begins to appear in various documents, nothing reliable is known about his career. Into this vacuum, some scholars have projected a mass of speculation, inspired by the complete works, much of it fanciful.

PART TWO, 1585–1593: SHAKE-SCENE

Five: 'The Very Cunning of the Scene'

p.49.   **helped legitimize a hollow crown** Brigden, op. cit., p. 386. I am indebted to this excellent account of Tudor England.

p.50.   **This tragedy, she snapped** There are many versions of this anecdote. The most recent occurs in Greenblatt, op. cit., pp. 20–22.

p.50.   **fraught with perils, many great** Brigden, op. cit., pp. 213–38.

p.51.   **The film studio of today** Christopher Isherwood, *Prater Violet* (London, 1946), pp. 47–8.

p.52.   **In this fusion of history** For Tudor England's consumers of paper and ink see *Love's Labour's Lost* [4.2.24].

p.52.   **Official curiosity, writes Phillips** See *Attention Seeking* by Adam Phillips (London, 2019), pp. 3–10.

p.55.   **the poet Robert Browning identifies** The lines come from *Bishop Bloughram's Apology*, 'Our interest's on the dangerous edge of things. The honest thief, the tender murderer, the superstitious atheist.'

p.57.   **an indecipherable millefeuille** See Sarah Lyall, *The Anglofiles: A Field Guide to the English* (London, 2009), p. 39.

p.60.   **The playwright David Mamet writes** See D. Mamet, *Some Freaks* (London, 1990), pp. 132–3.

p.60.   **diction of common life** See Samuel Johnson, Preface to *A Dictionary of the English Language* (1755).

p.61.   **change the way his audiences** Shakespeare would also captivate and celebrate his age in theatrical entertainment such as *The Taming of the Shrew* (1590–91), *Titus Andronicus* (1592), and *The Comedy of Errors* (1594).

Six: 'Hot Ice'

p.62.   **The man everywhere** Henry James, *The Tempest* (1907), from Roger Gard (ed.), *Henry James, the Critical Muse, Selected Literary Criticism* (London, 1987), pp. 428–43.

p.62.   **Shakespeare's dialogue conceals** See C. T. Onions, *A Shakespeare Glossary* (Oxford, 1911), passim. This volume celebrates many dialect treasures found in Shakespeare, such as *neaf* (a fist), *shog* (depart) and *yest* (foam).

p.63.   **snow, in Warwickshire** Such usages suggest that Sir Francis Bacon, an East Anglian, is a most unlikely candidate as the author of Shakespeare's plays.

p.63. **a virtuoso development** Ted Hughes, *Winter Pollen* (London, 1994), p. 106.

p.64. **an open doorway into a different world** Noble, op. cit., p. 139.

p.65–6. **If you cannot understand** Bernard Levin, *Enthusiasms* (London, 1983), pp. 167–8.

p.69. **scholar-writers like Sir Thomas More** Sir Thomas, fluent in Latin, popularized Latinate words in English such as *absurdity, contradictory, exaggerate, indifference, monopoly* and *paradox.*

p.70. **For the uttering sweetly** Philip Sidney. See A. C. Baugh and Thomas Cable, *The History of the English Language* (London, 1978), p. 207.

p.70. **My lady tongue** In *Love's Labour's Lost*, Rosaline has a sweeter response to Berowne's romantic language, merely observing that he has a 'fair tongue'.

p.72. **Snoop Dogg adapting the vernacular** Disputes about the size of Shakespeare's vocabulary continue to exercise a certain class of academic truffle-hunter. For an authoritative summary, see David Crystal, *Think on My Words: Exploring Shakespeare's Language* (Cambridge, 2008), p. 2.

p.72–3 **neuroscience at Liverpool University** For more on Philip Davis, see *Brain*, vol. 139, part 12, December 2016, pp. 3310–13.

p.73. **Davis and his team** Other examples of Shakespeare's grammatical daring include the following. A noun transformed into a verb: 'He childed as I fathered' (*King Lear*). A noun made into a transitive verb: 'He words me, girls, he words me that I should not be noble to myself' (*Antony and Cleopatra*).

p.74. **It's the detail of these observations** Shakespeare's Forest of Arden has become renewed in the twenty-first century by the 'Heart of England Forest' planted by the estate of the millionaire publisher Felix Dennis after his death in 2015.

Notes

Seven: 'The Death of Kings'

p.78.   **Perhaps as early as 1589** A play entitled *harey the vj* was performed at the Rose Theatre on 3 March 1592 by the Lord Strange's Men and was then performed at least fifteen times that year. Some scholars believe that it was written as early as 1589. In this new genre, Shakespeare probably collaborated with Thomas Nashe, George Peele and others. Soon, he was making the history play his own.

p.78.   **These dynastic dramas** Shakespeare's histories include *Henry VI* (parts 1, 2, and 3); *Richard III*; *Richard II*; *King John*; *Henry IV* (parts 1 and 2); and *Henry V*, all written and performed in the 1590s.

p.78.   **rendering of 'the times deceased'** See Richard Proudfoot, Ann Thompson, and David Scott Kastan (eds.), *The Arden Shakespeare: The Complete Works* (London, 1998), p. 495.

p.81.   **From Christopher Marlowe, he had learned** See Jan Kott, *Shakespeare Our Contemporary* (London and New York, 1966), p. 358.

p.81.   **Hytner concedes a moving target** Hytner, *Balancing Acts*, pp. 155–6.

p.86.   **a production of *Sir Thomas More*** For the full circumstances of this contentious script see Stanley Wells, *Shakespeare & Co.* (Oxford, 2006) pp. 115–17.

Eight: 'Upstart Crow'

p.92.   **Biographical guesswork** Among many fine biographies consulted, I gratefully acknowledge Honan, *Christopher Marlowe*; Anthony Holden's outstanding *William Shakespeare* (London 1999); see Holden, op. cit., pp. 66–7, 71 and 74; see also Stephen Greenblatt's bestseller *Will in the World* (London, 2004), pp. 212–13, 267–9.

p.92.   **a certain William Shakeshafte** Alexander Hoghton's will of 3 August 1581 requests his neighbour 'to be friendly to William Shakeshafte now dwelling with me'. Holden, op. cit., p. 53.

p.92.   **still just twenty-one** Holden, op. cit., pp. 64–71.

p.93.   **a matter of a goddess** Anthony Burgess, *Nothing Like the Sun* (London, 1964), pp. 3–5.

p.93.   **with lodgings in Bishopsgate** See Bearman, op. cit., pp. 61–3: 'From the little evidence we have – national tax returns – he appears in the mid-1590s, to have been lodging respectably but not extravagantly, in St Helen's Parish in Bishopsgate Ward.'

p.94.   **the Shakespeare scholar-detective Geoff Marsh** I am delighted to record my thanks to Dr Marsh, who first gave me his tour of St Helen's in 2017. Marsh has done some remarkable detective work on the composition of Shakespeare's Bishopsgate neighbours. See his *Living with Shakespeare* (Edinburgh, 2021).

p.94.   **scanning the proofs of a quarto** For the role of Richard Field in printing some of Shakespeare's poems and plays, see Stanley Wells and Paul Edmondson (eds.), *The Shakespeare Circle* (Cambridge, 2015), pp. 161–73.

p.97.   **Marlowe, by contrast, had grown up** Honan, op. cit., p. 191. See also Wells, *Shakespeare & Co.*, pp. 88–91.

p.97.   **Modern directors such as** Author interviews with Nicholas Hytner, and Trevor Nunn, gratefully acknowledged.

p.97.   **indifferent to the spelling of his name** Many variations include Shakespear, Shaksper, Shespeare, and even Saxpere, with or without a hyphen. The record is complicated by the fact that the writer himself signed his name in no fewer than six different ways.

pp.97–8. **Every surviving detail** Stephen Greenblatt, *Will in the World: How Shakespeare became Shakespeare* (London, 2004), p. 372.

p.98.   **the outstanding survivor** Lyly died in 1606;
          Marlowe in 1593; Kyd in 1594; Watson in 1592;
          Peele in 1596; and Nashe in 1601. The rising
          generation, writers like Ben Jonson, born in 1572,
          were all younger men.

p.99.   **snapper-up of unconsidered trifles** This must be an
          in-joke. Shakespeare had lifted the plot of *The
          Winter's Tale* from *Pandosto: The Triumph of Time*,
          a popular romance from 1588, by Robert Greene.

p.100.   **Polonius reads out** Greenblatt, op. cit., pp. 214–15.
          See also Holden, op. cit., p. 109, an incomparable
          biography, which also makes this connection.

p.100.   **one of the richest young men in England**
          Southampton's exact role in the emergence of the
          sonnets is unclear. Shakespeare's dedication proves
          the earl's patronage, but does not establish if a
          particular kind of work was requested.

p.101.   **coded commentary on Walsingham** See C. M.
          Andrew, *The Secret World* (London, 2018), p. 186.
          Richard III (1592) is believed to be the first play to
          use 'intelligence' in the sense of covert information,
          when Hastings declares 'nothing can proceed that
          toucheth us / whereof I shall not have intelligence'
          [*Richard III*, 3.2.20].

p.102.   **complex and rather pointless** Nicholl, *The
          Reckoning*, p. 311.

p.102.   **another Elizabethan spy** Ibid., pp. 306–7.

Nine: 'Dead Shepherd'

p.103.   **the only game in town** T. S. Eliot, 'John Ford',
          Selected Essays (London, 1932), p. 203.

p.104.   **in their mid- to late twenties** Both had plays
          presented at the Rose Theatre. For both – either as
          rivals or friends – the early 1590s were a time of
          severe jeopardy, exacerbated in Marlowe's case by his
          hot temper.

p.104.   **varieties of risk** Marlowe was implicated in the death of a man named Bradley after a sword fight in September 1589, but was soon discharged from prison, possibly through court connections. Wells, op. cit., pp. 81–2.

pp.104–5. **done her majestie good service** Honan, op. cit., p. 154.

p.106. **Awake, ye men of Memphis!** See Jorge Luis Borges, 'The Enigma of Shakespeare', in *The Total Library* (London, 1999), pp. 463–72. Borges singles out for special praise the 'perfection' of Marlowe's line in *Doctor Faustus*, his evocation of Helen of Troy, 'O thou art fairer than the evening air, clad in the beauty of a thousand stars.'

p.108. **If Shakespeare had died** Wells, op. cit., p. 78.

p.109. **at the heart of his own creative endeavours** The dates for the composition of the sonnets are contentious. We only know for certain that 138 and 144 had been written by 1598.

p.109. **a sequence of events began** Greenblatt, op. cit., p. 318.

p.110. **Marlowe was dead** Nicholl, op. cit., pp. 13–44. I am indebted to Nicholl for his account of these dramatic events.

p.110. **the official account of his death** Wells, op. cit., p. 100.

p.110. **Poley, Ingram Frizer and Nicholas Skeres** Nicholl, op. cit., decisively establishes how sinister and dangerous Marlowe's fellow diners were.

p.110. **in the defence and saving** Ibid., pp. 18–23.

p.111. **No one was quicker** Wells, op. cit., p. 102.

p.112. **His life he contemned** Nicholl, op. cit., pp. 59–69.

p.112. **written soon after** Mercutio in *Romeo and Juliet* and Bottom in *A Midsummer Night's Dream* both have lines, the latter parodic, that seem to make an allusion to Marlowe's style.

p.112. **by the memory of Marlowe** Harold Bloom, *Shakespeare* (London, 1999), p. 461.

p.113. **the only occasion throughout** Nicholl, op. cit., p. 86.

p.115. **About him a thousand corpses** See James Shapiro on 'plague' generally in *The Year of Lear: Shakespeare* *in 1606* (London, 2015), pp. 23–4. I gratefully acknowledge his account of plague years in Shakespeare's mid-life career.

p.117.   **first heir of my invention** Nicholl, *The Lodger*, p. 192.

PART THREE, 1594–1599: WORDS, WORDS, WORDS

Ten: 'Sin of Self-Love'

p.122.   **raucous, bawdy and, above all, popular** Brook, op. cit., p. 73.

p.123.   **Momentous change was in the air** See Arthur C. Danto, *Andy Warhol* (New York, 2009), p. 16.

p.125.   **How we weep and laugh** Montaigne was available for Shakespeare to read from its first appearance in French in 1580. Translated by John Florio, it was published in English in 1603. Florio was part of Southampton's circle; through him, Shakespeare had access to the latest European culture. See the outstanding translation, M. A. Screech (ed.), *The Essays of Michel de Montaigne* (London, 1991).

p.125.   **speaks directly to the playwright's obsessions** The comedies and tragedies of Shakespeare's first decade as a playwright include: *The Two Gentlemen of Verona* (1592–3); *The Comedy of Errors* (1593); *The Taming of the Shrew*; *Richard II* (1595/6) and *Richard III* (1592–3); *Titus Andronicus* (1593–4). He probably read Montaigne thanks to the translator John Florio.

p.125.   **we ought to consider** M. A. Screech (ed.), op. cit, pp. 262–5.

p.126.   **retain the ability to function** F. Scott Fitzgerald, *The Crack-Up* (New York, 1964), p. 69.

p.126.   **In this long poem** Shakespeare took the seventy-three lines of the Lucrece story from Ovid's *Fasti* and dramatized them in nearly 2,000 lyrical variations.

p.126.   **No one discovered Shakespeare** Katherine Duncan-Jones and H. R. Woudhuysen (eds.), *Shakespeare's Poems*, Arden edition (London, 2007).

p.127.   **awarded the ultimate accolade** Don Paterson,
          Reading Shakespeare's Sonnets (London, 2010), p. ix.
p.127.   **passionate, at times demented, exegesis** The classic
          example of this condition must be the sad case of the
          Tudor historian A. L. Rowse, and his obsession with
          the identity of 'the dark lady' during the 1970s.
          Rowse, obsessed by the sonnets, drove himself nearly
          mad with his quest to 'prove' Emilia Lanier's claims
          as the 'dark lady'. See Rowse, *Shakespeare, the
          Elizabethan* (London, 1977).
p.127.   **Nothing that he ever wrote** 'Nothing', in senses both
          sexual and nihilistic, recurs throughout Shakespeare.
          There is a library of books on the sonnets. Some of
          the best include Don Paterson's *Reading
          Shakespeare's Sonnets*; Michael Schoenfeldt (ed.),
          Companion to Shakespeare's Sonnets (London,
          2007); and also the edition edited by Stephen Booth
          (London, 2000).
p.127.   **The sweet, witty soul of Ovid** For Meres and
          Palladis Tamia, see Shapiro, *1599*, p. 18; and Wells,
          op. cit., pp. 61–3.
p.127.   **they would become pirated** See Duncan-Jones and
          Woudhuysen (eds.), op. cit., pp. 83–4.
p.128.   **The slippery 'Will'** See also sonnet 134.
          So, now I have confessed that he is thine,
          And I myself am mortgaged to thy will,
          Myself I'll forfeit, so that other mine
          Thou wilt restore to be my comfort still;
          [Sonnet 134, 1–4]
p.129.   **fifteenth-century Italian** Shakespeare's source, *The
          Tragical History of Romeus and Juliet* (1562) by
          Arthur Brooke, is itself a palimpsest based on a
          French prose version by Pierre Boiastuau (1559),
          which was in turn an adaptation of an Italian
          rendering by Bandello (1554), derived from Luigi da
          Porto's 1525 version of a tale by Masuccio
          Salernitano (1476).
p.130.   **this headlong lovers' tragedy** The tightly plotted

timescale of *Romeo and Juliet* unfolds over five days and nights.

p.135. **the huge army of the world's desires** Peter Holland (ed.), *Love's Labour's Lost* (New York, 2000), pp. xxix–xlii.

p.134. **Its premise is absurd** Holland (ed.), op. cit., p. xxxvi.

p.136. **Berowne and Rosaline become prototypes** Rosaline, like the 'dark lady', has 'a velvet brow, With two pitch-balls stuck in her face for eyes [3.1.191–2]', to which the king adds pointedly, 'Thy love is black as ebony [4.3.245].'

Eleven: 'Wood'

p.141. **within varieties of 'wood'** the etymology of 'wood' (originally 'wode') derives from the Middle English *wode*, and the Old English *wōd* meaning 'mad, raging, enraged, insane, senseless, blasphemous'. On this reading, P. G. Wodehouse has madness coded into his identity as a comic writer.

p.141. **Playing his words on stage** See Bernard Cornwell, *Fools and Mortals* (London, 2017), pp. 377–81.

p.143. **the words for me** Seamus Heaney on BBC One, in conversation with Patrick Garland, 1.10.1973. Quoted in Adam Nicolson, *The Making of Poetry* (London, 2019), Epigraph. The American writer Lorrie Moore expresses her version of this insight when she writes that Shakespeare 'explored the strangeness within the ordinary and the familiar within the strange – the task of every artist.' L. Moore, *See What Can Be Done?* (London, 2018), p. 216.

p.146. **the crudest sex machine** *Plays and Players*, 18, 1970, cited in Helen Hackett (ed.), *A Midsummer Night's Dream* (London, 2005), p. liv.

p.146. **Probably written around 1595** He had already touched on some of its themes (amateur theatricals and the love tangles of wooing couples) in *Love's*

Labour's Lost and *The Two Gentlemen of Verona*. See
Stanley Wells (ed.), *A Midsummer Night's Dream*
(London, 1967). Introduction by Helen Hackett, p. liv.

p.146. **On this occasion, without** He would return to 'The
Knight's Tale' in 1609, with *Cymbeline*.

p.148. **the director Richard Eyre** Richard Eyre, *National
Service* (London, 2003), p. 226.

p.149. **Bubonic plague stalked** Shapiro, *The Year of Lear*,
pp. 22–4.

p.150. **the loud groans of raving** For Dekker, see Wells,
Shakespeare & Co., p. 119.

Twelve: 'W. Shake-speare'

p.154–5. **The poet Richard Barnfield** Jonathan Bate and Eric
Rasmussen (eds.), *William Shakespeare: Sonnets and
Other Poems* (London, 2009), pp. 1–18.

p.155. **'the fat knight'** This was a pointed caricature of a
Protestant martyr. (See next.)

p.156. **Falstaff (formerly Oldcastle)** 'Sir John Oldcastle' was
a name revived from an old play, but recent history
also contained a genuine Oldcastle, a Lollard martyr
hanged in 1417. Eventually, his heirs at court
pressured Shakespeare to change the name, though the
Oxford edition of the *Collected Works* maintains that
'there is reason to believe that even after 1596 the
name "Oldcastle" was sometimes used on the stage'.

p.157. **manic, dissolute prose-poet** Kermode, *Shakespeare's
Language*, pp. 59–64.

p.158. **free artists of themselves** quoted in Bloom, op. cit.,
p. 271.

p.161. **having broken cover** Shakespeare uses 'humble
author' and 'bending author', respectively, in the
epilogues to *2 Henry IV* and *Henry V*.

p.162. **Ever since W. H. Auden** Giorgio Melchiori (ed.), *The
Merry Wives of Windsor* (London, 2000), pp. 56–71.
See also Humphrey Carpenter, *W. H. Auden* (London,
1981), p. 346.

p.164. **Thomas Kyd, Christopher Marlowe, and the rest**
Greenblatt, op. cit., p. 200.

p.164. **a slender quarto volume** Nicholl, op. cit., p. 86. This
record of Shakespeare's reaction is owed to Thomas
Heywood who recorded that Shakespeare was
'offended' that Jaggard, who was 'altogether
unknown to him', had 'presumed to make so bold
with his name'.

p.165. **adding two Shakespeare sonnets** 'When my love
swears' (number 138) and 'Two loves I have'
(number 144).

p.165. **still haunted Shakespeare's** See Duncan-Jones and
Woudhuysen (eds.), op. cit., pp. 4–9.

p.165. **the fallen former favourite** Brigden, op. cit., pp.
342–55.

p.166. **lacking in the good fortune** For one version of this
psychodrama see Strachey, op. cit. passim. See also
Shapiro, *1599*, pp. 57–66.

p.166. **kiss your fair hands** Strachey, op. cit., pp. 115–16, 150.

p.166. **so great an indignity** Strachey, op. cit., p. 175.

p.167. **battle against Tyrone** Shapiro, op. cit., pp. 283–9.

Thirteen: 'A Kingdom for a Stage'

p.168. **'*Shakespeare* among the English'** See Wells, op. cit.,
p. 107; also Holden, op. cit., p. 164.

p.169. **nothing worthy Her Majesty's** Strachey, op. cit.,
pp. 115–16, 150. For one version of this psychodrama
see Strachey, op. cit., passim. See also Shapiro, op. cit.,
pp. 57–66; Strachey, op. cit., p. 175.

p.170. **a conventional expression** See note to p. 161.

p.170. **All the news I can send** Quoted in Shapiro, op. cit.,
p. 21.

p.170. **To the poet John Weever** Shapiro, op. cit., p. 18.
Inter alia, Weever composed a sonnet in praise of
Shakespeare, which suggests he may have been one
of the privileged few who had seen a manuscript of
the sonnets.

p.171.   **to convert the wood** Holden, op. cit., pp. 166–7.

p.172.   **to Shoreditch to repossess the Theatre** This story is repeated in many Shakespeare biographies. A very good account occurs in Holden, op. cit., pp. 184–5. I am indebted to his version of the Globe saga. See also Shapiro, op. cit., pp. 1–5.

p.172.   **did riotously assemble themselves** C. W. Wallace, 'The First London Theatre', *Nebraska University Studies*, vol. XIII, 1913, pp. 278–9. Shakespeare's co-investors were William Burbage, John Heminges, Augustine Phillips, Thomas Pope and Will Kemp, a clown.

p.175.   **with D-Day looming** In the spring of 1944, the eve of D-Day, Lieutenant Laurence Olivier took leave from wartime service as a junior officer in response to an invitation from the Ministry of Information (MOI) to make a film of *Henry V* as part of the war effort. The idea, sometimes misattributed to Winston Churchill, was consciously daring.

p.175.   **Olivier had been persuaded** Hollywood commissioned surprisingly few Shakespeare films in the 1930s: *A Midsummer Night's Dream*, 1935; *Romeo and Juliet*, 1936. I am indebted to Philip Ziegler, *Olivier* (London, 2013).

p.176.   **whose riding I suspect** See Ziegler, op. cit, pp. 105–13. Ziegler's account of the production is definitive. See also 'War on Film: *Henry V*' by Taylor Downing (*Military History Monthly*, August 2018).

p.176.   **mid-twentieth-century patriotism** The film skirts the massacre of Harfleur and the notorious slaughter of French prisoners.

p.176.   **this is a beautiful tune** Ziegler, op. cit., p. 108.

p.176.   **how many fucking horses** Ziegler, op. cit., p. 109.

p.176.   **The poet James Agee** See Shapiro (ed.), *Shakespeare in America*, 'Laurence Olivier's *Henry V*', pp. 460–66.

p.176.   **It was the Chorus's** See Ziegler, op. cit, pp. 105–13. See also Downing, op. cit.

p.177.   **It doesn't date at all** Shapiro, op. cit., pp. 459–74.

p.177.   **half a century later** Hytner, *Balancing Acts*), p. 55.

p.179.   **maximize publicity for his cause** Shapiro, op. cit., pp. 116–17.

p.180.   **written without interruption** Shapiro, op. cit., p. 151.

p.181.   **in the straw-thatched house** Strachey, op. cit., p. 190.

p.182–3 **There was Elizabeth** Strachey, op. cit., p. 212.

p.184.   **old and out of use** There are many versions of this political drama: Tarnya Cooper in her NPG catalogue, *Searching For Shakespeare* (London, 2006); Shapiro, op cit.; Greenblatt, op cit.; or Holden, op. cit., pp. 184–6.

p.185.   **I owe God a death** Greenblatt, *Tyrant*, pp. 16–20.

p.185.   **I know my sins** Strachey, op. cit., p. 254.

PART FOUR, 1600–1609: SHAKESPEAREAN

Fourteen: 'Distracted Globe'

p.191.   **'brain-defying, logistics-confounding' transit** The director Dominic Dromgoole, quoted in Ann Thompson and Neil Taylor (eds.), Arden edition of *Hamlet* (London, 2008), p. 161.

p.192.   **For the Danish Shakespeare-lovers** *New York Times*, 'Hello, sweet prince', 02.09.2009.

p.193.   **two quarto editions** Q1, 'bad', 1603; Q2, 'good', 1604/5.

p.193.   **doubt and controversy** There are three distinct and significant dates for any Shakespeare play: of composition, first performance and first printing. In each of these categories, *Hamlet*'s beginnings are disputed. The editors of the latest 'revised edition' concede that 'we are no nearer than previous scholars to establishing a "precise date".' The consensus favours 1599–1600.

p.193.   **runs to about 4,000 lines** In the Riverside edition of the play, there are 4,042 lines. The text of *Hamlet* used here is from the Oxford Shakespeare *Complete Works*, but I also recommend Arden's excellent 'revised edition' of *Hamlet*, edited by Ann Thompson and Neil Taylor. The legend of Hamlet

(Amleth) in Saxo the Grammarian's twelfth-century *Danish History* was a principal source for Shakespeare that had already undergone adaptation in France (de Belleforest's *Histoires Tragiques*). See the Norton Shakespeare, pp. 1661–2.

p.194.   **his *Mona Lisa*** Several critics have made the comparison with the *Mona Lisa*. A fairly recent version is to be found in Kott, op. cit., p. 58: '[Hamlet's] name means something even to those who have never seen or read Shakespeare's play. In this respect he is rather like Leonardo's Mona Lisa. We know she is smiling even before we have seen the picture.'

p.194.   **the world's literature** In 1999, the Shakespeare critic Frank Kermode observed that the 1997 volume of *Shakespeare Quarterly* listed some 4,780 items, of which 342 were about *Hamlet*, 'almost one a day,' he noted. See Kermode, 'Writing about Shakespeare', in *LRB Selections 1*, p. 136.

p.194.   **as well constructed as any play** T. S. Eliot, 'Poetry and drama' in *On Poetry and Poets* (1943).

p.195.   **600 new words** See Alfred Hart, 'The Growth of Shakespeare's Vocabulary', *Review of English Studies*, vol. 19, no. 75, July 1943, pp. 242–54. These range from *gibber*, and *fanged*, to *remorseless*, *avouch* and *unpolluted*.

p.196.   **in the history of anglophone poetry** Frank Kermode, *The Age of Shakespeare* (London, 2004), p. 102.

p.202.   **It is dirt that gives the roughness** See Brook, op. cit., p. 76.

p.202.   **the popular boys' companies** The references in *Hamlet* to the 'eyrie of children' who are 'now the fashion' [2.2.340–42] allude to the 'war of the theatres' in which fashionable boy actors, known as the Children of the Chapel, challenged the livelihoods of the established theatre companies. From 1600 to 1604, Shakespeare, Burbage and their fellow actors became obsessed by this threat, which would eventually become regulated by the Privy Council, and further reduced by the plague of 1603–5.

Fifteen: 'What You Will'

p.207.   **literary London. Around 1600** The scholar and
           literary contrarian Gabriel Harvey made these notes
           in the margin of a new edition of Chaucer. See Wells,
           op. cit., p. 3.

p.207.   **Shakespeare himself had moved** The best edition of
           Twelfth Night is published in the Arden series, edited
           by Keir Elam (London, 2008). See also Holden, op.
           cit., pp. 200–1. After a private performance of
           Twelfth Night at the Middle Temple in 1602, a
           young lawyer named Manningham noted that the
           play resembled *The Comedy of Errors*, Plautus's
           Roman play *Menaechmi*, and an anonymous Italian
           play called *Gl'ingannati* (*The Deceived*).

p.210.   **first record of *Hamlet*** See Ann Thompson and Neil
           Taylor (eds.), Arden Shakespeare, *Hamlet*, revised
           edition (London, 2016), p. 55. The 'bad quarto' was
           registered on 26 July 1602.

p.210.   **The resonant importance of *Hamlet*** Shakespeare's
           younger contemporaries (John Marston, Thomas
           Dekker, Thomas Middleton, and Ben Jonson) made
           knowing, even parodic, references to the Gravedigger
           scene, and also to the Ghost.

p.210.   **In his study of 'Hamletomanie'** See Dickson, op.
           cit., pp. 24–5. I also acknowledge Ian Buruma,
           Voltaire's Coconuts: Anglomania in Europe (London,
           1999), a witty and comprehensive survey of
           European anglophilia.

p.210.   **fashionable Anglomania** Buruma, op. cit, p. 60.

p.210–11. **Tolstoy's claim** See Orwell, 'Lear, Tolstoy and the
           Fool', op. cit.

p.211.   **with the 'soul of *Hamlet*'** Buruma, op. cit., pp. 38–9.

p.212.   **When the great Romantic** Richard Holmes,
           Coleridge: Early Visions (London, 1989), pp. 261–8.

p.212.   **the poetic 'Imagination'** Richard Holmes, *Coleridge:
           Darker Reflections* (London, 1998), pp. 107–8.

p.212.   **Coleridge was less interested** Holmes, op. cit., p. 124.

p.213.　　inward excitement　Holmes, op. cit. p. 271.

p.213.　　**Feeling and Understanding**　Terence Hawkes (ed.),
　　　　　Coleridge on Shakespeare (London, 1969), p. 99,
　　　　　from a report of the lectures of 1811–12.

p.213.　　*Hamlet* **was the play**　Hawkes, op. cit., p. 157,
　　　　　recorded by Samuel Taylor Coleridge, 7 January, 1819.

p.213.　　**extraordinarily like Coleridge**　Holmes, *Darker
　　　　　Reflections*, vol. 2, p. 282.

p.213.　　**a smack of Hamlet**　Holmes, *Darker Reflections*, vol.
　　　　　2, p. 286.

p.214.　　**conceiving an Iago as an Imogen**　John Keats, Letter
　　　　　to Richard Woodhouse, 27 October 1818.

p.214.　　**The fire is at**　Robert Gittings (ed.), *Letters of John
　　　　　Keats* (Oxford, 1970), p. xix.

p.214.　　**Several things dovetailed**　Gittings, op. cit., p. 43, Keats
　　　　　to George and Tom Keats, 21, 27 December 1817.

p.215.　　**Negative Capability**　Letter to George and Tom Keats,
　　　　　21, 27 December 1817, in Gittings op. cit., pp. 42–3.

p.215.　　**We hate poetry**　Gittings, op. cit., p. 61, Keats to
　　　　　J. H. Reynolds, 3 February 1818.

p.215.　　**notably from Delia Bacon**　See James Shapiro,
　　　　　Contested Will (London, 2010), pp. 189–206. J.
　　　　　Thomas Looney was a very unappealing Shakespeare
　　　　　denier, a reactionary nationalist and a member of the
　　　　　Church of Humanity, another US cult.

p.215.　　**Shakespeare could not have written**　Shapiro's
　　　　　Contested Will makes the definitive refutation of
　　　　　these theories.

p.216.　　**strategic opacity**　Greenblatt, op. cit., pp. 323–5.

Sixteen: 'Tell Me Who I Am'

p.221.　　**The old humanists**　Marilynne Robinson, *The
　　　　　Givenness of Things* (New York, 2015), pp. 10–11.

p.222.　　**The first was a script**　Shapiro, in *The Year of Lear*,
　　　　　examines the gestation of both *King Lear* and
　　　　　Macbeth in rich, and circumstantial, detail. I
　　　　　gratefully acknowledge his scholarship.

p.222.   **published in a quarto** A copy of this quarto edition is now held by the British Library. The provenance of the play is further complicated by a record of *The moste famous Chronicle historye of Leire king of England and his Three Daughters*, which appears in the Stationers' Register on 14 May 1594, but never published.

p.222.   **Shakespeare's borrowing** Stephen Greenblatt, *Will in the World* (London, 2004), pp. 356–8.

p.222.   **A second, factual source** Nicholl, op. cit., p. 62.

p.223.   **One scene, in particular** In Sidney's version, the blind father wants his son to take him to a rock from which he can do away with himself, but his son refuses. Edgar's response to his father Gloucester's request is quite different. The extraordinary enactment on the cliff at Dover in *King Lear* is Shakespeare's dramatic invention.

p.223.   **The fusion of this theme** Shapiro, op. cit., pp. 49–50.

p.227.   **At the head of the title page** Shapiro, op. cit., pp. 47–63.

pp.227–8. **grotesque quality** Kott, op. cit., pp. 131–2.

p.228.   **The farther he goes** Harold Pinter, *Correspondence*, British Library, ADD MS 88880/7/2.

p.229.   **a big shit-show** *Guardian*, 01.04.2019.

p.229.   **Shakespeare, the Greatest Englishman** *Guardian*, 17.06.2019.

p.230.   **Mr Johnson was reaching** *The Times*, 21.12.2019.

p.230.   **At the close of *Henry IV*** See Martin Kettle, *Guardian*, 08.01.2020.

p.231.   **From Falstaff down, the red-blooded English** See Ben Macintyre in *The Times*, 23.05.2019.

Seventeen: 'Shameful Conquest'

p.236.   **two nations were made one** Wells, op. cit., p. 119.

p.237.   **freely to use and exercise** Holden, op. cit., p. 207.

p.237.   **Kitted out in the scarlet** Holden, op. cit., pp. 206–7. In the thirteen years between James's accession and

Shakespeare's death, the King's Men would act a play at court some 187 times (an average of thirteen performances a year, compared to the three per annum of Elizabeth's later years).

p.237.   **At the court of Elizabeth I**   The new king also paid twice as well as his predecessor, and thereby guaranteed his players an income even when the theatres were closed by the plague, as they often were during the 1600s.

p.239   **the outstanding non-event**   There are many excellent accounts of the Gunpowder Plot and the reign of James I. I have relied on Antonia Fraser, *The Gunpowder Plot* (London, 1996), and Roger Lockyer, *James VI and I* (London, 1998).

pp.239   **the State Opening of Parliament**   I acknowledge an
  –40.   important debt of gratitude to James Shapiro. *The Year of Lear*, brings together many connections between Shakespeare and the events of November 1605, especially in its account of the Midlands aspect of the plot.

p.240.   **More delay**   Fraser, op. cit., passim.

p.241.   **lodging on Silver Street**   Nicholl, op. cit., passim.

p.242.   **citizens on terror alert**   The Midlands' contribution to the Gunpowder Plot is described in fascinating detail in Shapiro, op. cit., pp. 105–25. My account relies on this narrative.

p.243.   **Some of these suspects**   Shapiro, op. cit., pp. 116–17.

p.244.   **from behind a screen**   Shapiro, op. cit., p. 174.

p.244.   **do not now equivocate**   Shapiro, op. cit., p. 176.

p.245.   **I do not know what**   Shapiro, op. cit., p. 178.

p.246.   **The 'Scottish play'**   Bardolatry comes in many guises. Since the late nineteenth century, *Macbeth* is often referred to by people who work in the theatre as the 'Scottish play', a thespian euphemism designed to ward off the bad luck said to be associated with the play. This superstition first appeared as a parody of the English antiquary, and gossip, John Aubrey (1626–97) by the celebrated English essayist and parodist

Max Beerbohm, in a review published on 1 October 1898 entitled '*Macbeth* and Mrs Kendal' (*Saturday Review of Politics, Literature, Science and Art*, 01.10.1898). In the course of praising Kendal's Lady Macbeth, Beerbohm observed, 'According to Aubrey, the play was first acted in 1606 at Hampton Court, in the presence of King James. It is stated that Hal Berridge, the youth who was to have acted the part of Lady Macbeth, "fell sudden sicke of a pleurisie, wherefor Master Shakespere himself did enacte in his stead".' Beerbohm's fabrication quickly attracted claims of *Macbeth*'s 'curse', notably several references to the Macready–Forrest feud which led to the fatal riot in Astor Place of May 1849 (see chapter 19.3).

p.249 –50. **This was the wonderful insight** See Thomas De Quincey, 'On the Knocking at the Hell Gate in *Macbeth*', in Robert Morrison (ed.), *On Murder* (Oxford, 2006), pp. 3–8.

p.250 **De Quincey was first inspired** In 1811, seven people from two separate households were found brutally murdered along the Ratcliffe Highway. News of the atrocities quickly spread across England, generating an extraordinary hysteria.

Eighteen: 'Brave New World'

p.255. **A whole country of English** Ben Jonson, John Marston, and George Chapman, *Eastward Ho!*. [3.2]

p.255. **great frequenter of plays** See Sir Richard Baker, *Chronicles* (London, 1643). American dreams filled the imaginations of many ambitious young men; Donne applied for a secretarial job in Virginia, but was turned down.

p.255. **And sailing towards her India . . . O my America!** Elegies XIII and XIX.

p.256. **had actually run aground** This ship is referred to variously as the *Sea Venture* and the *Sea Adventure*. See Kieran Doherty, *Sea Venture: Shipwreck, survival,* *and the salvation of the first English colony in the New World* (New York, 2008), and Holden, op. cit., pp. 280–82.

p.256–7. **the shipwrecked sailors** There are many versions of the *Sea Venture* saga. I have relied on Doherty, op. cit. and Holden, op. cit., pp. 280–82.

Nineteen: 'A World Elsewhere'

p.258. **Next to the Holy Bible** The first recorded volume of Shakespeare's plays to reach the thirteen colonies was a copy of the 1685 Fourth Folio, which arrived in Virginia in 1696. See Shapiro (ed.), *Shakespeare in America*, p. xxiii. I am indebted to this anthology in the writing of this chapter.

p.258–9. **The first American performance** Shapiro, op. cit., p. xxii.

p.259. **This experimental study** Professor John Jowett, in a programme note to the 2018–19 RSC production, *Timon of Athens*, directed by Simon Godwin.

p.259–60. **hardly a pioneer hut** Shapiro op. cit., p. xvii.

p.260. **her mightier Swan shall save** Shapiro, op. cit., p. 36.

p.260. **a history of America** Shapiro, op. cit., p. xxii.

p.262. **marked for special consideration** On Melville's 'marginalia', see Charles Olson, '*Lear* and *Moby-Dick*', *Twice a Year* , vol. 1, Fall–Winter 1938, pp. 165–89, and *Call Me Ishmael* (New York, 1947); F. O. Matthiessen, *American Renaissance: Art and Expression in the Age of Emerson and Whitman* (Oxford, 1941); Julian Markels, *Melville and the Politics of Identity: From* King Lear *to* Moby-Dick (Urbana, 1993); Geoffrey Sanborn, 'The Name of the Devil: Melville's Other "Extracts" for *Moby-Dick*', *Nineteenth-Century Literature* , vol. 47, September 1992, pp. 212–35; and 'Lounging on the Sofa with Leigh Hunt: A New Source for the Notes in Melville's Shakespeare Volume', *Nineteenth-Century Literature*, vol. 63, June 2008, pp. 104–15.

p.262. **Through the mouths of the dark characters** Shapiro, op. cit., pp. 129–30, from Melville, 'Hawthorne and his Mosses'.

p.264. **grim-visaged war** Shapiro, op. cit., p. xxvi.

p.264. **hardly a newspaper boy** See Stephen Marche, *How Shakespeare Changed Everything* (London, 2012).

p.265. **the duke . . . mighty soon** Mark Twain, *The Adventures of Huckleberry Finn* (London, 2014) pp. 177–8.

p.266. **He . . . drew the man of England** Twain, op. cit., pp. 117–18.

p.267. **From the 1880s to the 1940s** See Katherine West Scheil, *She Hath Been Reading: Women and Shakespeare Clubs in America* (Ithaca, 2012).

PART FIVE, 1610–1616: 'EXIT GHOST'

Twenty: 'Chaos Is Come Again'

p.271. **the setting was the American Civil War** Robert McCrum, 'Shakespeare and the American Dream' (two parts), BBC Radio 4, 19 and 24.04.2016.

p.272. **In January 1846** See Shapiro (ed.), op. cit., pp. xix–xx.

p.272. **very like a girl** Shapiro, op. cit., p. xix.

p.273. ***Othello* was understood as** Shapiro, op. cit., pp. 42–53.

p.274. **the plebeians' opposition** Kott, op. cit., pp. 141–2.

p.275. **These great issues** Michael Witmore in 'Shakespeare and the American Dream', BBC Radio 4, 24.04.2016.

p.276. **This, Witmore suggests** Ibid.

p.276. **Shakespeare remains at the centre** Shapiro interview for 'Shakespeare and the American Dream', BBC Radio 4, 19 and 24.04.2016.

p.276. **As 2019 ended** See James Shapiro, *Shakespeare in a Divided America* (London and New York, 2020).

p.277. **a Shakespearean-level tragedy** *Guardian*, 11.06.2019.

p.279. **Hawthorne helped Bacon** The heterodox views of Bacon, Looney, Hoffman, Ogburn et al. have been reheated in many ways, notably in Roland Emmerich's film *Anonymous* (2011).

p.279. **pet horse-boy** Shapiro, *Contested Will*, pp. 93–100. I have relied on this important, and entertaining, study for my account of the anti-Stratfordians.

p.279. **The case for Marlowe** Marlowe's life has provoked a range of enjoyable fictional responses, from Anthony Burgess's *A Dead Man In Deptford* (London, 1993) to *The Marlowe Papers* (London, 2012), a novel in verse by the poet Ros Barber.

p.279. **most improbable of all** For the hierophants of the Marlowe Society, their playwright was not murdered in a tavern (see chapter 9), but spirited away to France through court connections (Marlowe was a government agent). There, for the next twenty-odd years, he wrote the plays attributed to Shakespeare, smuggling them back to London through diplomatic channels.

p.280. **Freud's views are based** Looney would probably have been forgotten but for the appearance in 1984 of Charlton Ogburn's *The Mysterious William Shakespeare: The Myth and the Reality*. As well as marshalling the best evidence for the Earl of Oxford, Ogburn arranged for his 'case' to be formally tried by three US Supreme Court justices in September 1987. This stunt, which awkwardly went against Ogburn, persuaded the *New York Times* to ventilate the question, 'Who wrote William Shakespeare?'

p.282. **In 1602, within the College of Heralds** In the row between the two factions at court, Shakespeare himself became an object of ridicule. Ben Jonson, in his satire *Every Man Out of his Humour*, poked fun at him as a rustic buffoon who pays thirty pounds for a ridiculous coat of arms with the humiliating motto 'Not Without Mustard'.

p.282. **'the smoking gun'** Author interview with Heather Wolfe. See also *Observer*, 17.01.2017. In fairness to Dr Wolfe, she characterizes the significance of her find in the College of Heralds with some caution, claiming (correctly) that it provides evidence of Shakespeare (and not just his father) applying to obtain arms.

Twenty-One: 'Our Revels Now Are Ended'

p.284. **an astonishing sequence** The numbering of Shakespeare's 154 sonnets also makes a subtle allusion to the 150 psalms in the Book of Psalms, the first book of the *Ketuvim*, the third section of the Hebrew Bible. See Greer, op. cit. p. 252, for her theories about the publication history of the sonnets.

p.284. **plus a long poem entitled** A few scholars still question the authenticity of 'A Lover's Complaint'.

p.285. **Only thirteen first editions survive** Why, for instance, Shakespeare did not entrust the sonnets to Richard Field is unclear. A first-class edition from a printer he had known and worked with might have done better.

p.286. **replete with puzzles** The Victorian critic Edward Dowden, identifying 'depths of despair', hints at the poet's possible 'breakdown' during 1608. The pioneering Shakespeare scholar E. K. Chambers entertained a similar theory about a 'nervous breakdown', possibly an attack of plague, before rejecting his own speculation as 'conjecture'. See the indispensable Holden, op. cit., p. 264.

p.286. **More nonsense has been** W. H. Auden (introduction), *The Sonnets* (New York, 1964), p. xvii.

p.287. **the novelist used the occasion** One of Greene's stranger assertions in this lecture was his demand that a properly disloyal Shakespeare should have defected 'to the side of the poet Southwell disembowelled for so-called treason'.

p.287. **The writer is driven** Graham Greene, 'The Virtue of Disloyalty', address given at the University of Hamburg, 06.06.1969 (Hamburg, 1968 & 1969), Verheilung der Shakespeare Preise, p. 49.

p.288. **If only he had lived** Greene, op. cit., p. 50.

p.289. **The Blackfriars monastery, abandoned** I have relied for this account of the Blackfriars Theatre on Holden, op. cit., pp. 258–9.

p.289. **his investment brought him** Some twenty years after his death, this stake was still yielding his heirs about £90 per annum.

p.289. **abstract, and timeless, romance** *Cymbeline* and *The Winter's Tale* both date to 1609–11, and both were staged at the Globe in 1611. There is no consensus about which came first. See the Arden *Complete Works* (London, 1998).

p.290. **some famous absurdities** Samuel Johnson lost patience in a majestic fit of irritation: 'This play has many just sentiments, some natural dialogues, and some pleasing scenes, but they are obtained at the expense of much incongruity. To remark the folly of the fiction, the absurdity of the conduct, the confusion of the names and manners of different times, and the impossibility of the events in any system of life, were to waste criticism upon unresisting imbecility, upon faults too evident for detection, and too gross for aggravation.' Notes from Johnson's edition of *The Plays of William Shakespeare* (1765): see H. R. Woudhuysen (ed.), *Samuel Johnson on Shakespeare* (London, 1989).

p.290. **some heart-stopping poetry** It's tempting, after Samuel Johnson, to dismiss the work as a whole for its improbabilities. How is it, most egregiously, that Imogen's husband Posthumus can become exiled from Celtic Britain to Renaissance Italy? Why would Posthumus (now in Rome) want to become embroiled in Iachimo's ridiculous wager (that he can seduce the virtuous Imogen)? Later, after Imogen's disguise as 'Fidele', how is it that she can awake to believe that the headless body of her stepbrother Cloten, lying next to her, is actually Posthumus? Others question Jupiter throwing thunderbolts, and his descent on an eagle. For the record, two leading Romantics – Keats and Hazlitt – both placed

Cymbeline among their favourite Shakespeare plays.

p.292. **who says what to whom** Shapiro, *Contested Will*, p. 352.

p.294. **the crew of the *Sea Venture*** This vessel has been identified as both the *Sea Venture* and the *Sea Adventure*.

p.294. **This was followed by William Strachey** The letter was eventually published in 1625, two years after the First Folio.

p.295. **all in the space of three hours** For Samuel Johnson, this is nothing less than the artistic climax of genius, the perfectly 'regular' setting for a perfect plot which Shakespeare has made 'instrumental to the production of many characters, diversified with boundless invention, and preserved with profound skill in nature, extensive knowledge of opinions, and accurate observation of life. In a single drama are here exhibited princes, courtiers, and sailors, all speaking in their real characters.' See Woudhuysen (ed.), op. cit., p. 101.

p.295. **writes Peter Brook** Brook, op. cit., pp. 106–7.

p.297. **The language in which** Bate (ed.), *The Romantics on Shakespeare*, pp. 529 and 534.

p.297. **even paraphrases Ovid** Golding's translation of Ovid's *Metamorphoses* [7.197–209] begins: 'Ye airs and winds, ye elves of hills, of brooks, of woods alone, Of standing lakes, and of the night, approach ye everychone . . .'

p.298. **My ending is despair** *The Tempest* was first performed before the court at Whitehall on 1 November 1611 as part of the celebrations surrounding the marriage of Princess Elizabeth to Frederick, elector of Palatine.

Twenty-Two: 'Sans Everything'

p.299. **inverted this conceit** See Paterson, op. cit., pp. 204–6, who identifies 'the note of hapless despair that suffuses this poem', just one of many possible readings. Others comment on the poet's 'narcissistic smugness'.

p.300.   **For the substantial sum of £140** Shakespeare's purchase of the property in Blackfriars was executed in a way that raises some questions about his purposes for it. On 11 March 1613 he paid £80 in cash, with a further £60 as a mortgage until September. The title deeds list three co-purchasers, who were actually trustees, one of them Shakespeare's fellow actor John Heminges. For more on the details of this acquisition see Lois Potter, *The Life of William Shakespeare: A Critical Biography* (Hoboken, 2012), pp. 396–7.

p.300.   **the Thames by Puddle Wharf** Holden, op. cit., p. 303.

p.300.   **This new home mirrored** Nicholl, op. cit., p. 276.

p.301.   **Now was not the moment to retire** Some have doubted the substance of the senior writer's contribution, but to the other actors in the King's Men, *All Is True* (as it was known at the time) is authentic Shakespeare: the script would join the thirty-seven plays preserved for posterity in the First Folio. It seems clear that Shakespeare had not yet turned his back on the theatre.

p.301.   **Middleton, Wilkins and Fletcher** Wells, op. cit., pp. 194–223.

p.301.   **whole house to the very grounds** Greenblatt, op, cit. p. 279.

p.302.   **The record is patchy** *The Two Noble Kinsmen* was subsequently included in the Second Folio of 1679. Shakespeare's other late play, *The History of Cardenio*, is lost. We know it was performed by the King's Men in 1613, and was probably based on an episode from Cervantes' *Don Quixote* (first published in a translation by Thomas Shelton in 1612).

p.302.   **Their latest collaboration** Holden, op. cit., p. 301.

p.303.   **Burgess associates with** Burgess's first foray into Shakespeare's world occurred in 1964 with *Nothing Like The Sun*, a fictional version of Shakespeare's love life, partly driven by the claim that the poet's imagination had been inspired by syphilis. This became a film script, *The Bawdy Bard*, never produced, which morphed into his biographical essay, *Shakespeare* (London, 1970). Later, Burgess returned to Elizabethan fiction with a novel about Christopher Marlowe, *A Dead Man in Deptford* (1993).

p.303. **The mood of the tragedy** Burgess, *Shakespeare*, op. cit., p. 206, and Schoenbaum, op. cit., pp. 77–8.

p.303. **The latter part of his life** Stanley Wells, *Shakespeare, A Dramatic Life* (London, 1994), p. 389.

p.303. **A library of speculation** Greer, op. cit., pp. oo–oo.

p.304. **In November 1614** The William Combe case, a disagreeable dispute about enclosures and the consolidation of the 'yardlands' at Welcombe, that dragged on after Shakespeare's death, is fully described in Holden, op. cit., pp. 312–15.

p.304. **The playwright Edward Bond** See the introduction to Edward Bond, *Bingo* (London, 1974), p. ix.

p.304. **He could either side with the landowners** Bond, op. cit., p. x.

p.305. **a sleazy publican** A vintner who also failed as the proprietor of the Cage.

p.306. **Shakespeare mingles everything** For Charles Lamb's comment, see Kermode, *Shakespeare's Language*, p. 308. Shakespeare seems to have written Act One, and the first scenes of Acts Two, Three and Five, as well as the final scene quoted here.

p.307. **Shakespeare, Drayton and Ben Jonson** Schoenbaum, op. cit., p. 78. See also Salley Vickers' short story, 'A Merry Meeting', a witty and fanciful reconstruction of this event.

Twenty-Three: 'The Undiscover'd Country'

p.308. **the end of November 1623** For more on the First Folio, see Emma Smith, *The Making of Shakespeare's First Folio: Four Centuries of an Iconic Book* (Oxford, 2015). See also Dickson, op. cit., p. 109, for the cost of the First Folio (originally bound in plain calf, £1.00, unbound 15 shillings).

p.309. **In dedicating this magnificent volume** Two other facts about the First Folio are indisputable: both its value (somewhere north of $5m in rare books sales) and its comparative rarity (some 240 copies survive worldwide in public and private collections).

p.309. **as if he thought** Greenblatt, op. cit., p. 372.

p.310. **A labour of love** The treasury of the First Folio gave future readers not just a cast of immortals (Rosalind, Lady Macbeth, Prospero et al.), but also a heap of new words (*catastrophe, assassinate, indifference, monopoly* etc.).

p.310. **Notably, it collected some thirty-six plays** *Pericles* and *The Two Noble Kinsmen* were accepted later, making a total of thirty-eight canonical plays.

p.310. **'a self-satisfied pork butcher'** The description is Shakespeare scholar John Dover-Wilson's.

p.311. **the identification of Shakespeare** Cooper, op. cit., p. 54.

p.311. **For years to come, Freud** Freud's anxieties are engagingly described in Shapiro, op. cit., pp. 184–6.

p.311. **its four rival contenders** For a full account of these portraits, see Cooper, op. cit.

p.311. **a fog of speculation and misattribution** Emma Smith, *Shakespeare's First Folio* (Oxford, 2016) is indispensable reading.

p.312. **We need not repine** Burgess, *Shakespeare*, op. cit., p. 239.

p.313. **'the fever of the mad'** *The Tempest* [1.2.210].

p.313. **the curious case of England's** See Robert McCrum, 'To hell and back: the story of an obsession', *Guardian*, 27.10.2018. I record my thanks to Carol Hughes for commissioning the lecture that inspired this research into Hughes's struggle with *Shakespeare and the Goddess of Complete Being* (London, 1992).

p.314. **Arthur Phillips would probably** See 'Shakespeare and the Will to Deceive', *New York Times*, 28.04.2011.

p.315. **this exceptional pastiche** I gratefully acknowledge an email interview with Arthur Phillips about *The Tragedy of Arthur*.

p.315. **Definitely Shakespeare** *New York Times*, Q & A with Phoebe Waller-Bridge, 22.11.2019.

Epilogue: 'Remember Me'

p.317. **the Club launched its blog** There is some dispute about this date: none of us is quite certain about the timing. Predictably, when I recently clicked on the Club's site I found this message: *Oh no! You're looking for something which just isn't here! Fear not, however, errors are to be expected, and luckily there are tools on the sidebar for you to use in your search for what you need . . .*

p.318. **Iago's 'Demand me nothing'** *Othello* [5.2.309].

pp.320 **Creativity always comes** Albert O. Hirschman's essay
–21. 'The Principle of the Hiding Hand' is cited in 'The Gift of Doubt' by Malcolm Gladwell, *New Yorker*, 17.06.2013.

p.321. **Everything that was essential** This Chekhov quotation comes from *Reading Chekhov* by Janet Malcolm (New York, 2002), pp. 36–7. I gratefully acknowledge this source, and also Ms Malcolm's translation.

p.322. **There's something a little irritating** W. H. Auden, *The Dyer's Hand* (New York, 1962). See also W. H. Auden, *Lectures on Shakespeare* (Princeton, 2000).

p.322. **I'm a writer, he declared** Harold Pinter, *Plays* 4 (London, 1981), Introduction, pp. ix–xi.

Postscript

p.367. **another new Shakespearean meme** See 'Shakespeare in Lockdown' by Andrew Dickson, the *Guardian*, 22.03.2020. And see also Emma Smith, *New York Times*, 29.03.20, 'What Shakespeare teaches us about living with pandemics'.

ACKNOWLEDGEMENTS

Shakespearean was first suggested by Oskar Eustis' cele-brated 2016 'Shakespeare in the Park' production of *Julius Caesar*, and my Radio 4 documentary, *Shakespeare in America*, produced by the incomparable Maggie Ayre. Thereafter, a book of this kind has many mentors and friends to whom I owe a huge debt of gratitude. First in my thanks is the Shakespeare scholar Professor James Shapiro at Columbia University, together with Michael Witmore and Heather Wolfe at the Folger Shakespeare Library. Sara Kestelman shared many insights into Peter Brook's famous production of *A Midsummer Night's Dream*. At Boughton Hall, Richard, Duke of Buccleuch and Queensberry, and his artistic adviser/curator Paul Boucher, opened my eyes to the importance of the Earl of Southampton. My friend Geoff Marsh took me on a mem-orable tour of St Helen's, Bishopsgate. The film maker John-Paul Davidson has a rare and wonderful under-standing of The Kings' Men. The indefatigable Shakespeare biographer Anthony Holden shared several invaluable readings, and made many helpful suggestions. At the Beckett Foundation in the University of Reading, Steven Matthews, William Davies and their colleagues gave me a remarkable year in which to reflect on the dialogue between

Acknowledgements

sixteenth- and twenty-first-century theatre. I also acknowledge with gratitude my conversations with directors Nicholas Hytner, Adrian Noble and Trevor Nunn. I am particularly glad to thank Nick Dennys for his help with Graham Greene's lecture, and Jon Snow for giving me privileged access to the Heart of England Forest. Further, I am indebted in so many ways to my American posse, Deborah Needleman, Jacob Weisberg and Malcolm Gladwell, as well as to Joanna Kavenna and Margreta de Grazia. My daughter Isobel used more of her time at Brown University than was probably scheduled to investigate Shakespeare's retirement to Stratford. I must also record a special thank you to Arizechi Ogwueleka at A2Z Computer Solutions, Simplified IT, who rescued the final draft of my digital text from the brink of oblivion. At the close, my friend and former *Guardian/Observer* colleague, Andrew Dickson, also provided some generous and fruitful comments. And finally, to the Shakespeare Club, 'let us be thankful for that which is'. As we 'go off', we must, of course, 'bear us like the time'.

SELECT BOOK LIST

Bate, Jonathan, *Soul of the Age* (London, 2008)

Bearman, Robert, *Shakespeare's Money* (Oxford, 2016)

Bloom, Harold, *Shakespeare: The Invention of the Human* (London, 1999)

Brigden, Susan, *New Worlds, Lost Worlds* (London, 2001)

Brook, Peter, *The Empty Space* (London, 1968)

Burgess, Anthony, *Shakespeare* (London, 1970)

Conrad, Peter, *Shakespeare: The Theatre of our World* (London, 2018)

Dickson, Andrew, *Worlds Elsewhere: Journeys around Shakespeare's Globe* (London, 2016)

Fraser, Antonia, *The Gunpowder Plot* (London, 1996)

Greenblatt, Stephen, *Will in the World* (London, 2004)

—— *Tyrant* (London, 2018)

Greer, Germaine, *Shakespeare's Wife* (London, 2007)

Holden, Anthony, *William Shakespeare* (London, 1999)

Honan, Park, *Christopher Marlowe, Poet and Spy* (Oxford, 2005)

Hughes, Ted, *Shakespeare and the Goddess of Complete Being* (London, 1993)

Hytner, Nicholas, *Balancing Acts* (London, 2017)

Kermode, Frank, *Shakespeare's Language* (London, 2009)

Kott, Jan, *Shakespeare Our Contemporary* (London, 1966)

Select Book List

Nicholl, Charles, *The Reckoning: The Murder of Christopher Marlowe* (London, 1992)

—— *The Lodger* (London, 2007)

Noble, Adrian, *How To Do Shakespeare* (2010)

Onions, C. T., *A Shakespeare Glossary* (Oxford, 1911)

Paterson, Don, *Reading Shakespeare's Sonnets* (2010)

Schoenbaum, S., *Shakespeare's Lives* (Oxford, 1993)

Shapiro, James, *1599: A Year in the Life of William Shakespeare* (London, 2008)

—— *The Year of Lear: Shakespeare in 1606* (London, 2015)

Smith, Emma, *This Is Shakespeare* (London, 2019)

Steiner, George, *Language and Silence* (London, 1967)

Wells, Stanley, *Shakespeare & Co.* (Oxford, 2006)

INDEX

Admiral's Men   170–1
Aeschylus   194
Agee, James   176
Allen, Giles   171, 172–3
All Is True (film, 2018)   36
All Is True see Henry VIII
Almeida Theatre   80
American Civil War   264, 271, 273
Americas   255–7, 258–67, 271–8, 280–1, 283
   see also United States
Annesley, Sir Brian   222
'anti-Stratfordians'   279–80
Antony and Cleopatra   18, 26, 72–4, 194, 237–8, 288
Apuleius   146
Arden, Mary   243
Arnold, Matthew   215–16
Arouet, Jean-Marie (Voltaire)   210
As You Like It   103, 114, 129, 151–2, 208, 238
   and the First Folio   310
   homage to Marlowe   112, 136
   inspiration for   98
   and old age and death   299
   'we are all players' metaphor   169

Athenaeum (literary magazine)   30
Aubrey, John   15
Auden, W. H.   162, 286, 321–2
Austen, Jane   28–9, 30

Bacon, Delia   215, 278–9
Bacon, Sir Francis   22, 61, 278
Bandello, Matteo   232
Bannon, Steve   44–5
'bardolatry'   26, 27, 31–2, 36
Barnfield, Richard   154–5, 165
Barnum, P. T.   20, 261
Beale, Simon Russell   161, 201, 218–19
Beaumont, Francis   266, 284
Becket, Thomas à   104
Beckett, Samuel   32, 122, 123, 227–8, 259, 316
Beerbohm Tree, Herbert   201
Berlioz, Hector   29
Bermuda   256–7
Birmingham   30
Bishopsgate   93–4, 98, 115
Blackfriars   171
Blackfriars gatehouse   300
Blackfriars Theatre   171, 289–91, 294, 302
Blackwater   167

Blake, William 29
Bloom, Harold 157–8
Blount, Edward 308
Boccaccio, Giovanni 232
Boleyn, Anne 51
Bond, Edward 304
book trade 68–9, 121
Booth, John Wilkes 44, 264
Booth brothers 276
Borges, Jorge Luis 15, 312
Boston Common 34
Boswell, James 27
Branagh, Kenneth 36, 37, 191, 201
Brecht, Bertolt 259
Brexit 10–11, 229–31, 234–5
Bridge Theatre 21
British Broadcasting Corporation (BBC) 36–7, 54
British Empire 29
British Library 35
Britishness, transition to 236, 252
Brook, Peter 32, 122, 146, 202, 295
Brooke, Ralph 282
Brown, Gordon 229
Browning, Robert 55
Brunel, Isambard Kingdom 37
Bull, Eleanor 109, 110
Burbage, Cuthbert 171–2
Burbage, Ellen 172
Burbage, James 171, 172
Burbage, Richard 82, 171–2, 174, 236–7
Burbage family 289
Burgess, Anthony 93, 303, 312
Burghley, Lord 108
Burton, Richard 191

Bush, George W. 11
Byron, Lord 154

Cambridge 104
Canterbury 103, 104
Carlyle, Thomas 21–2
Cassidy, John 42
Catesby, Robert 243
Catholics 87, 92, 115, 240–2, 243, 287
Caxton, William 68
Cecil, William 50
Centennial Park, Nashville 271
Central Park, New York City 42–4, 276
Chaplin, Charlie 22, 278
Chapman, Graham 174
Charles, Prince 36–7
Charles I, King 25
Chaucer, Geoffrey 142, 146, 212, 306
Chekhov, Anton 321
Chettle, Henry 15, 99
Churchill, Sir Winston 36
Cleese, John 174
Clinton, Bill 9
Clinton, Hillary Rodham 10–11
Coke, Edward 244–5
Coleridge, Samuel Taylor 13, 29, 60, 212–13, 296
Collected Works (Shakespeare) *see Complete Works*
College of Heralds 282
Collins, Francis 305
Collins, Colonel Tim 177
Comedy of Errors, The 168, 253, 255–6, 294
Comey, John 42
Commonwealth Shakespeare Company 34

Index

Complete Works of William Shakespeare, The 17, 19, 23, 27, 29, 35, 210, 229, 258, 262, 263, 287, 308, 313

Condell, Henry 174, 257, 275, 302, 308, 316

Confederates/Confederacy 264, 271, 272, 273

Conrad, Peter 37

Conservatives 230

Coriolanus 16, 90–1, 159, 194, 258, 287
  allusions to the plague 288, 325
  and the 'authorship question' 280
  and characterization 125
  and historical geography 228–9
  and identity 210
  mobs of 90, 205
  Tom Hiddleston's 161
  and the United States 174, 278
  and the vernacular 61

Cornwell, Bernard 141

Corpus Christi, Texas 272–3

Cotter, Patrick 277

Covid-19 pandemic 9, 322, 325

Crick, Francis 221

Cumberbatch, Benedict 19, 201

Curtain playhouse 171

Curtain Road Theatre, Shoreditch 93, 115

Cymbeline 256
  Blackfriars' staging 290–1
  genre 220
  inspiration for 81
  setting 229
  and the vernacular 63

D-Day (1944) 175–7

Dante 194, 322

Danto, Arthur 123

Davenant, Sir William 26

Davis, Jefferson 264

Davis, Philip 72–3

De Quincey, Thomas 250

de Tocqueville, Alexis 259–60

de Vere, Edward, Earl of Oxford 22, 279–80

Declaration of Independence 259, 272

Dekker, Thomas 115, 150, 236

Delacorte Theater 43

Denmark 192

Depp, Johnny 44

Dethick, Sir William 282

Devereux, Robert, Earl of Essex 115, 127, 165–7, 169, 172–3, 179–80, 182–6, 194, 204, 216, 248, 253, 318

Diana, Princess of Wales 36

Dickens, Charles 30, 261

Dickson, Andrew 210

Dixon, W. Hepworth 30

Donmar Theatre 57

Donne, John 255, 279

Donnellan, Declan 219

Doran, Greg 160

Drayton 307

Droeshout, Martin 311

Dromgoole, Dominic 191

Dryden, John 25–6

East India Company 210

Edward III 22

Einstein, Albert 221

Eliot, George 62

Eliot, T. S. 31, 103–4, 122, 194

Elizabeth I 36, 49–51, 61, 86,
    319
    and the 'authorship question'
      22, 279
    death 49, 204, 235
    and the Earl of Essex 115,
      165–7, 169, 182–6, 204
    and Falstaff 162
    favourite clown 171
    and the granting of coats of
      arms 282
    and Henry Garnet 243
    plots for the deposition of
      183–7, 204
    and Shakespeare 49–50,
      237
    succession 102, 114–15,
      235–6
Elizabeth II, Queen 37, 86
Elliott, Marianne 219
Emerson, Ralph Waldo 12–13,
    265–6
Emmerich, Roland 280
England, condition of 233,
    234–6, 241, 246, 248,
    252
Engels, Friedrich 162
English Civil War 123
English nationalism 71,
    230–2
Englishness 29, 38, 66, 138,
    143–4, 236, 271, 319,
    322
espionage 101–2, 104
Essex House 184, 185
Euripides 194
Eustis, Oskar 42
Eyre, Richard 148

Faber & Faber 121
Falstaff, Sir John 29, 64, 66,
    75, 78, 82, 124, 156–64,

    165, 169, 170, 230, 231,
      307
Faulkner, William 66
Fawkes, Guido 240, 242–3
Federal Bureau of Investigation
    (FBI) 42
Feilgrath, Ferdinand 212
Ferguson Riots 2016 274–5
Field, Richard 68, 94, 116,
    181
Fiennes, Ralph 80
First Folio (*Mr William
    Shakespeares Comedies,
    Histories & Tragedies
    Published according to the
    True Orginall Copies*)
    (1623) 13, 22, 25, 160,
    174, 220, 257, 275, 278,
    286, 296, 302, 308–14,
    316
Fitzgerald, F. Scott 126
Fleabag (TV series) 54, 55,
    56–7, 315
Fletcher, John 266, 284, 301,
    302, 306
Florio, John 232
Flower, Edward 30
Folger Shakespeare Library,
    Washington DC 275–8,
    280
Ford's Theatre, Washington DC
    276
Forrest, Edwin 263
Founding Fathers 257
Fourth Folio 25
Fox News 43–4
France 210, 232
Frederik, Crown Prince of
    Denmark 192
Freud, Sigmund 22, 280, 311,
    313
Frizer, Ingram 110

Gambon, Michael 160
Game of Thrones (TV series) 77
Garibaldi, Giuseppe 30
Garnet, Henry 243–4
Garrick, David 27, 30, 201
Gentleman's Magazine 28
German Shakespeare cult 210–12
Gibbon, Edward 33
Gielgud, Sir John 191, 201
Gilliam, Terry 174
Globe Theatre (contemporary), Southwark 20–1, 191, 219
Globe Theatre (original), Southwark 34, 173–5, 177–87, 194, 196, 222, 236–7, 254, 289–91, 294, 311, 319
  burnt to the ground (1613) 173, 301–2, 316
  and *Hamlet* 193, 198–9, 207
  and *Julius Caesar* 180–2
  and *Macbeth* 248
  motto 174
  premiere (1599) 173, 177–9, 180
  and *Twelfth Night* 208
Globe Theatre (second reconstruction), Southwark 302
Godard, Jean-Luc 32
Goold, Rupert 80
Grandage, Michael 219, 225–6
Grant, Ulysses S. 272–3
Greenblatt, Stephen 41, 45–6, 216, 309
Greene, Graham 55, 287–8
Greene, Robert 97, 98, 99–100, 108, 117, 164, 291
Griffin, Bartholomew 165
Guardian (newspaper) 230
Gunpowder Plot (1605) 239–45, 248, 252, 253

Hall, John 305
Hall, Peter 219
Hamlet 7, 14, 17–19, 22, 29, 49, 123–4, 127, 129, 191–213, 236–7, 287, 300, 319, 323
  Andrew Scott's performance (2017) 21, 35, 161
  and the audience–play interaction 53
  Coleridge and 213
  Davenant's 26
  Elizabethan political influences on 186–7
  establishment 210
  first foreign performance 210
  ghost character 34, 194, 197, 198, 202, 204, 299, 303
  Globe Theatre production (2015) 191
  and Goethe 211
  and Greene's criticism 100
  Hamlet's madness 21, 194, 199–200, 203–6, 207–8
  and immersive technology 33–4
  initial reactions to 207
  and introspection 196, 198–200, 204–5, 213, 218
  language of 66, 68, 195
  narrative rule-breaking 60
  and the New World 262, 264–5

Hamlet *(cont.)*
  parodies 40–1
  performance marathon of
    219
  Player King character 201–3
  revenge theme 197–8,
    204–5
  uncut text 193–4
  undercurrent of danger 8
  violence of 79
  'we are all players' metaphor
    169
Hamlet 360: Thy Father's Spirit
  34
Hathaway, Anne 5, 92, 281,
    301, 303–4
Hawthorne, Nathaniel 261–2,
    278–9
Hazlitt, William 29
Heaney, Seamus 143
Hegel, Georg Wilhelm Friedrich
    157–8
Helsingor 192
Heminges, John 174, 257,
    275, 302, 308, 316
Henry, Gregg 42
Henry IV 81–2, 114, 155,
    156–60, 162–3, 168, 230
  all-female productions 220
  and characterization 124
  Greg Doran's production
    (2014) 160
  National Theatre
    performance (2005) 160
Henry IV Part 1 37, 60, 64–5,
    157, 159–60, 165
Henry IV Part 2 12, 35, 37,
    49–50, 51, 60, 75, 92,
    112, 158, 160–1, 169–70
Henry V 37, 60, 82, 161–4,
    168, 175, 194
  Chorus 175, 176, 178, 179

  at the Globe (1997) 20–1
  Hytner's National Theatre
    production 177
  Nashville Centennial Park
    production (2015) 271
  premiere in the Globe (1599)
    173, 177–80
  and the United States 271,
    278
  violence of 79
Henry V (film, 1944) 175–7
Henry VI 60, 87–90
  and characterization 81
  and Marlowe 108
  mobs of 88–90
Henry VI Part 3 91, 100,
    232
  and Shakespeare's fame 78
  violence of 79
Henry VIII (or *All Is True*)
    254, 300–301
Herbert, Philip 309
Herbert, William, Earl of
    Pembroke 286, 309
Herder, Johann Gottfried
    211
Hiddleston, Tom 161
Hirschman, Albert O. 320–1
History of Cardenio, The 22
Holden, Anthony 172
Holinshed, Raphael 82, 235,
    314
Holmes, Richard 213
Honan, Paul 97
Hughes, Ted 32, 63
  *Shakespeare and the Goddess
    of Complete Being*
    313–14
Huguenots 241
Huxley, Aldous 66
Hytner, Nicholas 21, 81–2,
    97, 146, 177, 219

372

iambic pentameter   141
Idle, Eric   174
Inns of Court   25
Ionesco, Eugène   227
Ireland   166–7, 169, 179, 182
Irving, Henry   31, 201
Isherwood, Christopher   51–2

Jackson, Glenda   161
Jacobi, Derek   161, 218,
    225–6
Jaggard, William   164
James, Henry   19, 22, 62
James I and VI, King   102,
    183, 204, 216, 222,
    235–40, 244–8, 252, 254,
    279, 288, 298, 302, 319
Jamestown   255, 256, 294
Jefferson, Thomas   259
Jesuits   243–4
Johnson, Boris   157, 230
Johnson, Samuel   26–7, 29,
    60–1
Jones, Terry   174
Jonson, Ben   70, 95, 97, 111,
    124, 160, 236, 254–5,
    266, 284, 307–8, 310–12
Joyce, James   122, 322
Jubilee, The, Theatre Royal
    28, 30
Julius Caesar   19, 35, 62, 114,
    124, 161
  all-female productions   220
  Bridge Theatre production,
    2018   21
  and characterization   197
  and the First Folio   310
  ghost character   299
  mobs of   90
  and the New World   264
  premiere at the Globe (1599)
    180–2

'Shakespeare in the Park'
    productions   42–4
  and the United States   277,
    278
  violence of   79
  Voltaire's   210

Kean, Edmund   201
Keats, George   214
Keats, John   13, 29, 30,
    214–16, 320–1
Kempe, Will   171
Kermode, Frank   196
King James Bible   36, 286
King John   16, 18, 75, 81,
    230–1
King Lear   17, 58, 123, 161,
    194, 222–9, 235, 275,
    320, 326
  allusions to the plague   149,
    288
  the author behind   15
  and the 'authorship question'
    280
  and characterization   125
  cinematic version   32
  Donmar production (2010)
    218, 225–6
  Ian McKellen's production
    (2007)   122
  and identity   210
  inspiration for   81
  and introspection   125
  language use   18, 73
  madness theme   122, 218,
    223–7
  marathon performance of
    219
  narrative rule-breaking   60
  National Theatre production
    (2014)   218–19
  and the New World   262

King Lear (cont.)
  and the plague 325
  and Shakespeare's fame 155
  violence of 79
King's Men (formerly the Lord
    Chamberlain's Men)
  115, 227, 236, 287, 289,
  300, 302, 316
Kinnear, Roy 19
Kott, Jan 145–6, 227–8
Kurosawa, Akira 32
Kyd, Thomas 95, 98, 102,
  109, 164

Laing, R. D. 32
Lamb, Charles 306
Law, Jude 19, 192, 201
Lawrence, D. H. 22, 122
Le Carré, John 315
Leir, King 222, 227
Levin, Bernard 65
Life of King Henry the Eighth,
  The (All is True)
  (Shakespeare and Fletcher)
  301, 305–6
Lincoln, Abraham 44, 263,
  264, 276
Lloyd, Phyllida 219–20
Lodge, Thomas 98–9
London 14, 30, 46, 60, 63,
  67, 69, 76, 80, 89, 91,
  93–8, 124, 126, 129, 139,
  149, 164, 169, 173–4,
  182, 183, 184, 185, 193,
  205, 207, 209, 236, 241,
  243, 288, 294, 300, 303,
  304, 319
London Olympics (2012)
  37–8
Longstreet, James 272
Looney, Thomas 280
Lord Admiral's Men 173

Lord Chamberlain's Men 113,
  115, 154, 171–5, 182–4,
  236
  see also King's Men

Lord Strange's Men 104,
  170–1
'Lover's Complaint, A'
  (Shakespeare) 284
Love's Labour's Lost 16–17,
  58, 114, 121, 134–9, 151,
  155, 168
  and landscape 142
  language use 69, 72, 142
  published in *The Passionate*
    Pilgrim 165
  Raleigh characterization 17,
    253
  and the United States 278
Love's Labour's Won 22
Ludgate 185
Lyall, Sarah 57
Lyly, John 98

Macbeth 186, 194, 229, 234,
  239, 241–2, 244–52, 287
  the author behind 15
  and the 'authorship question'
    280
  and characterization 29,
    59, 125
  and the First Folio 310
  ghost 299
  inspiration for 81
  and language use 63, 66,
    95
  narrative rule-breaking 59
  and the New World 263,
    264
  and the plague 325
  violence of 79
McCrum, Michael 4

Index

McKellen, Ian 121–2
Macready, William Charles 263
Magruder, General ('Prince John') 272
Malcolm X 264
Malone, Edmond 26
Mamet, David 60
Mandela, Nelson 9, 35
Marlowe, Christopher 3–7, 61, 81, 95, 97–9, 103–14, 164–5, 266
  and the 'authorship question' 22, 279
  death 109–14, 151, 196
  Doctor Faustus 106–7
  dramatic revolution of 122
  Edward II 108, 125
  greatness 108
  high culture 123
  'portrait' 3–5, 310
  and Shakespeare 108, 111–13, 115–16, 125, 130, 135–6, 297
  and the spy game 101–2, 104
  stardom 105
  Tamburlaine the Great 105–8, 112
  wild lifestyle 105
Marsh, Geoff 94
Marx, Karl 162
Mary, Queen of Scots 51
Mayflower (ship) 257, 258
Measure for Measure 58, 126, 209, 220
Mediterranean 254, 257
Melville, Herman 122, 261–3, 312
Mendes, Sam 218–19
Merchant of Venice, The 16, 108, 114, 288

Meres, Francis 127, 168, 170
Merry Wives of Windsor, The 49, 162, 232
Mexico 272
Meyrick, Sir Gelly 183–4, 186
Middleton, Thomas 284, 301
Midsummer Night's Dream, A 19, 72, 98, 114, 134, 139–40, 142–51, 151, 168, 200–1
  Bridge Theatre production, 2019 21
  Brook's, 1970 32
  criticism 26
  homage to Marlowe 112
  and the influence of Chaucer 306
Millais, John Everett 29
Milton, John 25, 212, 322
Monomoy Theatre, Chatham (Mass.) 141
Montaigne 79, 125, 232
Monty Python's Flying Circus 174
More, Sir Thomas 69, 82, 84
Mozart, Wolfgang Amadeus 221, 318
Much Ado About Nothing 19, 28, 58, 70, 74, 136
Mueller report 277
Murakami, Haruki 9

Nashe, Thomas 98, 111
National Endowment for the Arts 44
National Portrait Gallery 310–11
National Theatre 57, 160, 177, 218–19
nationalism 71, 230–2
New Place, Stratford-upon-Avon 300, 304, 308

Index

New World   252, 253–7,
    258–67, 271–8, 280–1,
    283
New York City   259, 263
New York Times (newspaper)
    33–4, 37, 41, 43, 314,
    315
New Yorker (magazine)   42
Newton, Isaac   36
Nicholl, Charles   112
Nixon, Richard   278
Noble, Adrian   34, 64, 97, 219
Nonsuch Palace   182–3
Norman, Marc   279
North, Thomas   180, 181
Nunn, Trevor   97, 219

Obama, Barack   9–10, 274–5
Observer (newspaper)   20, 21,
    121
Olivier, Laurence   175–7, 191,
    201
Orwell, George   310
Othello   29, 161, 194, 271–5,
    318
    and characterization   125
    narrative rule-breaking   60
    and the New World   262
    Voltaire's   210
Ovid   100, 113, 116, 127,
    146, 232, 297

Palin, Michael   174
Paris Accord (2015)   11
'Parody on the Soliloquy of
    Hamlet' (anonymous)   40
Passionate Pilgrim, The
    (volume)   164–5
Paterson, Don   127
Peele, George   98
Pembroke's Men   170–1
Pepys, Samuel   26

Percy, Thomas   240–1
Pericles   22, 220
Philadelphia   259
Phillips, Adam   52–3
Phillips, Arthur   313
    The Tragedy of Arthur by
        William Shakespeare
        314–15
Phillips, Augustine   186
Pilgrim Fathers   271–2
Pinter, Harold   228, 322, 324
plague   95, 100, 108–9, 115,
    124, 126, 139, 149–50,
    236, 288–9, 301, 325–6
Plath, Sylvia   32
Platter, Thomas   181–2
Plutarch   180, 181, 232
Poley, Robert   102, 109, 110
Pope, Alexander   26, 122, 212
Porter, Cole   261
Privy Council   104, 109, 171,
    184, 186, 239
Protestants   87, 287
Proust, Marcel   66
Pryce, Jonathan   201
Public Theatre, New York
    42–4
Puritans   25, 95, 202, 258,
    261

Quincey, Thomas De see De
    Quincey, Thomas   250
Quiney, Thomas   305

Raleigh, Sir Walter   17, 61,
    86–7, 105, 184–5, 253,
    258, 279
Rape of Lucrece, The   109,
    126, 285
Red Dragon (ship)   210
Redgrave, Vanessa   22, 32, 161
Reformation   71, 289

Renaissance   5, 63, 71, 129,
    279
Restoration   25, 26
Richard II   60, 77, 114,
    154–6, 168, 234, 244
    the author behind   15
    and characterization   78,
        124–5, 196–7
    deposition scene   184, 186
    excitement of   81
    homage to Marlowe   108,
        112
    language use   70–1
    nationalist sentiment   231
    productions at the Globe
        (1601)   184
    and the United States   278
    violence of   79
Richard III, King   80
Richard III   15, 28, 41, 56,
    60, 78, 80–4, 154, 155,
    168, 264
    Almeida Theatre production
        80
Robinson, Marilynne   221
Romantics   13, 29, 210, 213,
    214, 215
Romeo and Juliet   7, 114,
    129–34, 139, 151, 154,
    168, 194, 197
    and characterization   124
    homage to Marlowe   112
    inspiration provided by   29
    and language use   72
    New York production (1730)
        259
    violence of   79
Romeo and Juliet (film, 1968)
    32
Rose Theatre   171, 222
Roth, Michael   229
Roth, Philip   24

Rotunda, Stratford-upon-Avon
    27
Rowe, Nicholas   303
Royal Festival Hall   220
Royal Shakespeare Company
    (RSC)   33, 45, 162

St Paul's Churchyard   94, 244
Scarborough, Adrian   161
Schiller, Friedrich   211
Schillinger, Liesl   278
Schlegel, A. W.   212
    Dramatische Werke   211
Schoenbaum, Samuel   33
'School of Night'   105
Scofield, Paul   201
Scotland   233, 235–7, 245–6,
    248
Scott, Andrew   19, 21, 35,
    161
Sea Venture (ship)   256–7, 294
Second Folio   25
September 11 terror attacks,
    2001 (9/11)   8, 9
Shakespeare, Hamnet (son)
    92, 194, 305
Shakespeare, John (father)
    194, 281, 326
Shakespeare, Judith (daughter)
    92, 301, 305
Shakespeare, Mary (mother)
    326
Shakespeare, Susanna (daughter)
    92, 301, 305
SHAKESPEARE, WILLIAM
    accent   97
    and the ageing mind *in
        extremis*   220–1
    American performances
        252, 258–9, 263, 271–4
    annus mirabilis (1599)   114
    anonymity   99–100, 316

Index

SHAKESPEARE, WILLIAM *(cont.)*
appearance 15
archetypal nature of his
human dramas 29, 42,
114
arrival in London 46
attention-grabbing tactics
34–5, 65, 73, 83–5
and the 'authorship question'
22, 215, 278–82, 311
biography 280–2
birth 4, 49
and the birth of his children
92
birthday 30
birthday anniversaries
30–2, 276
bisexuality 114, 128
and the book trade 68–9
'borrowings' 98–9, 108,
117, 291–2, 306
bourgeois life of 53
and characterization 29, 42,
59, 78, 81–5, 87–8, 124–5
and the clash of the people
and the state 90–1
coat of arms 281–3, 288
and the condition of England
233, 234–6, 241, 246,
248, 252
conservatism 288
contemporary relevance 6,
7, 16, 30, 46
creative privacy 316, 321
creative risk-taking 15, 23,
40, 53–5, 60, 104, 121,
140, 217, 220, 238, 250,
292–3, 307, 318, 320–1
curiosity 52–3, 56, 60, 78,
220, 238, 253, 319
death 6, 299, 307
death anniversaries 24, 191

and the death of his son
194
detailed observations of
16–17, 74–5
dramas of history 60, 77–9,
79–84, 87–91, 158
and dramatization of the self
124, 126–8, 218, 220
and Elizabeth I 49–50, 237
elusive nature 6–7, 15, 36,
92–3, 97–8, 214–15
Englishness 29, 38, 66,
138, 143–4, 236, 271,
319, 322
and the exercise of royal
power 51–2
failing health 305
first London property 300
fluidity and mobility of his
work 123–4
as 'free man' 319
genre-switching 114
given his own playhouse
153, 173
greatness 5–7, 115, 121,
126, 318
at the head of his profession
168
Henley Street residence 28
and identity 209–10, 217,
218, 220, 294
and the imagination 24, 29,
38, 73, 82–3, 125, 138,
140–1, 144, 157, 319
insight 15–16
instinct for drama 52
and the interaction of the
mundane and the
theatrical 56–7, 145
and introspection 124–6,
128–9, 196, 198–200,
204–5, 213, 218, 220, 290

Index

and jeopardy/peril 14–15,
41, 51–3, 55, 60, 95,
114–15, 151, 174, 216,
233, 238–9, 257, 295
and the King's Men 287
and landscape 142–4
and language 61, 62–76,
123, 125, 133–4, 139,
142, 143, 157, 158, 169,
195, 238, 251, 320
last will and testament 304,
305
'late' style 292
location choice 142–4,
228–9, 254, 257
lost plays 22
the 'lost years' (1585–92)
92–3
love triangles 128
and Marlowe 108, 111–13,
116, 125, 130, 135–6, 297
marriage 5, 92, 281
as member of the Stuart
royal household 237–9,
288
modesty 322, 323
nationalist credentials
230–2
and 'negative capability'
215–16, 320–1
and negligent ambiguity
208, 216–17, 232, 237,
271, 295, 321
new interpretation of reality
162–3, 206
and the New World 252,
254, 255–7, 258–67,
271–8, 280–1
nihilism 205, 229, 247,
295, 298, 306
and old age 223–6,
299–300

omnipresent nature 13, 36
and originality 15, 23, 40,
60–1, 116, 121, 127–8,
140, 320–1
personality 15, 31, 214
as playwright for his people
122
as poet of historical
disruption 40–1
popular nature of his theatre
122
portraits 310–11
as practical man of theatre
34
quits London theatre scene
for Stratford 302–5, 308
receives patronage from the
Earl of Southampton
109, 117, 129, 183, 253–4
rising fame of 154–5,
164–5
rule-breaker 59–60
and the self 124, 126–8,
218, 220, 316, 319, 322
and sex 95–6
and sexual jealousy 7, 162,
211, 292
social and cultural paradigm
shift of 122–4
social mobility 281–3
spelling of his name 97
and the vernacular 61,
62–7, 74–5, 123, 169,
238
and violence 78–9
vocabulary 71–2
Warwickshire youth and
language 62–4, 75–6,
133–4, 139
'we are all players' metaphor
169
and wit 136

SHAKESPEARE, WILLIAM *(cont.)*
see also *specific works*
Shakespeare Apocrypha   22
Shakespeare Birthplace Trust
275
'Shakespeare Club'   19, 21,
57–8, 85–6, 121–2, 129,
141, 160, 192, 218–19,
231, 314, 316–17
Shakespeare Clubs, American
267
'Shakespeare criticism'   26
'Shakespeare industry'   28
'Shakespeare Jubilee', Stratford-
upon-Avon (1769)   27–8
Shakespeare in Love (film,
1999)   103, 116, 209,
279
'Shakespeare in the Park'
productions   42–4
Shakespeare Prize   287, 322
Shakespeare statue, Central
Park, New York City   276
'Shakespearean' myth   36, 93,
284, 286, 298, 303
Shakespearomanie   211, 215
Shapiro, James   45, 180, 260,
276–7, 283
Shaw, George Bernard   22,
313
Sher, Anthony   160
Shoreditch   54, 73, 98, 102,
171–2
Sidney, Sir Philip   70, 222–3
Simpson, Bart   264
Simpson, Homer   264
Sir Thomas More
(collaboration, 1590s)   86
Skeres, Nicholas   110
Smith, Emma   229
Snoop Dogg   72
Sondheim, Stephen   264

sonnets (Shakespeare)   109,
114, 126–9, 164–5, 284–6,
289, 299
sonnet 64   8, 12
sonnet 71   299
sonnet 81   154
South Africa   35
Southwark   171–3
Southwell, Robert   287–8
Spanish Armada   87, 105, 239
Spenser, Edmund   61, 142
Sprague, Charles   260
Star Chamber   183
Stationers' Company   284
Steiner, George   7, 33
Stoppard, Tom   116, 279
Stormzy   34–5
Strachey, Lytton   166, 182–3,
292
Strachey, William   294
Stratford-upon-Avon   14, 27–8,
30, 33, 62, 66–7, 69, 73,
75, 88, 92, 103, 130, 142,
144, 164, 242, 280–3,
288, 302–5, 308, 311,
319, 326
'Stratfordians'   281
Street, Peter   172, 180
Stuarts   220, 235, 236, 252,
310, 357
Summers, Sir George   356
Swan playhouse   171

Taming of the Shrew, The   19,
74–5, 95–6
Tempest, The   17, 37–8,
58, 66, 140–1, 161, 195,
258, 290, 294–8, 300,
308, 313
and the 'authorship question'
280
classical unities of   294–5

Index

Davenant's version   26
and the First Folio   310
genre   220
Henry James' 1907
   introduction   19, 62
homage to Marlowe   112
and identity   210
and the New World   257,
   263
RSC production (2013)   33
Tennant, David   19, 201
Terry, Ellen   31
theatre   129
   attendance figures   173–4
   closure and the plague   100,
      109, 126, 288–9
   and immersive technology
      33–4
   popular (rough)   202
   and the Puritans   25, 95,
      202
   restrictions   108
Theatre, The, Shoreditch   50,
   171–3
Theatre Royal, Drury Lane   28
Third Folio   25
Thorpe, Thomas, 'Shakespeares
   sonnettes'   284–5
Time magazine   176
Times, The (newspaper)   31,
   212, 230
Timon of Athens   220, 223,
   259, 262, 303, 325
Titus Andronicus (with Peele)
   71, 79, 98, 154, 223,
   254
Tolstoy, Leo   21–2, 194,
   211
Tower of London   181, 183,
   185–6, 243
Tresham, Francis   243
Troilus and Cressida   19, 49,

63, 101, 124, 159, 278
Trump, Donald   11, 41, 42,
   44, 277, 278
Tudors   51, 80, 81–2, 86, 142,
   168, 176, 235, 236, 257,
   310
Turner, J. M. W.   29
Twain, Mark   22, 122, 264–5,
   278, 313
Twelfth Night   19, 24–5, 49,
   73, 75, 207–9, 216–17
Twitter   44, 52
Two Gentlemen of Verona, The
   70, 168
Two Noble Kinsmen, The
   (Shakespeare and Fletcher)
   22, 58, 302, 306–7
tyrants   45–6, 52
Tyrone, Earl of   166–7, 169,
   182

Ulster   166–7, 182
United States   8–11, 40–5,
   257, 263–7, 271–8, 280–1,
   283
Upstart Crow (TV comedy
   series)   36
US Army   272–3
US Presidential Election 2016
   11, 39, 41

Venus and Adonis   49, 83, 99,
   109, 111, 116–17, 124,
   126–7, 207, 285, 291
Verdi, Giuseppe   29
Virgil   194
Virginia Company   256, 294
Voltaire *see* Arouet, Jean-Marie

Waller-Bridge, Phoebe   54–5,
   315
Walsingham   101, 115

Index

Walter, Harriet   161, 220
Walton, William   176
war on terror   9, 273
Wars of the Roses   77, 81, 87
Warwickshire   5–6, 14, 62–3,
    75, 94, 133, 148, 242,
    243
Washington DC   264, 275–8,
    280
Watson, Thomas   98, 229
Weever, John   170
Welles, Orson   31–2, 278
Wells, Stanley   108
West Indies   255
Westminster Abbey   110
Wheeler, Margaret   305
White House   44, 277–8
Wilde, Oscar   31, 286
Wilkes, John   276, 301
Wilson, Benjamin   28
Winter's Tale, The   17, 93,
    194–5, 284, 290–4

and the 'authorship question'
    280
borrowings of   99
genre   220
and language use   67–8, 73,
    75–6
Winthrop, John   258
Witmore, Michael   275–6,
    277–8, 280
Wodehouse, P. G.   30
Wolfe, Heather   280–1, 282–3
Wolff, Michael   44
Wood, John   160
Woolf, Virginia   18
Worcester, Earl of   184
Wordsworth, William   212
Wriothesley, Henry, Earl of
    Southampton   100, 109,
    117, 129, 169, 170, 183,
    185–6, 254, 256, 286

Zeffirelli, Franco   32